PRAISE FOR *19 AND 20*

"*19 and 20* is a book-event that has becom[...]
the world. In it, Colectivo Situaciones pract[...]
ing (escucha) and experimentation that translates the powerful mobilizations that
took the streets to end neoliberal plundering (saqueo) into an inspiring and crucial
praxis of thinking. Learning from the events instead of imposing old categories on
their singularities, this book is a crucial source of inspiration on militant research
and situated thinking. A singular work of pedagogy from below, this new edition
comes in a timely moment where the deepening of the neoliberal expropriation
of life that the pandemic has made so explicit meets with the tenth anniversary of
the global uprisings of 201. Today, once again, *19 and 20* offers a crucial map for
experimenting in the situated praxis of political thought."

—**Susana Draper**, coeditor of *Feminicide and Global Accumulation* and author
of *Afterlives of Confinement* and *1968 Mexico*

"Assemblies may become thinking machines. And experiments of resistance may
give rise to alternative experiences of sociability. Colectivo Situaciones develops
out of these findings, that emerged within the 2001 resurrection in Argentina, a
powerful reflexive research: a truly magnificent effort to explore the potentialities
of a future beyond capitalism."

—**Stavros Stavrides**, author of *Towards the City of Thresholds*

"This is a book born in the barricades, neighborhood assemblies, and factory occupations of Argentina's 2001 uprising against neoliberalism. Written by movement
participants, it's an inspiring account of the rebellion and a grassroots model of how
to research and theorize a movement that forged a new way of doing politics from
below. The English translation of such a classic book that's been passed around revolutionary circles for decades is a cause for celebration and hitting the streets!"

—**Benjamin Dangl**, author of *The Five Hundred Year Rebellion: Indigenous
Movements and the Decolonization of History in Bolivia*

"Twenty years ago, Argentina erupted in blockades and assemblies, occupations,
demonstrations, and communal kitchens. In both its circumstances and forms,
the 2001 uprising presaged the protests of 2011 and the struggles of our time.
Colectivo Situaciones' *19 and 20* provided both the sharpest analysis of that moment and a model of theoretical practice: nimble, dialogical, embedded in the
movements with whom it thought, made in common. To rediscover it today is to
do more than reconnect with the recent past; it is inevitably also to ask how it il-
luminates what we have lived since, and how we can continue to extend its lessons
into the future."

—**Rodrigo Nunes**, author of *Neither Vertical nor Horizontal: A Theory of
Political Organization*

"A long decade before Occupy Wall Street, Argentineans poured into the streets to reject austerity and short the circuits of neoliberal capitalism, proving that state violence was no match for popular refusal. But this is not a book about Argentina or even Latin America as a whole, a brutal laboratory where neoliberalism was imposed in blood and fire. It's about a way of thinking that is also a doing, about what the concrete experience of rebellion teaches us about how the world moves, and how to turn that movement into thought. Find yourself in this book."

—**Geo Maher**, author of *A World Without Police* and *Spirals of Revolt*

"The 2001 uprising in Argentina is a major flashpoint in a wave of popular struggles that repudiated the neoliberal capitalist order and authored new forms of non-capitalist social construction. Colectivo Situaciones gives us important analyses of the uprising and its legacies, the roots of Argentina's financial and political crisis, and changes in contemporary forms of anticapitalist mobilization and resistance. Their close attention to grassroots practices of resistance, political organizing, and world-making is emblematic of their method of militant research, which itself has been an inspiration to so many. Those interested in contemporary social movements, political theory, and the history of Argentina and the region will find much to appreciate in this wonderful new edition. "

—**Jennifer S. Ponce de León**, author of *Another Aesthetics Is Possible: Arts of Rebellion in the Fourth World War*

"Why, more than two decades later, does the shouting '¡Qué se vayan todos!' still resonate in our minds and hearts? How did these new forms of organizing and organizations that emerged in the early 2000's change the way we understood democracy and made us believe that everything is possible? This book is a must read for the ones who are trying to understand not only the new cycle of collective action driven by movements that started twenty years ago, but who are also looking at the long path that since then—social movements in Argentina in particular and Latin America in general—has been walked until today. Memory can also be a space for resistance."

—**Marcela Olivera**, water commons organizer based in Cochabamba, Bolivia

19 AND 20

Brooklyn, NY

19 AND 20

NOTES FOR A NEW INSURRECTION

COLECTIVO SITUACIONES

Translated by Nate Holdren and Sebastián Touza

19 and 20: Notes for a New Insurrection
Colectivo Situaciones

Translated by Nate Holdren and Sebastián Touza
Afterword translated by Anna-Maeve Holloway
Edited by Jay Blair, Malav Kanuga, and Stevphen Shukaitis

This edition © 2021 Common Notions

19 y 20: Apuntes para el nuevo protagonismo social
Spanish language edition printed in Argentina in April 2002.
First edition released 2011 with Autonomedia and Minor Compositions

www.autonomedia.org | info@autonomedia.org
www.minorcompositions.info | minorcompositions@gmail.com

ISBN: 978-1-942173-48-9 (print)
ISBN: 978-1-942173-60-1 (eBook)
LCCN: 2021947331

Common Notions   Common Notions
c/o Interference Archive   c/o Making Worlds
314 7th Street   210 South 45th Street
Brooklyn, NY 11215   Philadelphia, PA 19104

www.commonnotions.org
info@commonnotions.org

Cover design by Morgan Buck / Antumbra Design www.antumbradesign.org
Layout design and typesetting by Morgan Buck and Margaret Killjoy

For Sebastian Touza, in loving memory amid grief and outrage

Printed in Canada

ACKNOWLEDGEMENTS

THE POLITICS OF THE QUOTATIONS AND INTERVENTIONS IN THIS BOOK are not innocent: through them, we have involved friends and compañeros, for whose thought and generosity we are thankful. Against our will, all the people who write here must be absolved of any responsibility other than being authors of the lines they sign. We would like to thank very specially María Pía López and Guillermo Korn, who devoted themselves to reading, revising, criticizing, and expanding the manuscripts of this work. To Florencia Lance for supervising, as always, every step of *Ediciones De Mano en Mano*. To Carlos "Cucho" Fernández, who nurtures and animates, with his aesthetic thinking and graphic art all the publications of this collective and to Lucía Scrimini for her longstanding collaboration and support, and to Diego Ortolani for his lucid presence. To the comrades of Colectivo Situaciones whose constant work make possible and valorize these initiatives. We also would like to note the circumstantial absence of Marcelo Matellanes who, nonetheless, is present here with his ideas.

ACKNOWLEDGEMENTS FOR ENGLISH EDITION

THIS TRANSLATION AND PUBLICATION WAS A LABOR OF LOVE THROUGH-out. There are many people without whom this would have never occurred, more than can be easily thanked. The editors and transla-tors offer our thanks to all our compañeros who have supported us. We thank the Colectivo Situaciones. We give particular thanks to the Institute for Anarchist Studies for the initial funding of the transla-tion. The intellectual interest and encouragement was equally impor-tant. Thanks to Jon Beasley-Murray for his comments. And thanks to the Micropolitics Research Group from Goldsmiths for organiz-ing the "Studies in Transversality I: Militant Research" gathering with Colectivo Situaciones in London (held October 12–16, 2009. Many comrades from the Aut-Op-Sy discussion list and the Notas Rojas col-lective contributed to this project in indirect but nonetheless mean-ingful ways. We thank as well Massimo De Angelis and everyone in-volved in the Commoner (www.commoner.org.uk), ephemera (www.ephemeraweb.org), Richard Day, Mark Coté, Greig de Peuter, Michael Hardt, Antonio Negri, Charles Weigl, the Free Association, and the Turbulence collective.

The translators wish to thank Malav Kanuga for his input and sup-port and to give particular thanks to Stevphen Shukaitis for his encour-agement, his engagement and work, and for his patience. We are espe-cially grateful to our partners Cecilia and Angelica. This project would not have happened if not for them, and this is only a tiny piece of what they have given us and for which we are endlessly grateful. We also wish to thank our children Matilda and Kit, born during the life of this project; we look forward to someday discussing these ideas with you.

CONTENTS

TRANSLATOR'S PREFACE

By Nate Holdren & Sebastián Touza

FOUR SPANISH WORDS BECAME PART OF THE UNIVERSAL LANGUAGE OF RE-
bellion after a multitude of Argentineans occupied the streets the evening
of December 19th 2001: *¡Que se vayan todos!* All of them out! The words
were thrown at every politician, functionary, economist, journalist and at
nobody in particular, by thousands of people banging pots and pans and
chanting in response to a state of siege declared by the government. The
following day, after three dozen had died in street fights with the police,
president Fernando de la Rúa resigned. The period opened by the revolt
was of intense social creativity. Hundreds of popular assemblies were created across the country. The unemployed workers movement, whose force
had been growing since 1996, acquired a new visibility. Many factories
and businesses that had gone bankrupt were taken by their workers and
began to run under their control. Several of these initiatives came together
forming circuits of trade based in solidarity principles helping to provide
the necessaries of life for the millions who had been marginalized from an
economy crippled by its servile obedience of the dictates of IMF inspectors.
The event cut a threshold in history, a before and an after for Argentina that
would find a wave of resonances around the world.

The revolt surprised analysts, always ready to judge the new with
reference to their old interpretive grids. But for many of its protagonists, it had long been foretold. Argentina had been one of the testing
grounds for neoliberalism since 1975, shortly before a dictatorship, initially commanded by General Jorge Videla, institutionalized the repression of revolutionary activism, while launching a package of economic
reforms that began undoing the labor rights and welfare state policies
that had been the result of decades of workers' struggles. Over 30,000
people were tortured, murdered, or disappeared by the regime.

After eight years of dictatorship electoral democracy finally returned in 1983. The repression and the military's large-scale process of

social engineering had been successful in demobilizing the population. Neoliberal reforms could now be imposed by consensus. In the 1990s, president Carlos Menem and his finance minister, Domingo Cavallo, in alliance with the labor bureaucracy, undertook sweeping structural adjustment reforms, privatizing nearly every state-run company at every level of government, deregulating labor and finance markets, pegging the peso to the dollar, and leaving nearly forty percent of the population unemployed or underemployed.

During the Menem era, a new generation of activists and new forms of protest slowly emerged. H.I.J.O.S., the organization of the children of the disappeared, came about in 1995 and introduced the practice of *escraches* creative forms of collective action denouncing the unpunished torturers of their often-revolutionary parents and preserving their memory. In 1996, unemployed workers began to protest blocking roads. Their multiple movements, known as *piqueteros*, spread throughout the country very quickly. All the attempts of the Peronist government to co-opt the movement proved unsuccessful. To find alternatives to the recession, barter clubs were created in different points of the country, giving rise to a massive underground economy based on the principle of solidarity.

In 1999 Fernando de la Rúa became president with a promise of change, but kept the neoliberal reforms intact in the name of preserving "governability." When the failure to repay the (now massive) foreign debt brought the national economy to the verge of collapse, de la Rúa recruited Cavallo. By July 2001, the pace of events had become dizzying. The numerous *piquetero* movements, which so far had acted mostly in isolation, started coordinating entire days of roadblocks throughout the vast Argentine geography. In the mid-term elections of October 2001 voters massively submitted spoiled ballots, and voter abstention rates were unprecedented. In November, Cavallo froze withdrawals from bank accounts to prevent a drain on reserves that would force the government to unpeg the peso from the dollar. People from all walks of life suddenly found themselves without money to meet their most basic needs. On December 19th, 2001, the people of Argentina took to the streets in protest.

Two years before that December, Colectivo Situaciones formed in Buenos Aires.* Previously they had been involved in El Mate, a student group notable for creating the Che Guevara Free Lectureship. The

---

* For a more detailed history of Colectivo Situaciones and the activist milieu in which the group came together see chapter 5 of Sebastian Touza's unpublished dissertation Antipedagogies for Liberation, http://summit.sfu.ca/item/8902 (accessed November 15, 2011).

Lecturship was an experiment oriented toward recuperating the memory of the generation of Argentinean and Latin American revolutionaries of the 1960s and 1970s that began at the faculty of social sciences at the University of Buenos Aires and quickly spread throughout several universities in Argentina and abroad.

Colectivo Situaciones came into being motivated by the search for a form of intervention and knowledge production that 'reads' struggles from within, trying to move away from the modalities established by both academia and traditional left politics. This method springs from the recognition that "…as much potential as thought and practice have, they cannot reach their full potential if not based in a concrete situation," as Colectivo Situaciones elaborated in an interview with Marina Sitrin.* Reading from within, they argue, "gives rise to what Gilles Deleuze said: 'creation as resistance, resistance as creation.'" Situaciones regards itself as "an experience of resistance and creation, to create resisting in the area of thought, linked to practice." The two days of street fighting on the 19ᵗʰ and 20ᵗʰ and the alternative forms of life that appeared afterward—including neighborhood assemblies and factory occupations—formed such a concrete situation, revealing what Colectivo Situaciones calls the thought of the multiple, a form of thinking of the multitude that rejects all centralized forms of power.

In the immediate aftermath of the December events, Colectivo Situaciones began to write this book, which lays bare some of the core values and principles Colectivo Situaciones invoke in their definition of themselves as militants. This has led us to reflect on our role as translators and made us want share with the reader our urge to dispel any mythical (mis)understanding of the transparency of language. We share Colectivo Situaciones' conviction that abstraction inevitably impoverishes experience. Translation adds one more layer of abstraction. In this sense, we assume the full significance of the Italian adage *traduttore, traditore*. Every translation is a betrayal of a sort. Awareness of that is central to our attempt to keep faith with the concrete situation in which the experience being communicated unfolds. In a way, the perspective of Situaciones is against a certain idea of a book offering something, but the book does make an offer. What the book offers is less a matter of directions or recipes and more along the lines of a handshake or a letter. The book offers a look at how some people have made sense of important events in their locations, and asks that readers seek to act in

---

* Marina Sitrin, "The Shock of the New: An Interview with Colectivo Situaciones," translated by Chuck Morse and Marina Sitrin, *Perspectives on Anarchist Theory*, Fall 2003.

their own locations. In the rest of this introduction, we detail some of the difficulties we had in doing the translation, in the effort to bring the reader closer to the work of Colectivo Situaciones.*

A number of Colectivo Situaciones' core concepts posed translation difficulties. For instance, the term *militancia de investigacion*. This phrase can be translated into English as either "research militancy" or "militant research." We do not mean to take words too seriously (always a risk in translation) but these two expressions bear reflection. "Militant research" implies continuity with other examples of militant research.** "Research militancy" may sound strange to the English speaker's ear and it is less immediately clear what the term means.

The grammatical difference between these two phrases is a matter of which word defines the activity and which word qualifies it; which word will be the predicate of the other. There seems to be more than a difference of emphasis. Does the Spanish phrase refer to knowledge production that happens to be radical in some way (militant research)? Or does it refer to radical activism that happens to take the form of knowledge production (research-militancy)?

In our indecision, we asked Colectivo Situaciones which expression they felt more comfortable with. To our surprise—or perhaps not, given their penchant for refusing simple answers—the response was "both." "We think of our practice as a double movement: to create ways of being militants that escape established a priori political certainties and embrace politics as research (in this case, it would be 'research militancy'), and at the same time, to invent forms of thinking and producing concepts that reject academic procedures, breaking away from the image of an object to be known and putting at the center subjective experience (in this case, it would be 'militant research')."

---

* We feel compelled to note that this book draws on a range of thinkers too numerous to mention. Among the more important in shaping the work of Situaciones are Alain Badiou, Miguel Benasayag, Gilles Deleuze, and Jacques Rancière. Some readers will be familiar with these and other figures. We insist, however that Colectivo Situaciones do not simply apply the thought of others. They think and in doing so they reconfigure concepts. This is fundamentally what they offer to and ask of readers. As such, we do not provide an overview of the theorists whose work informs this book. Indeed, contributing to an academic dialog among adherents of great individual theorists would be among the least interesting things that could be done with this book.

** See for instance Stevphen Shukaitis and David Graeber, Eds. (2007) *Constituent Imagination: Militant Investigations // Collective Theorization.* Oakland: AK Press.

The Argentinean social landscape in which the men and women of Situaciones forged their ideas early on was a desert swept by neoliberal winds, in which only a few movements of resistance could stand up by themselves. Those were times in which dilettante post-modern thinkers had come to the conclusion that social change was a relic from the past and in which people involved in politics could only see their activity through rarely questioned models. Research militancy was a response to the need to rebuild the links between thought and the new forms of political involvement that were rapidly becoming part of the Argentinean reality.

In "On Method," the prologue to *La Hipotesis 891*, a book Colectivo Situaciones wrote together with the unemployed workers' movement of Solano, the authors distinguish research militancy from three other relations to knowledge: academic research, political activism, and humanitarianism.* Academic research inevitably reifies those it constructs as objects. Academics cannot help leaving outside the scope of their investigation the function of attributing meaning, values, interests, and rationalities of the subject who does the research. Universities require this of academic research and academic researchers. Traditional political activists involved in parties or party-like organizations usually hold that their commitment and involvement makes their relation to knowledge more advanced than the work done by academics. But their activity is no less objectifying, in the sense that it approaches struggles from a previously constituted knowledge framework. Struggles are thus regarded not for their value in themselves, but rather in terms of their contribution to something other than themselves—the coming socialist or communist society. A third figure, the humanitarian activist, also relates to others in an instrumental fashion—in the justification and funding of NGOs (nongovernmental organizations)—and takes the world as static, not subject to being radically changed (thus, the best one can hope for is the alleviation of the worst abuses).

Research militancy does not distinguish between thinking and doing politics. Insofar as we see thought as the thinking/doing activity that de-poses the logic by which existing models acquire meaning, this kind of thinking is immediately political. And, if we see politics as the struggle for freedom and justice, all politics involves thinking, because there are forms of thinking against established models implicit

---

* MTD of Solano and Colectivo Situaciones. *Hipótesis 891: Más Allá de los Piquetes*. Buenos Aires: De Mano en Mano, 2002. [Hypothesis 891: Beyond the Roadblocks] An updated version of this passage appears as an article in the book *Utopian Pedagogy*, edited by Richard Day, Mark Coté, and Greig de Peuter (Toronto: University of Toronto Press, 2007).

in every radical practice—a thought people carry out with their bodies. Movements think. Struggles embody thought.

This brings us to a second translational and conceptual difficulty. Colectivo Situaciones have much to say about and with two Spanish words *poder* and *potencia*. Unfortunately, both translate as the English word "power." Generally speaking, we could say that *poder* expresses power as "power over" (the sense it has, for instance, when it refers to state or sovereign power) and *potencia* is defined as "power to," the type of capacity expressed in the statement "I can."* To continue with the generalization, it is possible to say that *poder* refers to static forms of power, while *potencia* refers to its dynamic forms. *Potencia* always exists in the here and now; it coincides with the act in which it is effected. This is because *potencia* is inseparable from our capacity—indeed, our bodies' capacity—to be affected, individually and collectively. This capacity cannot be detached from the moment, place, and concrete social relations in which *potencia* manifests itself. This means that anything said about *potencia* is necessarily an abstraction. Whatever is said or communicated about it can never be the *potencia* itself. Communication of and about *potencia* might then be said to require an indirectness and a literary quality. Description and narration may allow us to approach *potencia* in a side-winding manner whereas a direct approach leaves *potencia* always receding, like the horizon.

Since research militancy is concerned with the expansion of *potencia*, a simple descriptive presentation of its techniques would necessarily lead to an abstraction. Such a description might produce a "method" in which all the richness of the *potencia* of research militancy in the situation is trimmed off to leave only that part whose utilitarian value makes it immediately transferable to other situations. The thought of practices is thought with the body, because bodies encounter each other in acts that immediately define their mutual capacities to be affected. Miguel Benasayag argues that act and state—to which correspond *potencia* and *poder*—are two levels of thought and life.** None of them can be sub-

---

* For further discussion of this distinction see John Holloway, *Change the World Without Taking Power* (London: Pluto Press, 2002). Translators of works by French and Italian philosophers inspired by Spinoza usually run into similar difficulties. See the translator's introduction written by Michael Hardt in Antonio Negri, *The Savage Anomaly: The Power of Spinoza's Metaphysics and Politics* (Minneapolis: University of Minnesota Press, 1991).

** Miguel Benasayag, a former member of the Argentinean Guevarist guerrilla army PRT-ERP, is now philosopher and activist residing in Paris. He participates in the collective Malgré Tout and played an important role in the early life of Colectivo Situaciones.

sumed under the other. Either one takes the side of *potencia* or the side of *poder* (or of the desire for *poder*, as expressed in militants who want to "take power," build The Party, construct hegemonies, etc.).

Potencias found in different forms of resistance are the foundation of "counterpower," but the terms are not the same. Counterpower indicates a point of irreversibility in the development of resistance, a moment when the principal task becomes to develop and secure what has been achieved by the struggle. Counterpower is diffuse and multiple. It displaces the question of power from the centrality it has historically enjoyed, because its struggle is "against the powers such as they act in our situations" (*La Hipotesis 891*). To be on the side of *potencia* is to recognize that the state and the market originate at the level of the values we embrace and the bonds that connect us to others.

Potencia defines the material dimension of the encounter of bodies, while *poder* is a level characterized by idealization, representation, and normalization. Colectivo Situaciones avoid a name to define their political identity, which would fail to convey the fluid multiplicity of militant research. "We are not autonomists, Situationists, or anything ending with ist," they once told us. Identities have normalizing effects: they establish models, they place multiplicity under control, they reduce the multiple dimensions of life to the one dimension of an idealization. They make an exception with *Guevarism*, because in their view Che Guevara preferred to stay on the side of *potencia* and opposed those who calmed down concrete struggles in the name of ideal recipes on how to achieve a communist society.* This preference also reflects Situaciones roots in the experiences of El Mate as we described above.

An investigation into the forms of *potencia* and the social relations that produce it can only be done from a standpoint that systematically embraces doubt and ignorance. If we recognize that the practical thought of struggles is an activity of bodies, we have to recognize again that nobody knows what a body can do. To do research in the realm of *potencia*—to investigate that which is alive and multiple—militant researchers have to abandon their previous certainties, their desire to encounter pure subjects, and the drive to recuperate those subjects' practice as an ideal of coherence and consistency. In this regard, we can say that Colectivo Situaciones seek to concretely embody two Zapatista slogans: "asking we walk," and "we make the road by walking," such that, the act of questioning and collective reflection is part of the process of constructing power. It bears mentioning as well that this process and practice of research, if

---

*   See Miguel Benasayag and Diego Sztulwark. *Política y Situación: De la potencia al contrapoder* (Buenos Aires: Ediciones de Mano en Mano, 2000), p. 217-21.

successful, will find little success in the commercial and academic capitalist marketplaces of ideas. The degree to which institutions of capitalist society begin to recognize and reward militant researchers would be the degree to which militant research would become less important for radicals.

Research militancy is a form of intervention, a practice that accompanies other practices, or *experiencias*. This is our third translation difficulty. Colectivo Situaciones, like many other activists belonging to the wave of new protagonism in Argentina, uses the word *experiencia* to refer to singular, more or less organized groups, with flexible boundaries, involved in an ongoing emancipatory practice. Examples of *experiencias* with whom Colectivo Situaciones have practiced research militancy include H.I.J.O.S. (the human rights group formed by children of the disappeared),* MoCaSE (a campesino group), and MTD of Solano (a movement within the larger *piquetero* movement, formed mainly by unemployed workers), Grupo de Arte Callejero (a street art group that works very close to H.I.J.O.S), the educational community Creciendo Juntos (a free school run by militant teachers), and a number of other *experiencias* in Argentina, Bolivia, Uruguay, and Mexico. The word *experiencia* connotes both *experience*, in the sense of accumulation of knowledges of resistance, and *experiment*, understood as a practice that is both creative and exploratory. In the book, when the word *experiencia* has this double connotation we have translated it as *experience/experiment*.

We keep these words together because we find it important to keep present the experiential dimension to which the word *experiencia* makes reference. An *experiencia* can have territorial characteristics, such as MTD of Solano, whose roots were in a shanty town located in the south of greater Buenos Aires, or it can be more deterritorialized, like Colectivo Situaciones. But in all cases, *experiencias* are defined by a certain form of life, a particular quest to redefine the bonds that form that group of people as a collective, and to redefine these bonds in such ways that they produce, in that situation, social relations that are superior to those of capitalism. The construction of a noncapitalist sociability is a key activity for the *experiencias* Colectivo Situaciones works with. For MTD of Solano, for instance, the production of subjective bonds that are different from those of the state and the market was a defining moment of their concept of autonomy. The material basis of support for both the market and the state are the bonds produced at the local level. Thus, one of their most important activities of self-reflection involves the critique of individualist values, contractual relations, and the instrumentalization

---

* See *Genocide in the Neighborhood*, by Colectivo Situaciones (translated by Brian Whitener), Chain Links, 2010.

of life as they appear at the most basic and concrete level. It is here, on the same level, in the same time and space, that *potencia* exists. There are certain types of social bonds that make *potencia* stronger. Others make it weaker. The research militancy theorized and practiced by Colectivo Situaciones is committed to producing bonds at that concrete level and weaving them in such way that they allow for maximum *potencia*.

Militant research as practice aims at amplifying the elements of a non-capitalist sociability. This requires Colectivo Situaciones to develop a particular type of relation with the groups and movements they work with. Following Spinoza, Colectivo Situaciones calls this relation "composition." Composition does not refer to agreements established at a discursive level but to the multidimensional flows of affect and desire that relationships put in motion. Thus, research militancy becomes immanent to the *experiencias* it works with. This concrete relation is not something one achieves on one's own by thinking and writing in isolation; it is not achieved through conscious understanding, but by a collective process of becoming open to the dynamics of affect that define the possibility of *potencia* in the situation.

Here, Colectivo Situaciones moves away from a certain truism pervasive in much of contemporary activist culture, both in Argentina and in North America: the idea that a certain type of communication (be it the use of the Internet, grassroots filmmaking, or any other medium) has an inherent emancipatory effect on people. Communication produces abstractions of experience. Experiences can only be lived. Even though there is *potencia*, for instance, in the activism that carries out grassroots communication experiments, the *potencia* such as it exists in the situation cannot be communicated. In this sense, perhaps Colectivo Situaciones would agree with the thesis put forward by Michael Hardt and Antonio Negri, according to which there is no circulation of struggles.* Except that, for Colectivo Situaciones, this is not just the case for this point in history. Struggles do not communicate their *potencia*, they never did and they never will. There is, however, the possibility of resonances between struggles and points of resistance, but that is something entirely different. There are resonances between struggles when there are "shared epochal problems" and they face similar obstacles, making possible the transference of "certain knowledges, feelings, and declarations." Thus, there could be resonances between, for instance, Argentinean *piqueteros* and migrant workers in Western Europe, even if there is no actual exchange of words between them.**

---

* Michael Hardt and Antonio Negri. *Empire* (Cambridge, Mass. And London, U.K.: Harvard University Press, 2000), pp. 52-9.

** For a discussion of the notion of resonance see John Holloway, "Dignity's

Colectivo Situaciones makes a crucial distinction between the abstract perspective of "global thinking," and the thought of the situation, for which the experiential dimension is the concrete form of existence of the world. Here, as the Malgré Tout Collective puts it, the choice is clear: either world or situation.* The global standpoint is one in which we look at the world as spectators, the mass-mediated outlook that turns us into concerned individuals, concerned about issues that come to us only as representations. The constricted sphere of the situation, however, is one whose configuration we are responsible for. We produce and are produced by the situations we inhabit. Either our practices are those of the individual-spectator, and thus keep in place certain values, bonds, and affects that reproduce the centrality of state power and the pervasiveness of market relations, or we are the persons in situations who are open to producing and maintaining the bonds that assemble a different, noncapitalist sociability.

Research militancy takes an immanent commitment to the situation. The situation, as Colectivo Situaciones understands it, is a space and time that defines its own meanings and subtracts itself from the meanings produced by the state and the market. The working hypotheses of research militants are direct elaborations on the exigencies of the situation. In contrast with the academic researcher, the traditional militant, and the humanitarian activist, who are "extra-situational," the militant researcher thinks and acts in the situation.

There is a challenge at the heart of militant research, which we share in our attempt to introduce this book to others. How to write about the *potencia* of an experience/experiment knowing that its *potencia* will not be transferred in the writing? What kind of writing can at least look for resonances? Certainly, not a writing that presents itself as a blueprint, as an outline, as a forecast. A writing like this has to be antipedagogical. Militant

---

Revolt," in Holloway, John and Eloína Peláez *Zapatista! Reinventing Revolution in Mexico*(London: Pluto Press, 1998), and the essays in The Free Association, *Moments of Excess: Movements, Protests, and Everyday Life*(Oakland: PM Press, 2011).

* "Manifeste," Collectif Malgré Tout. Available online at http://1libertaire. free.fr/malgretout02.html (English translation http://es.scribd.com/ doc/49144478/Manifiesto-Malgre-Tout-final-pdf). In 1999, El Mate (Colectivo Situaciones had not appeared yet), Malgré Tout, Mothers of Plaza de Mayo, along with other collectives from Latin America and Europe, gathered in Buenos Aires to form the Network of Alternative Resistance. Their joint declaration outlines several of the principles of Colectivo Situaciones' philosophy. An English translation can be found in this website: www.voiceoftheturtle.org/library/nar_manifesto.php

research does not teach, at least not in the sense of an explication which assumes the stupidity and powerlessness of those to whom it explains.* Research militancy is a composition of wills, an attempt to create what Spinoza called joyful passions, which starts from and increases the power (*potencia*) of everyone involved. Such a perspective is only possible by admitting from the beginning that one does not have answers, and, by doing so, abandoning the desire to lead others or be seen as an expert.

As translators we have been inspired in part by the work of Red Notes in the 1970s, which translated news, analysis, theory, and agitational materials from Italian social movements of the time. The earliest English translation of writers like Antonio Negri were carried out by Red Notes, not for prestige or pay but in the effort to enrich cycles of struggles by trying to contribute to a resonance with other struggles. We would like to think that our translation of this book is in the same spirit. We believe that this book is a significant resource for all of us who live within (and despite) our current moment, as well as for understanding the important events of December 2001. These are not distinct: navigating the opportunities and challenges within a moment of crisis is aided greatly by immersing one's self in the details of other such moments, though as we discuss above, this is much more a matter of resonance than of direct transmission. That conviction about the importance of resonance between struggles, and the view that the events described in this book are a particularly important resource for people in struggle, is what led us to translate this book.

The work of the Colectivo Situaciones has much to offer radicals around the world, in terms of the content of their political views, their philosophical views, and their efforts at engaging with the intellectual life of movements in an attempt to help movements enrich their own collective abilities to think independently. For ourselves we can say that Colectivo's work has been formative to our intellectual and political outlooks. We have been tremendously gratified over the past few years to see other translations of Situaciones' writings appear and we would like to think we played some role in encouraging these translations. There is much left untranslated, however, by Colectivo Situaciones certainly as well as numerous other authors. We urge others to take up the tasks of translating radical texts, despite barriers posed of professional

---

* On this point Colectivo Situaciones are strongly influenced by the work of Jacques Rancière, a figure who has become quite important to our own thought via Situaciones' influence. We highly recommend Rancière, *The Ignorant Schoolmaster: Five Lessons In Intellectual Emancipation*, Stanford University Press, 1991.

qualification (or lack thereof), academic publishing markets, intimidation, or anything else. Segmentation of struggles by language weakens all of us. Colectivo Situaciones refer to an adage from the philosopher Spinoza, "nobody knows what a body can do." The same applies of translation. Radicals have greater abilities to translate than they think they do; more people should use that ability. It is our fervent hope that doing so, that circulating materials produced by one cycle of struggles can increase the collective ability to do that resides, repressed, among the networks of all exploited and oppressed people globally.

We have tried in this preface to take responsibility for the singular perspective each translation implies. Any definitive reading is a matter of force or authority, because words and ideas and writings are open fields subject to multiple uses. Single meanings and monopolies of uses are only ever the product of power relationships; they are not inherent to texts. This applies to translators and to authors' own understanding of their work. In this sense, no translation is definitive. Every translation is *a* reading. In closing this preface we would like to argue that a certain reversal of this statement is also true: every reading from a perspective of *potencia* is *a* translation.* Ten years after Argentina's 19th and 20th, dozens of destituting revolts have taken place around the world, from Iceland's pot and pan bangers, to the Arab Spring in North Africa, to the Spanish Indingados, and the Occupy movement in different cities around the world. In our view these movements have proceeded via a logic of resonance, in a fashion which Colectivo Situaciones describes. We hope this translation will inspire some people involved in those movements. Doing so will require that readers will create their own translation of our translation. In our view, being conscious and aware of this re-translation effort to be the best way to avoid an abstract, codified appropriation of this book which might establish dead equivalences between the struggles in Argentina ten years ago and those of today. The reading that looks for resonances is not an act of communication between struggles, but one of translation in situation. In this sense, the greatest fidelity to the struggles discussed in this book can be kept only if any possible stabilization of the meanings produced by the Argentine struggles is avoided. To translate a translation involves the difficult but fundamental act of establishing connections and convergences not between words, but between *potencias*.

---

*   On this view of translation see Colectivo Situaciones and Sandro Mezzadra, "Gubernamentalidad: frontera, código y retóricas del orden," in Colectivo Situaciones (ed.) *Conversaciones en el impasse: dilemas políticos del presente.* Buenos Aires: Tinta Limón, 2009.

We have lived a long time with this translation. We began it several years ago when the events of December 2001, were still fresh. We had hoped to see this book finished and into the hands of like-minded readers much sooner. There is an uncomfortable irony in our slow process translating a book written rapidly in the heat of the moment shortly after that December. Since then the world has seen several cycles of struggles and much instability in the capitalist system. In our view these cycles and crises, with their tensions between repetition of departure from past patterns, make this book still relevant to the present.

We have had much time—perhaps too much!—to ponder what this book asks of and offers to readers. What this book asks and offers is fundamentally political. It will be clear by now that we as translators believe there is much that is important about the work of Colectivo Situaciones. In particular, we share with them a political outlook, one that does not want to replicate itself or accrue followers, like a party line. It is not a matter of receiving correct ideas that they transmit, as if copying recipes from a cookbook. Rather, it is a matter of learning to recognize and amplify the *potencia* in our own situations, and so to act in a way that resonates with the practice of Colectivo Situaciones. This means that it is not up to us or to anyone to dictate what is to be done with this book. At the same time, lest this laissez-faire attitude give a misleading impression, one thing must be made clear: this book was written by militants, during and about a process of tremendous upheaval and possibility. The book is not an attempt to break into the niche market of academic publishing, or the unpaid labor market of traditional activist organizations. Of course, as a book that is political and theoretical it must attempt to engage with and navigate both of these arenas, for the alternatives are few and far between. The book does not seek to build commitment or convince anyone. It assumes militancy as its starting point. This book was written by militants who want to understand and in the process to build, to construct relationships with others, other militants, with whom to think and attempt to mutually enrich attempts at acting in specific contexts. If this introduction and this translation facilitate such processes then we will count our efforts as successful.

* * *

Sebastián Touza died from COVID-19 in April 2021. Magdalena Day, a student and collaborator of Sebastián's at Facultad de Ciencias Políticas y Sociales, National University of Cuyo (Mendoza, Argentina) offers these words:

Sebastián Touza was a researcher, a teacher, a brilliant intellectual, and the warmest human being. In the last years he was concerned with how our attention is increasingly diminished in the digital world of social media, and with the micropolitics of desire in cybercapitalism. His Sociology of Technology seminar, taught in 2016 with Cecilia Díaz Isenrath, showed us what a privilege it was to have him in Argentina, and especially in Mendoza, his hometown. Nevertheless, what made him so important for many of us was that he gave space in his research groups to what you might call "outsiders": anyone from developers and digital experts to educators and biologists would meet social scientists for an analysis of technology.

He indirectly invited some of us to deconstruct our own labor as digital workers starting a path in research—in a smooth manner, as he would never dictate a course of action. We talked on several occasions about creating a structure that would address all our diversity and needs as doctoral students. There was, and there still is, the problem of the tough conditions for anyone interested in having a life aligned with intellectual labor. He wasn't in a hurry to give shape to such a structure, but he would always invite everyone to participate as he didn't look for power and wasn't interested in hierarchies. Nevertheless, he was the person with whom we all would talk about this. We naturally gravitated towards him due to his generosity and his consistency as a committed thinker. After his passing, I understood that his vision was rather rhizomatic: yes, it was a challenge to generate a common ground for thought, but why would you give a name or any kind of form to affective relations constituted around ideas? After all, those of us grieving and missing him right now found an open door, a mentor, and a friend in Sebastián without even asking.

Sebastian believed deeply that a better world was possible and dedicated himself to that belief as an intellectual and a militant, a pair of terms he was not comfortable in either conflating or separating. The virus and the fucking system that made the virus a pandemic robbed him of getting to see that world, and stole Sebastian from his family, friends, students, and comrades— who loved him dearly. We are all poorer for his passing. He leaves behind a rich repository of thinking, both in the objectified form of the words he committed to the page as a writer and translator, and in the living form of the relationships he helped knit together and the individuals whose lives he enriched. Our hope is that this book continues to serve that knitting. This new edition is dedicated to his memory and to the renewal of the project of destroying the world that stole him from us.

PREFACE TO THE FIRST EDITION

by Michael Hardt

"COME TO ARGENTINA," A EUROPEAN FRIEND URGED ME IN EARLY 2002, "it's the Paris Commune of our generation!" The insurrection that had exploded a month earlier was the wide social expression of both economic protest—against the neoliberal paradigm—and political unrest. The rebellion was aimed against not a single political figure or party but rather the whole political class and the entire political system: "que se vayan todos" (all of them must go) was an emblematic slogan of those days. The revolt overthrew one government after another and cast the entire political system in crisis. And even more inspiring than the intensity and radicalism of the revolt were the new practices of protest and experiments in democratic organizing that were woven together throughout the society. While the poor and unemployed paralyzed cities with pickets and large segments of the middle class banged pots and pans in protest, large assemblies formed as new decision-making structures, barter systems spread, workers occupied and ran themselves factories set to close, amid myriad other original experiments. Argentina had become a laboratory to test new forms of insurrection and democracy, indignation and autonomy, refusal and self-government.

Well, if the insurrection in Argentina that began in December 2001 was our Paris Commune, then Colectivo Situaciones fits well in the position of Karl Marx. As Friedrich Engels was fond of saying, one of Marx's many talents was to analyze the historical importance of political events as they took place. This book by Colectivo Situaciones, written in the heat of action, certainly demonstrates that same talent in full, delving into the complexity of concrete events while simultaneously stepping back to recognize how our political reality has changed. The authors give us not only an excellent historical introduction to and examination of what happened in Argentina during these months but also, and perhaps more importantly, an investigation of what kinds of political subjectivities we could become now, in its aftermath. This new political situation did not begin suddenly on the 19th and 20th of December 2001, but perhaps it was revealed more clearly then. And it is by no means isolated to Argentina or even Latin America but extends well beyond.

One of the novelties of our era that Colectivo Situaciones emphasizes is the potential of a new political subjectivity. Being represented in government is not the best we can hope for. "Our dreams do not fit in their ballot boxes" according to another slogan of the times. In the insurrection emerged instead horizontally organized subjectivities that insisted on not being represented by politicians but maintaining and developing their own powers of political expression. These subjectivities did not spring forth from nothing in the days of revolt, the authors explain, but rather were prepared in the work of numerous groups across Argentine society. The insurrection gave them an extraordinary acceleration, brought them together and consolidated them. It is important to recognize too that this multitude was not formed spontaneously but rather grew through a wide variety of organizational experiments.

It is appropriate, then, that the analysis of these events comes to us not from a single Karl Marx but a multiplicity of voices. Colectivo Situaciones are masters of collaborative writing. All of their books are expansive in the sense that they engage the voices of others through what they call militant research. This kind of collaboration and research starts from a position of humility: listening to and respecting the intelligence and power of expression of others. But these expressions are always put to the test by and linked together with the intelligence and voices of the members of Colectivo Situaciones. In this book to the plurality internal to their own writing collective they add chapters written in collaboration with an elected politician, university professors, and an activist organization of the unemployed. The different expressions are organized not as point and counterpoint, as if constructing a debate but rather as a chorus of distinct but overlapping voices. Form follows content: only such a plural method of writing can grasp the potential of an emerging plural political subjectivity.

Another wonderful quality of this book, which I admire in all the writings of Colectivo Situaciones, is the ability to bring together some of the most complex and abstract theoretical analyses with the most immediate, practical concerns. In their hands the work of not only Karl Polanyi but also Michel Foucault and even Baruch Spinoza carry real importance in debates in the streets. This is not really the unity of theory and practice, which so many have longed for. Instead Colectivo Situaciones has a remarkable capacity to listen for and understand theoretical interventions at widely different levels. They know that the kinds of theoretical reflections that go on in social movements are just as intense and valuable as those in university classrooms; and they know that political activists without university degrees are just as intelligent and capable of political reasoning as their better educated comrades. But this does not lead them either to a stance against professional intellectuals. Instead they manage to hold the two levels of political thinking together, forming a bridge that allows them to communicate. And what results are some of the richest and most satisfying political arguments. This kind of multi-level theorizing would not be possible without Colectivo Situaciones' extraordinary talents for collaboration.

So, today, ten years after the events analyzed in this book, was my friend right that it was our Paris Commune? I know, historical analogies like this end up distorting the present, as if we always have to measure up with the past. But they do help us sometimes get a new perspective. Like the Paris Commune, the insurrection in Argentina was an explosion of political creativity and experimentation with new forms of democracy, and like the Paris Commune it was defeated. The defeat in Argentina was not as swift and bloody as it was for the Communards. Two and a half years after the insurrection began a stable representative government was in place and the organizations and new social forms described in this book were slowly diluted and sucked back into the dominant political system. But also like the Commune, this seeming defeat turned out to be a victory of sorts. The new political subjectivities formed in such moments of social creativity do not disappear but transform over long periods and eventually find new outlets of expression.

More generally I would say that the 2001 insurrection in Argentina was one of the events that inaugurated a decade of extraordinary political creativity in Latin America as a whole. Throughout the continent powerful social movements and explosive revolts overthrew neoliberal governments and led to the election of progressive governments, which at times have recuperated the energies of and, at others, have been contested by those same social movements. The multitudinous political subjectivities analyzed by Colectivo Situaciones at the beginning of the decade were the protagonists of this entire adventure. Perhaps defeat and victory, then, are not the right terms here. What seems more central to me is the possibility of a new form of political subjectivity that Colectivo Situaciones grasp in the tumult of the events. That potential has only grown over the past decade, as we have seen in the rebellions and democratic experiments across Latin America, which have served as inspiration for others throughout the world. In this respect, the process that Colectivo Situaciones saw opening in the insurrection has still not been closed. The subjectivities in struggle they recognized emerging—a powerful multitude capable of autonomy, horizontal organization, and democratic expression—still today define the horizon of our political potential. Those days in December 2001 are not yet really finished and past, but rather form an essential part of the living political history of our present.

PREFACE TO THE SECOND EDITION

By Marcello Tarì

19 AND 20: NOTES FOR A NEW INSURRECTION REMAINS A "CLASSIC" IN THE revolutionary literature of recent decades. What is a classic? It is many things, but especially it is a work that expresses a certain truth of the time and a truth, however small it may be, always contributes to changing reality. As far as the last twenty years are concerned, it seems to me that of the texts that have marked in depth an alternative interpretation of contemporary history and that have acted within movements as propellers of practical imagination, we can remember three: *Empire* by Michael Hardt and Antonio Negri, which actually closes the decade of the 1990s and the parable of what was called the antiglobalization movement; *19 and 20* by Colectivo Situaciones, which was born from an insurrection that inaugurated a new cycle of world struggles whose motives have not yet been consummated; *The Coming Insurrection* of the Invisible Committee, which stands as the heir of the previous cycle and at the same time as its implacable critic, relaunching the conflict on a level as much material as metaphysical.

The fact that the last two books are signed not by their own names but by a collective or a committee is a first revealing sign of what had changed in the transition to the 2000s and had been preparing for some time, both as a way of doing theory and as a strategic indication. As far as the first question is concerned—theoretical reflection—that is, the "logical" conclusions of Foucauldian and Deleuzian propositions were being drawn, already developed by Maurice Blanchot and which, in reality, go back to the first romanticism of *Athenaeum*, on the problematic nature of the author's function and on focusing on the event instead of the subject. In this case it means that a book that comes from within a movement, that reflects on the world from that position and succeeds in expressing a truth, is an event of thought that increases everyone's power to act, therefore it is an impersonal force that interprets and crystallizes the intensities that circulate among people in a given historical moment, rather than the product of one or more individuals. I think this is particularly valid for periods in which there are great telluric movements at work in the world that require from those who think inside them particular forms of asceticism, including the renunciation of one's name and face. Once the movement has passed or been reabsorbed, people generally return to producing their texts individually and signing them with their own names.

As far as strategy is concerned, proceeding without proper names or organizations but as lines of intensification of a collective process, this is an indication that came directly from the struggles and that Colectivo Situaciones was able to synthesize very effectively in their writing. It is not about anonymity as a reference to "clandestinity" but a gesture of deposition of the traditional figures of politics, even revolutionary ones. Today it is something taken for granted that the great movements are "leaderless," as for example we can easily see with regard to the Gilet Jaunes in France or #blacklivesmatter in the United States, but during the antiglobalization movement it was not like that at all.

Colectivo Situaciones, from the materiality of the piqueteros' organization, understood that the only way for a leadership to exist in the movement is in being something fleeting, anonymous, temporary and reversible—a radically *situational* leadership, thus allowing multiplicity, the quality that effectively defines a movement, to persist, spread and deepen, instead of being disciplined and emptied through centralized and personalized representation. From then on, no one can *represent* anyone else.

The other lesson of the Argentine insurrection that Colectivo Situaciones delivered to the movements is in fact the critique of centralization, which was one of the main legacies of Marxism and especially Leninism, preferring to it the notion of the "diffuse network," which does not operate through a command from the center that goes to the other nodes but spreads by *resonance*—through events, meetings, and compositions of various kinds that allow the composition of the movement to go "from the dispersed to the multiple," without the need to create a false organicity of the whole. I believe that these are irreversible acquisitions for movements, even if there is still a great need for experimentation in order to understand how to properly avoid the volatility that often afflicts the compositions that are created during periods of struggle and that often fail to last beyond it. And again, to experiment with how to recognize the authority of a situational or community leadership without ever confusing it with a power structure, and on this point I believe that the reflections of Italian feminism of difference (from Carla Lonzi to Luisa Muraro) have developed some very interesting proposals. Unlike power, in fact, according to Muraro, authority is not based on the violence of law but on the strength of the symbolic, not on command but on relationship, it does not have an external but an internal foundation: authority as a "mystical force" that expresses itself through words and gestures.* In order to give an archetypal example, Muraro points to the mother-child relationship, and it is inevitable to think of the role of the Mothers of Plaza de Mayo in the Argentina of those years, but we could also mention that of friendship. That which is created and binds us in a common truth.

At the heart of the elaboration of Colectivo Situaciones was the concept of "destituent insurrection" which, as I have already written, was not properly understood at the time of the book's publication.** It was only after the worldwide explosion of the 2007–2008 crisis and the subsequent uprisings that the paradigm of *destitution* reached its readability. Among the reasons for that prophetic anticipation there is the devastating financial crisis of Argentina in 2001. Argentina was the laboratory in which neoliberalism experimented on a local level what a few years later would differently affect our entire global space. At the same time, Argentina was also the laboratory of new forms of resistance and antagonism that over the years have emerged everywhere in the world. To give an example, the "flow blockade" would perhaps never have become a technique of global struggle if there had not been the example of the piqueteros. It is also very important that Colectivo Situaciones defines the destituent insurrection as the opening of a field of possibilities because it allows us to think of destitution not so much as a new paradigm of "politics," that is, as the management of the existing, but as a power that proceeds from the imagination of the masses, an imagination that operates by destructing the old forms of politics as well as of everyday existence, acting in particular on temporality, that

---

*   Luisa Muraro, *Autorità* (Turin, Itlay: Rosemberg and Sellier, 2013)

**   See Marcello Tarì, *There Is No Unhappy Revolution* (Brooklyn, NY: Common Notions, 2021)

is, transforming not only the present but also the past and the future.

In any case, the slogan of the Argentinean insurrection, ¡Qué se vayan todos, *que no quede ni uno solo!* has become in these twenty years the slogan of every revolt, of every insurrection, of every movement that has set itself as an interruption of the catastrophic course of the present state of affairs, and remains an exceptional document of the desire and determination that are proper to every people that finds their dignity.

"The unfolding of popular powers in the city actualized the recurrent image of the commune."* In this way Colectivo Situaciones, which reasoned from the popular practices that spread in those years in the Argentine metropolis, gave us a question that today is probably the most urgent, necessary, and strategic: namely, the question of the *commune*. It is wrong however to think of it as a simple and repeated citation of the Paris Commune and its theoretical interpretations: the current references of a commune are also multiple, both historically and geographically. But especially they respond to different existential needs.

I believe that the commune is *the* main theme today, since the global pandemic, among other things, has definitively shown how and to what extent "society" is something extremely abstract, incapable by definition of being a place of sharing, mutual aid, and popular organization. The "parties," for their part, are by now nothing more than the crystallization of private interests and their politics are synonymous with corruption and insensitivity. But the *commune,* precisely, can no longer be understood as "the finally discovered political form" of the government of the people or of the workers, as Marxism wanted, since it too functions first and foremost as a *situation*, territorial, cultural, existential and spiritual, expressing all that *is not governance*. Every commune is a tear in the nation, a secession from government, an exodus from the dominant value system.

The experiences of mutualism, which multiplied in different countries during the pandemic, were the only ones that practically challenged the so-called "social distancing," which is a notion that is by no means innocent, given that it originated in American sociology to measure the relations between whites and other ethnic and racial groups. At their most advanced, these new experiences of mutualism insist on the fact that the real "cure" consists in the reconstruction of the community, of its internal relations and of those that can be entertained with other communities, beyond the state. Care that intervenes on multiple levels: health, economic, existential, and political.

---

* See page 4.

Tiqqun, in the same period in which the text of Situaciones was written, wrote: "*How is it to be done?* They suggest that military confrontations with the Empire have to be subordinate to the intensification of the relationships inside our party. This means that politics is just a certain degree of intensity *within* an ethical element. Thus, revolutionary war must not be confused with its representation: the raw moment of combat." A good example of the relationships inside our party, intended as "historical party," are those potentials embryonically developed in our neighborhoods by the activities of collective care that have been unfolding in these months. It is very important that Tiqqun underlines that the "real war" is never the military confrontation, not only because by focusing only on that in the end we will always lose, that is we will lose the war and the soul, but because the spiritual, ethical, and material growth of the community is the only real way to oppose imperial colonization: the form of life of the commune *is* the form of combat. We need new examples, new inspirations, new words and gestures that communicate to the heart before the head and hands.

For this reason, it is urgent that transnational research, both practical and spiritual at the same time, be launched around the question of the commune. This research should be able to learn from the defeats, liberating the past, illuminate all that is powerful but hidden in the present, emancipating it from depression, and keep open the narrow door through which salvation comes. All power to the communes!

"Cor unum et anima una"

Marcello Tarì
Rome, February 2021

KEEPING 2001 OPEN

by Liz Mason-Deese

"2001 DOES NOT REFER TO A YEAR, BUT TO AN ACTIVE PRINCIPLE, AN INTER-pretive key for understanding this decade" read the invitation to a series of events organized by Colectivo Situaciones and friends in 2011 to celebrate and interrogate the ten-year anniversary of the events of that 19th and 20th of December. The invitation continued: "For us, 2001 is almost a method, a way of looking at things seeing them in motion. In this sense the crisis becomes a premise, with its multiple meanings: instability and creation, worry and uncertainty, opening and changing the calendar. . . . Both when it is visible and when, as in these times, when it runs as a subterranean cur-rent underneath a 'normal' society or in a 'serious' country."

Ten years on, the landscape had already mutated significantly from the moment of crisis in 2001. The years of the crisis were years of experimen-tation, experimentation in forms of social, political, and economic organi-zation—the proliferation of neighborhood assemblies, of barter clubs, of unemployed workers' organizations—and of ways of thinking, of relating thought and practice. After ten years, the political landscape had changed considerably, it was the moment of the "Pink Tide," of a "progressive" gov-ernment that was transforming Argentina into a "serious" country as Cristina Fernandez de Kirchner claimed. On the one hand, this government was a result of that uprising in 2001, only possible due to the space opened up by the revolt, on the other hand, many of the most creative experiences of the revolt were left aside as movements became subsumed into an institutional-ized logic that centers the state as the primary site of politics.

This did not mean that all the experimentation and openness of 2001 was lost, it continued to resonate in often unexpected ways and unexpected subjects. At that moment, those subterranean lines could be found in the movements of migrants, of young precarious workers, in campesinx and land struggles. And it was those subjects who were invited to participate in the event to commemorate the ten-year anniversary and, most importantly, to contribute to ongoing research about new modes of labor, alternative forms of living, and insurgent subjectivities.

Now twenty years later, we could ask: what does it mean to keep 2001 alive as a premise, in its multiple meanings, especially when that current seems more subterranean than visible? Retaining fidelity to that sense of 2001 means asking about the production of new forms of life in the present, those ways of living differently that are perhaps not those in the foreground of our common images of revolution, but that emerge from unexpected places, generating something that often does not fit into our prior conceptions of revolutionary activity.

Then, in thinking about how to keep 2001 open as a premise, I think there are three lines that are worth elaborating on and following. The first has to do with the transnationalism of the uprising, its immediate links to struggles around the world, in a way that emphasizes both the singularity and the universality of the revolt; it cannot be subsumed under global concepts, it is uniquely tied to a concrete situation, yet it resonates everywhere. Second, the concept of militant research/research militancy is essential—not as an abstract practice, but as one intimately interwoven into the specific situation of revolt—for remaining open to learning from, and truly participating in, the uprising in process without imposing prior definitions or predetermined notions of what that uprising should look like. Finally, what the analysis of 2001 elaborated throughout this book, from a perspective of research militancy, shows us is that the revolt did not take place on the basis of a particular subject—"the insurrection had no author," as Colectivo Situaciones reminds us. Rather, new subjectivities are produced in the process of the uprising itself. Thus, keeping 2001 open requires cultivating the emergence of insurgent subjectivities wherever they may arise.

RESONANCES BEYOND BORDERS

I FIRST ENCOUNTERED the work of Colectivo Situaciones, in the months following the uprising of the 19th and 20th, as their texts began circulating more widely in certain circles of the global justice movement around the world. I encountered their work through collective translations that were freely distributed online, printed out and distributed at events, and discussed in small activist reading groups in North Carolina where I lived at the time or at the counter-summits of the global justice movement. I met members of the Unemployed Workers' Movement of Solano as they traveled across the US, visiting college campuses and activist groups, on their way to the protests against the Free Trade Area of the Americas in Miami in 2003. Thus, we connected with the texts not only in intellectual or theoretical terms, but through shared embodied experiences, *acuerpamiento* as we say now, embodying the struggle and putting our bodies on the line together.

These texts were thus essential not only for learning about the revolt that had taken place in Argentina, and the novelty of it, but also for sharing the way of thinking and writing that accompanied it, not only the content of the writing, but the method of analysis-action, that was interwoven in the proposition of *research militancy*. This method—which perhaps could be crystallized in the Zapatista *caminar preguntando* —was a fundamental feature of that wave of global struggles. These struggles opened up questions about the revolutionary subject, class composition in the contemporary moment, the form of revolutionary action and organization, the meaning of revolution itself. Around the world new tactics were invented—and linked to strategies and ways of producing analysis—that emphasized a *not-knowing*, experimentation, something like humility, it formed what could be considered an *ethos* of that globally connected movement.

In this way, the work of Colectivo Situaciones immediately entered into a constellation of texts, conversations, concepts, that traced a geography from Seattle to Genoa, from Chiapas to São Paulo. It was also directly connected to a number of encounters, such as *Enero Autónomo* in Argentina, in which activists traveled to participate in assemblies and events with participants of Argentina's autonomous movements. These events did not aim to replicate the experience of the 19th and 20th in other countries, the forms of organization and movement that gave rise to the revolt or emerged in its wake, because that would have been absurd. Yet, they were based on a fundamental conviction that we can learn from one another, that encounter can open up new questions and paths and can resonate elsewhere.

Thus, while the reading presented in this book of the 19th and 20th is, fundamentally, a situated reading, immanent to the event itself, and drawing on specific genealogies of Argentinean and Latin American Marxist thought, it is also inserted in transnational circuits and conversations, as the events themselves are. This led to a specific way of reading the Argentine uprising, of understanding it as a revolt against neoliberalism, against financialized capital, that both emphasized the singularity of the revolt and connected it to global and particular struggles elsewhere.

MILITANT/INVESTIGATION

Within Argentina, Colectivo Situaciones stands out for their relationship with the 2001 revolt in comparison to others engaged in intellectual and theoretical production. Many intellectuals at the time downplayed the importance of the uprising, criticizing it as "spontaneous," "unorganized," and "prepolitical." In other words, it did not fit into their ideas of what a "revolution" should look like nor did it confirm their already-existing theories or follow the playbook they had devised. Therefore, much of the uprising remained illegible to those sorts of intellectuals and ways of thinking. Colectivo Situaciones, on the other hand, adopted a different approach. Without claiming to understand the uprising, they knew that it had to nevertheless be participated in, that first and foremost one had to be on the streets, at the barricades and roadblocks, and in the assemblies. Rather than judging the ongoing revolt according to some predetermined criteria, their role as a collective was to dig deeper and follow the threads of an insurgent subjectivity running through it.

This conviction that knowledge is produced in struggle—that struggles, mobilizations, rebellions are productive both in terms of new ways of understanding a situation and through new encounters between subjects and experiences—is a fundamental feature of Colectivo Situaciones' methods and politics of knowledge. Thus, the militant researcher is immanent to the situation at hand, not an external and neutral observer, but immersed in and of the struggles themselves, following and contributing to that insurgent knowledge produced in struggle. There is another element as well, knowledge is itself productive. Thus, militant research is not characterized by description, limited to the deployment of sociological categories and frames *of* analysis, but rather productive of new concepts, relations, encounters, and *potencia*.

Militant-researcher, research militancy: both call into question hegemonic forms of academic and intellectual research and dominant forms of activism and militancy. They call into question the very presumption of a research subject who conducts research, separate from the situation, and the object of research, passively being researched. But nor are they referring to a new form of action-research or participatory research or the like, forms that generally do not challenge the epistemological claims of hegemonic research, that continue depending on the established positions of researcher and participant, and often only lead to more extractive forms of knowledge production. Yet it also challenges dominant forms of activism and militancy, which assume the answers, the necessary tactics and strategies, the required forms of organization, the desired way of living, are *already* known. Research, in the productive sense described above, is an essential part of politics, not only for understanding our situations, but also to give rise to new encounters and new becomings, and to avoid getting stuck in reified ways of thinking and being in the world.

Fundamentally, research militancy is characterized by that position of immanence to the situation at hand and ultimately, research militancy points to the self-abolition of both the researcher and the militant as independent, fixed subjects. What was seen in the uprising in 2001 was that this practice of militant research was not embodied in a few specific subjects, even if the texts included here have names attached to them. Research militancy was a characteristic of the uprising itself, spread throughout the social field and put in practice in an insurrection that was more about inventing new forms of acting and being together than implementing predefined plans and programs.

SUBJECTIVITIES ARE FORMED IN STRUGGLE

IT IS THIS question of the subject—of the revolutionary subject and its relation to revolution—that is the final line that is important for keeping the premise of 2001 open. As the interventions contained in this book confirm, the revolutionary subject does not pre-exist the revolution; it is not a matter of identifying or shaping the subject and creating the conditions and *then* producing the revolution. Revolutionary subjects are shaped through collective, revolutionary action itself. The uprising involves the unmaking and remaking of subjectivities.

This book highlights this production of subjectivities through struggles in several cases, such as neighborhood residents coming together in assemblies or barter clubs. These were not necessarily activists or members of an organization, in fact what characterizes 2001 most of all is that it completely overwhelmed existing organizational forms. Leftist parties, trade unions, other established organizations were left playing catch up to the masses taking the streets who were defying a state of siege, fighting the cops, establishing barricades. The moment of insurrection was also a moment of generating new capacities, not only in terms of tactics for street battles, but also for collective decision-making and cohabitation.

Perhaps the most emblematic case is that of the unemployed workers who come to see themselves not in terms of merely lacking jobs, but active producers of other forms of living. They do not define themselves according to a sociological category or in relation to the hegemonic norms (waged employment). In other words, being unemployed does not automatically make one a piqueterx. Rather, being a *piqueterx* is a subjective position, no longer being a passive victim to an exploitative regime, but actively taking up the tools of struggle and seeking the creation of new relations. This can be seen also in the subsequent developments of the MTD of Solano, as, in the years following this publication, turned away from identifying as *unemployed* to name themselves according to their multiple, collective projects, starting a housing cooperative, engaging in various land takeovers, farming and gardening projects, small productive enterprises, feminist collectives, and so on. In all these processes, they specifically emphasize the need to deconstruct the desires that capitalism has produced and actively produce new ways of relating to ourselves and each other.

Thus, rather than confirming a politics automatically corresponding to fixed identities, the premise of 2001 emphasizes the—collective—production of new subjectivities through struggle and a different understanding of subjecthood itself. The very idea of this uprising representing a "new subject" is questioned, because it is not a matter of a single, fixed, consistent subject that emerges. Rather, that subject is discussed as *multiple, situated, eccentric*. That subject cannot be taken for granted, is not predetermined by existing identities or life experiences, but is actively constructed in the struggle. This necessarily has implications in the form that political struggle takes. How could such a multiple, *eccentric* and *inconsistent* subject be represented? Clearly, a politics of representation is not sufficient. But, what does it mean to take the production of subjectivity seriously in political struggle? This is where the insistence on the uprising as a moment of *fiesta*, of joy, of coming together, of encounter, is fundamental. But it also refers to the struggle as a moment of generating new capacities and new ways of living together.

TWENTY YEARS LATER

WHAT, THEN, DOES it mean to read this work twenty years later with the objective of keeping 2001 open as a premise? Those twenty years have seen a profound transformation of the political, social, and economic fields: many of the movements and organizations that emerged with the insurrection were later incorporated into the Kirchnerist governmental project while the alternative economic activities reached a mass level with the expansion of the popular economy, as people individually and collectively *invented* forms of income generation to survive during the crisis.* This was also accompanied by profound shifts in political subjectivities, with the neoliberal government of Mauricio Macri (2015–2019) and a proliferation of microfascisms from below, increased competition, and violence at all levels of society.

Thus, rather than remaining tied to the organizations, forms of mobilization and protest that were practiced in 2001, keeping 2001 opens means engaging in inquiry-action, of searching for and cultivating insurgent subjectivities. It requires immersing ourselves in the struggles of the moment, recognizing the knowledges produced within them and keeping that sense of indeterminacy alive. This perspective shows that, more than anything, it is the feminist movement(s) that has taken up the mantle of the spirit of 2001 in the ways discussed here. Organized territorially, through assemblies, through encounters in different places and at different scales, it is not encapsulated in a single organization or campaign. It is a transformation that occurs simultaneously on the macro and micro, molar and molecular, levels: winning the right to legal, free, and safe abortion for women and people with the capacity to gestate, driving the use of gender-neutral language across society, bringing labor unions to address gender discrimination in the workplace and in the organization itself, winning important legislative victories for non-binary and trans folks, and organizing massive transnational feminist strikes.

---

* Verónica Gago, *Neoliberalism from Below: Popular Pragmatics and Baroque Economies* (Durham, NC: Duke University Press, 2017).

The feminist movement has been able to do this through a process of situated investigation, starting from specific bodies that serve as entry points for producing a point of view that allows for understanding the whole. The work of weaving together different situations and struggles—in assemblies where women and trans and non-binary people share their own trajectories to put them in relation with others—produces a political cartography for comprehending the relations between different forms of violence and creates unexpected alliances. It connects households imploded by domestic violence to lands razed by agribusinesses and assassinated campesina and environmental activists, with the wage gap throughout industries and academia and invisibilized care work; it links the violence of austerity and budget cuts to women's protagonism in popular economies and to financial exploitation through public and private debt.* This is the work of militant investigation today: uncovering and cultivating these emerging insurgent subjectivities in order to keep the premise of 2001 open.

---

* Lucí Cavallero and Verónica Gago, *A Feminist Reading of Debt* (London: Pluto Press, 2021)

THE BALLAD OF BUENOS AIRES

by Antonio Negri

THIS BOOK DISCUSSES THE EVENTS OF THE 19TH AND 20TH OF December 2001 in Argentina, when the inhabitants of Buenos Aires took to the streets and aimed themselves at Congress, forcing the flight of the President, and the successive resignation of the government. But not just that: it also speaks of before and after the insurrection, it talks about the new political and social situation that was determined since the military dictatorship of 1976–83 and the neoliberal decade (1989–1999). The book—*Piqueteros. La rivolta argentina contro il neoliberismo* [Piqueteros. The Argentinian revolt against neoliberalism], Colectivo Situaciones tell us was thought with urgency, written and published in the space of less than three months. The original subtitle is "Notes for a New Social Protagonism." In fact, it treats in the form of notes, theoretical notes and syntheses of discussion by assemblies, the theory of organization of struggles and the critique of lived experiences. "Writing in situation" finds here an example in all ways innovative: the capacity to combine critical reflection and investigation materials reaches a level of true theoretical innovation. Those who, on the other hand, want to have proof of the newness of this political writing have to do no more than to find the materials that the Colectivo Situaciones have published frequently since 2001 until the end of 2002 (as a summary of all these materials one can look over all *Hypothesis 891. Beyond the piquetes*). In all these writings, then, the reflections of the collective cross with that of the grand assemblies of struggle. Above all with the Movement of the Unemployed Workers (MST) of Solano.

But fine, what is this Argentinean experience? Do these writings of the Colectivo Situaciones speak to us about a new configuration of revolutionary subjects? Do we find ourselves in front of a new Paris Commune? It is always dangerous to assimilate ideology to reality: but perhaps in this case it is worthwhile. Here there is something new: it is the act of violence of engagement with power that permitted, at the time, the unmaking of the continuity of social and political relations that have contained Argentine development, and giving rein to new particular apparatuses and subjects that constructed new realities of resistance and desire, of counterpower. Argentina, the struggles of its proletariat, the paradoxical confluence of sectors of the middle class with them, has convulsed the picture of the traditional analysis of class struggles and preferred the creation of new, unexpected, and untimely behaviors to the customary rituals of the left. As Marx, in the "Class Struggle in France," counterposed the communards to the socialist synagogue of Luxemburg, today from Argentina we find an example of new constitution of the multitude. The example of the constitution of the multitude (what we have seen and continue seeing is also its internal transformation) has to be seen essentially in the struggles that "Piqueteros" documents. To a radical institutional crisis ("all of them must go!" was a cry that denounced and registered the minority condition to which the traditional political parties were reduced), to a consequent lapse of the legitimation of the representative function (involving generalized public and private corruption), to a political crisis (demonstrated by the incapacity to reproduce customary models of constitutional alliance between social classes and bourgeois hegemony over the system), to a financial crisis (of payment of the debt and of inversion of the flows between the periphery and the center) and finally to a very profound social crisis that destroyed capacities productive (extreme unemployment, savage precarization of labor) and reproductive (crisis of public education and health), to all this responded a "multitudinary counterpower" that organized itself in autonomous systems of production, of interchange and political organization, in completely original forms. From workers' self-management of the factories to the generalized occupation of public buildings on the part of the neighborhood assemblies, from the construction of a new exchange from below (and a new market and new modalities of exchange) to the revolutionary and legitimate exercise of force on the part of the piquetes, there appears here a capacity of autonomous constitution of the multitudes, that bear an energy of universal conviction and of egalitarian social recomposition. The martyrdom of the generations destroyed by the military dictatorship of '70-'80 and the desperation of peoples that rebelled against neoliberal globalization in the '90s, find here the truth of a new experience of radical social construction.

When today it is said "a new world is possible," if we don't want to be imbeciles that scratch our bellies while telling lies, it is necessary to have the courage to imagine the possibility of a new world, of not trembling before the threats of the capitalist apologists, of inventing the possibility of a new currency, of its utilization, of thinking that it is possible to organize labor, a "dignified labor," autonomously, of deciding the common.

Is it possible to change the world without taking power, or better, is it not the way of destroying power? Isn't this imagination in action of the piqueteros and of the MTDs the true and only line that can be counterposed as a real alternative to the couplet reformism-terrorism that the global powers counterpose to the multitude?

I don't know what can happen in Latin America during the next decade. I know only that in Latin America a social laboratory, extreme and effective, is developing. The distance there is between the Argentine piqueteros and the Brazilian Lula, beyond what really will be and how it will be perceived subjectively, is in every way minimal: the Latin American laboratory rises against the unilateralism of US and global capitalism in an effective manner. Mutatis mutandi, in Latin America a subversive breach is being constructed within and against globalization, and this breach corresponds to that which the movements in Europe are producing. The social and political experimentation in Argentina, with its incredible recompositions between the organized unemployed and elements of the middle class impoverished by the IMF, show on the one hand the construction of the multitude and on the other the impossibility of opposing resistance within the bounds of the Nation-State. This is how in the South, civil but very poor, and in the North, rich but socially disintegrated, piquetes of resistance are formed.

This book by Colectivo Situaciones composes the fragments of a global discourse, founding on the basis of the experiences of the Argentinean struggle a style of inquiry that is directly organization of struggle. The communist political contents of these struggles are evident (it is evident also that the western European media give almost no information on this matter). What remains is that from here we can and should start again. When one assumes the problem of counterpower and takes it, beyond anarchist or spontaneist experiences, to the present crisis and to the world in which exodus (which is one of the figures of counterpower) can develop; when one becomes aware of the enormous asymmetry that there is between the forms of repression and the insurrectional development of the multitude; when then the problem of the "dualism of power" is reproposed in biopolitical conditions, is when we begin placing ourselves in "situation." Thanks to the Argentinean piqueteros that invented extraordinary forms of protest and of organization from below, thanks to the popular assemblies that are reinventing the forms of monetary exchanges and of management of social services, thanks to the militants that organized new networks of subversive communication, thanks, finally, to Colectivo Situaciones, who know, in the vital interchange with the multitudes, to give us critical information and hopeful reflections.

INTRODUCTION

by Colectivo Situaciones

THIS IS A BOOK ABOUT THE EVENTS OF DECEMBER 19TH AND 20TH OF 2001 in Argentina, but not exclusively. Such events, we believe, revealed in concentrated form the emergence of a new social protagonism. But the 19th and 20th cannot be taken as an excuse—nor, in any way, as a demonstration—to show something that *already* existed. Not even to mark a *degree zero* of Argentina. Our motives are otherwise.

The events of December tore down the *Nunca Más* democratic truce.[1] Since then, situations that were believed to have been conjured away appeared on the scene: levels of resistance willing to confront state power became visible and the threat of a military coup returned. In this sense, we believe they mark the end of the genocidal dictatorship that began in 1976. Or, in other words: the insurrection of December managed to escape the threatening double bind of all those years: *dictatorship or democracy.*

The traditional role of the state was severely overturned during these appearances: the declaration of a state of siege the night of December 19th and the ongoing rumors of a coup conspiracy sought to reestablish terror, but they were not enough, at any moment, to stop popular unrest.

The events of December force us to think of novelty and not just to inscribe the "facts" in an already existent totality of meaning. That is why our attempt is to think what the 19th and 20th opens in its singularity. That is, the *practices of fidelity* to such processes as were unfolding in the context of 2001 and of which this book seeks to be part. The events unleashed by the insurrection remain open. This indeterminacy, how-ever, is not an obstacle to the writing of this book. On the contrary, we intend to develop a style of thought constituted not by the preexistence of its object but by its interiority with respect to the phenomenon we are thinking about. In this way, thought abandons all positions of pow-er over the experience in which it participates. The classical separation between subject and object is left aside in order to turn thought into another dimension of experience. Thinking becomes a risky activity: it consists not in producing representations of objects, but rather in as-suming the theoretical dimension that is present in each situation. Nor is it about producing a final conjecture about the process still in motion, but about intervening in the current discussions, under the heat of the events. For that same reason, this is a book of urgencies. Neither predic-tions nor prophecies will be found in these pages. The goal of this work is to think the opening inaugurated in December from within itself: the possibilities of mobility and visibility of the bodies and knowledges that such events activated. But also to think how the experiences of struggle previous to the 19th and 20th were transformed. Summarizing, to think *in* the effects and not *about* them. To think without objectifying. To think without capture and appropriations. To think with the convic-tion that the moments we lived will inspire struggles and experiences to come. And that, in consequence, the task of thought is not neutral.

The hypothesis from and upon which we work here is constituted as a site of polemics, ruptures, and continuities with respect to the strug-gles of the seventies and the post-dictatorship period. We affirm the emergence of a collection of practices and languages that give way to a new type of intervention in the social and political sphere. Here we find a social protagonism that operates by bringing together dimensions of existence in their entirety; this is a consequence of a more significant historical rupture with respect to the myths of determinism and prog-ress characteristic of modernity.

Four decades ago, John William Cooke wrote his *Apuntes para la militancia*.* The fact that they were "notes" was not a sign of improvisa-tion; it was an immanent modality of writing in relation to the ongoing insurrectional phenomena. And "militancy" did not designate a group of readers *to* whom those notes were destined, but the very condition of

---

* The title of the book translates as *Notes for militancy*. John William Cooke (1919–1968) was a Peronist politician and intellectual who became widely influential among the Peronist youth and the left of the 1960s and 1970s generation of revolutionaries. (Tr.)

Cooke's thinking. *19 and 20: Notes for a New Insurrection* attempts to recover that spirit. The chapters of this book are also *notes*. Each of them can be read as an essay almost independent from the rest. Nevertheless, all have something in common: they constitute a specific approach to the same interrogation. What allows us today to substantiate a new modality of political intervention? How to account for this emerging *social protagonism*? What are the obstacles we encounter at the time of understanding this emergence? How are the events of December 19th and 20th inscribed in the journeys of this protagonism? How do we think through the effectiveness of these resistances?

Specifically, the kind of intervention we propose consists in displaying in these pages the advances of a *militant research*. Many threads comprise the fabric of this text. We mix narratives, chronicles, revised writings on the conjuncture, testimonies, theorizations, and interviews as modalities capable of producing an ethical reflection in the sense expressed by the Argentine philosopher León Rozitchner when he analyzed the American invasion of the Bay of Pigs: "The theme of every ethic deals precisely with the moment in which human acts express themselves in a world-defining material action, vindicating the values they promote and doing so amongst those who oppose the existence of this new modality of being. In its decisive, and also fleeting, moment, the singular knows that its action is established in the universal, that the course of the world converges in that act."[2]

In this sense, there is something we would like to highlight about our *methodology* or, rather, about our work: militant research has commitment as its presupposition, as the only possible way of taking on the epochal and generational demands to which we are challenged by our quest for justice and the struggles of the past. This means that we are skeptical about any purism of knowledge, any academic consideration, and discard any pretension to objective description. In fact, we believe that one of the *innovations* of the social protagonism is to tie an ethic of knowledge (*saber*)* to the concrete forms of existence. And this is nothing but a question: how to inhabit each situation by embracing our own capacities to produce and reappropriate the world?

We assume thought as a practice of fidelity to struggles of liberation. And such fidelity is not the straight and narrow path that promises brilliant futures, but one that talks to us about the men and women who, from the present, practice the urgent transformation of existence,

---

* In Spanish there are two words for knowledge: *conocer* and *saber*. The original expression is indicated between brackets. (Tr.)

making of their own lives the material foundation for such possibility.

The Argentine insurrection produced a spatial and temporal interruption from which there is no return, which has nothing to do with either interpretive pessimisms or optimisms. The unfolding of popular powers in the city actualized the recurrent image of the *commune*. This appearance inscribed an ethical ideal that only materializes itself—as an exigency—in the multiplicity of experiences that work everyday to bring into existence, to overhaul, and to unfold the possibilities opened (both symbolically and materially) in the days of December.

In *chapter one* we deal with the context of the ongoing transformation and its importance for thinking the new forms of resistance: the old state/disciplinary society has entered into a crisis and its mechanisms of domination, even without disappearing, have been rearticulated by market forms of domination and the mechanisms of biopower. The dominant subjectivity is no longer *political subjectivity*, but that of the *consumer-customer*. Inside this form of domination new modalities of resistance emerge that are not strictly "political" in the sense that they do not have resistance against a central state as a priority, but their preoccupations expand and become heterogeneous simultaneously with the disarticulation of the representations of the Fordist world of work. The challenge of contemporary struggles is to inquire into the forms of subjectification that are possible in market conditions.

The events of the 19th and 20th bring those challenges up to date once more. This is the point of departure of *chapter two*. The multitude does not present itself as people—agent of sovereignty. Nor does it operate according to its instituting power. We believe that the powers (*potencias*) of this *new type* of insurrection function in a "destituting" way, as in the battle cry "*¡Que se vayan todos!*" (all of them must go). Obviously, this slogan must not be reduced to its pure literality: the insurrection of 19th and 20th consisted of an immediately positive "no." The power (*potencia*) of the multitude does not allow itself to be read from the classical theory of sovereignty, but from the becomings it brings into being. The revolt was violent. Not only did it topple a government and confront the repressive forces for hours. There was something more: it tore down the prevailing political representations without proposing others. The mark of this insurrection on the social body is a major one. It cannot be inscribed in the tradition of classical insurrections: there was no leadership; nor was there a proposal to take over state power. Every strata of Argentine society was shaken and each of us wonders what is to be done with the effects of those events. The new social protagonism seeks neither homogeneity nor models; it only raises questions. It exists as a counteroffensive expressed in struggles that are multiple and in forceful dilemmas.

The sociologist Horacio González and the philosopher León Rozitchner, two professors who have turned the University of Buenos Aires and their lives into an adventure of thought, intervene in this chapter. Both accepted being submitted to lengthy and affectionate interviews that we edit here as short articles. We found this way of editing useful because it brings together discussions and personal chronicles which we insert as reflections on the issues that remain autonomous in terms of their elaboration, but essential to our own thought. Finally, our comrades from the political magazine *La Escena Contemporánea** also participate through a collective text that reflects upon the continuities and ruptures that the 19th and 20th mark in the modes of thinking and practicing politics.

In *chapter three* we deal with *political subjectivity*, which, in our view, is the greatest obstacle for the advance of this multiple and diverse movement. It is supported by classical (centralizing and hierarchical) epistemology that leads to the separation and reproduction of relations of domination inside popular organizations. Insofar as it strives to find a single and consistent subject, the gaze of political subjectivity leaves the elements of emerging counterpowers in a blind spot. There is a double nature to this obstacle: it operates by both obstructing the perception of changes in the forms of domination and hampering the emergence of the multiple forms of today's resistance. Moreover, this position emphasizes confrontation as the essence of resistance. Thus, a "reactive" conception of struggle is shielded, without grasping the power (*potencia*) of its self-affirmative forms. Summarizing: this is a politicism—which is at times also an economism—that preserves the image of social change based upon attaining control of the state apparatus. The discussion becomes more relevant amid the scenario posed by a climate of social unrest. The diagnosis of the *return of politics* since the 1970s is used to encourage all kinds of "political illusions" and to strengthen those tendencies that seek to "accelerate" this activism, expounding fantastic dilemmas to the experiences of counterpower.

This is one of the problems about which the Movimiento de Trabajadores Desocupados de Solano (Unemployed Workers' Movement of Solano)—from the south of greater Buenos Aires—reflects upon in *chapter four*. They tell us how they lived the 19th and 20th, how they participated, and how they see the rise of the neighborhood assemblies and the reality that opens in front of them. They explain the current

* The name of this group translates as *The Contemporary Scene*. (Tr.)

problems of the unemployed workers' movement or *piqueteros*. Unlike other organizations, MTD* of Solano, one of the most important piquetero experiences in the country, works from a situational perspective that allows it to slip away from the times and demands for a generalizing view, and instead strengthens itself by affirming the sovereignty of its concrete experience. From there, this group of piqueteros succeeds in escaping from the dilemmas of classical political subjectivity such as *reform or revolution* and, above all, from an ideology of *inclusion*.

Chapter five works through the experience of Comunidad Educativa Creciendo Juntos (Education Community 'Growing Together'): an alternative school in a poverty-stricken neighborhood of the Moreno district, in the province of Buenos Aires. There the 19th and 20th were hours of looting of supermarket chain stores and confrontation. Parents and teachers recount the situations that these circumstances open: a *postdisciplinary* society that empties traditional institutions of their meaning. If school, then, no longer derives its meaning either immediately from modern myths nor from the state institution, a challenge unfolds: its possible meaning will have to be constituted from a subjective operation founded in the self-production of community; and by community we understand here the space of meaning that is created from an ethical interrogation (which in this case is carried out in conditions of fragmentation and rupture of the social bond).

What is going on with "politics"? That is the question that structures *chapter six*. We begin from what is evident: the logic of "representation" appears deeply questioned. Here we appeal to "the logic of expression" in order to understand the forms of the new protagonism. The logic of expression and power (*potencia*) found "another politics," an ethics. While representation operates at the level of "political subjectivity," "expression" operates at the level of the new protagonism. The logic of expression allows us also to understand the relation between politics and management (*gestión*): *"the political"* as an expressive instance, among others. We understand politics and management from a new dialectic in which none of the poles can simply be negated. Management is finite and "represents" tendencies that exist at the basis of the nation. The chapter ends with Deputy Luis Zamora, a movement protagonist and elected public official, reflecting upon his practical experience of confronting the paradoxical possibility of questioning representation

---

* The movements of unemployed workers that were not affiliated with any major political party or union were usually referred to as MTD, from Movimiento de Trabajadores Desocupados (Unemployed Workers' Movement). (Tr.)

from inside representation itself. The text is the result of an extended conversation that we edited, preserving the fundamental points.

If anything new was produced by the 19th and 20th, it was the neighborhood assemblies that multiplied throughout the city of Buenos Aires and later throughout the suburbs and several cities of the interior of the country. The hypothesis in *chapter seven* is that the assemblies constitute a concrete mechanism to sustain the meaning of the insurrectional events. At the same time, they constitute themselves as operations capable of conveying local forms of counterpower. Their most insistent questions are in the crux of these experiences: how to do politics beyond "politics" and administration? What is the meaning of the events of the 19th and 20th? How to unravel it? How to give rise to non-capitalist forms of sociability once the party has been destituted* as a subject of change? In these assemblies, the same complexity as in the piquetes appears: there are tendencies, counterposed positions and heterogeneous attempts. On these themes, Horacio González writes again.

Finally, in *chapter eight* we deal with the problems posed by the articulation of networks once the classical political theory of party organization has been abandoned. We also discuss practices of *self-affirmed marginalization* as subjective processes capable of constructing non-capitalist modalities of socialization; that is, activities that create solidarity values that go beyond the "society of the individual" and that, consequently, begin to alter the landscape organized by the as yet still prevailing economic forces. Here we also develop the theme of circulation and reappropriation of knowledges (*saberes*) of resistance that—as is the case with the *escraches* of the organization H.I.J.O.S.,** later appropriated by the assemblies—imply a situational process of re-elaboration.

---

* We have chosen to use destituent as a translation of the Spanish word *destituyente,* which makes reference to the power that unseats a regime, in order to preserve the resonances that connote a power opposite to that which institutes. (Tr.)

** H.I.J.O.S. (Hijos por la Identidad y la Justicia, contra el Olvido y el Silencio—Sons and Daughters for Identity and Justice, against Forgetting and Silence) is a human rights organization created by the children of those "disappeared" and murdered by the 1976–1983 dictatorship. An *escrache* is a particular organizational form that consists of demonstrating in front of the house of former military officers in order to expose their ongoing impunity, occupying public space with colorful signs, graffiti, and street artists. (Tr.)

Insistence can bore and even drive to despair; we hope this is not the case. We trust the powers (*potencias*) of striving, to the point that this book is a play of repetitions, of variations on a similar argument we owe to Baruch Spinoza. The argument the philosopher turned to in order to lay the foundations for his ethics, which says: experience is not replaceable by abstract knowledge (*saber*)—the problem of morality—and striving to exist implies a labor of encounter with one's own capacities. The operation is complex: it begins with the first attempts to subtract ourselves from the original circumstances in which we find ourselves fully subjected to external forces. Our blindness impedes us from rapidly fleeing from these uncomfortable circumstances. We are condemned to coexist with and fight against this passive and sad modality of existence. But these first attempts to flee from the "arbitrary order of encounters" can give rise to a theoretical and practical research into the forms of affirming ourselves in our powers (*potencias*). This game of passions, reasons and capacities acts as a material base for the ethical process whose goal is that each body experiments* for itself what it is capable of. Each of the chapters of this book exposes this reasoning and attempts to show the political presence of ethics as an existential foundation.

NOTES

1. The *Nunca Más* (*Never Again*) report was elaborated by CONADEP at the request of Alfonsín's government and, since then, this slogan names the rejection of struggle as an element of politics. See "Psicoanálisis y política: la lección del exilio" by León Rozitchner in *Las desventuras del sujeto* (Buenos Aires: El cielo por asalto, 1996) and "La democracia de la derrota," by Alejandro Horowicz in *Los cuatro peronismos* (Buenos Aires: Planeta, 1991).

2. León Rozitchner. *Moral burguesa y revolución*. Buenos Aires: Tiempo Contemporáneo, 1969.

---

* In the usage given here, the Spanish verb *experimentar* connotes both experiment and experience. (Tr.)

CHAPTER 1
THE GREAT TRANSFORMATION

WE ARE INTERESTED IN DESCRIBING AN EPOCHAL SHIFT: NAMELY, OF the ruptures that we are witnessing. We don't seek to be exhaustive. The sole criterion is to situate the significance of the changes of the material conditions in which the world is inhabited and produced in order to interrogate the meaning of our own existences. This work, we announce, proposes to think the emergence of a new social protagonism. From this standpoint we aim to understand the constitution of the contemporary *market society* and of a fabric of *postdisciplinary* power that *spontaneously* produces *subjected subjectivities*—as the philosopher Louis Althusser called them—although no longer in the form of interpellation by state institutions, as was the case previously, but through the direct intervention of capital flows, forms of consumption and the society of the spectacle. This perspective permits us to rapidly describe the *landscape* over which the new social protagonism carries out an ethical operation.[1] This means a passage—a laborious one—toward the reappropriation of these conditions of departure such that these *original* circumstances no longer operate as a determination, but rather as conditions to be assumed that permits us a passage to the *act*. This sovereignty over the situation itself implies as well a certain capacity to cut out a space-time. This cutout is, in turn, the condition—and product—of the emergence of *sense* (it is this operation that we call *situation*).

FROM THE MARKET AS UTOPIA TO BIOPOWER

1. THE GREAT TRANSFORMATION (KARL POLANYI)

IF WE REVISIT Karl Polanyi's hypothesis[2] we can trace a genealogy: the *great transformation* is that which *fully* constitutes a *market society*. The formation of this "neoliberal" dispositif* of social domination was not constituted all at once. It traveled a long way until it acquired its current physiognomy, though in each period it had a different efficacy. This process can be summarized in the following: the unfolding—in space and time—of a metonymy that reduces "real" humanity to only one of its multiple existential motivations, namely the economic. Such a principle, applied as a retrospective gaze, rewrites history.[3] For example, in ancient trade relations among cities it finds the existence of the first attempts to form a foreign trade that would later be constituted by national states. However, here it *forgets* that, in earlier times, foreign commerce had much more to do with the idea of adventure and travel, with visits and exchange of gifts, with war and piracy, than with a purely mercantile exchange.[4]

A good part of Marxism shared this same fiction: any non-economic human motivation (aesthetic, religious, amorous)—any "non-material" motivation, to follow this tradition—was immediately termed idealistic. This ontological dualism—the economic and the "non-economic"—only reproduces the classical scission that accompanies the entire metaphysics of modernity: the rational versus the irrational; and at the limit, the civilized and the barbaric. In turn, inside this process we find the origin of the separation, characteristic of capitalist societies, between two spheres of social life: the economic and the political.[5] This separation, peculiar to capitalism, excludes direct coercion from the productive sphere and circumscribes it to the state, a separate sphere—deemed the political—that administrates both the law and repressive force. If in precapitalist formations economic and political domination

---

* The original word is *dispositivo*, a concept that Colectivo Situaciones uses in the tradition of Michel Foucault. It could be translated as "mechanism" or "device," but it also means (both in French and in Spanish), deployment of troops, police agents, etc. In other words, relays of force that operate at a situated level. The use of the original French expression has gained acceptance in English translations of Foucault and among authors that follow this philosopher. For this reason we prefer to use this term and not "mechanism," "device," or "deployment," none of which has the breadth of meaning of the original. (Tr.)

appeared visibly together, the separation between the economy and politics produces a phenomenon both novel and effective for domination: the *fetishism* of the state. Thus, the economic relations are supplemented by a "neutral" and "external" space with alleged capacities to organize the chaos produced in the sphere of the market. Politics, understood as the sphere of state articulations, far from being an ordering counterweight, accentuates the separation producing the conditions for capitalist accumulation.

The explanation of the passage from societies *with* markets to market societies[6] supposes one more element: the emergence of individualism together with the intensification of monetary circulation and the commercial exchange boom. Individualism is the anthropological substratum over which it is possible to convert exchange relations into utilitarian exchange. Individuals become personifications of the commodity and every type of noncontractual social organization (kinship, creed, occupation) becomes either subsumed under the primacy of work as a sphere separated from the rest of existence or commodified.[7]

The force and the historical specificity of capitalism thus produce, in Polanyi's terms, a *civilizing process*. Nevertheless, *market society*, Polanyi announces to us, "does not make sense" by itself, to the degree that the anthropology it founds, *homo aequalis*—the abstract equality of capitalism—is nothing but a fiction secured and produced by means of very concrete forms of sustained violence. As Polanyi suggests, this repression of anthropological forms and motivations sustained the Nazi reaction.[8] In this way, it is possible to notice the degree to which totalitarianism was present in the genesis of social-economic modernity: in the emergence of the market as self-fulfilling prophecy. That is why, for Polanyi there was another *great transformation*: the *resocialization* of the economy imposed by the political-economic crisis between 1930 and 1945. The "postliberal" economy—Keynesianism and the so-called Social Welfare State of the industrialized countries—incorporates elements of "state control or socialism" as values that regulate and limit the liberal utopia. In the 1950's, Polanyi observes that humanity produces all sorts of "arrangements" in order to undo the *liberal transformation*.

2. CRISIS OF CIVILIZATION (MARCELO MATELLANES)

If Polanyi attempted to give an account of the transformation set in motion by the domination of the market, Marcelo Matellanes[9] continues this line of thought until it coincides with present times. He concludes that neoliberalism expresses a *civilization-wide crisis*: "the new state project supposes, in the short term, the abrupt interruption—no longer only rationalized, but rather ideologically naturalized—of the mechanisms of social reproduction itself: the state disengages itself progressively from populations and territories; in short, from social cohesion." Thus, the present crossroads would not be as much a dilemma over how to resolve the existence of the economic crisis as one of how to think from the irresolvable fact that the crisis became the *norm*. The crisis, then, is of an ethical order or, in Matellanes' words, it is about "the socializing failure of capitalism." Neoliberalism can be understood as a *failure* since "the historical process of the last twenty years for which capitalism has been losing at an exponential rate (with increasing difficulties to revert this process) the possibility of actualizing its constitutive and constituent promise: that of securing social reproduction in a politically liberal, formally democratic, socially inclusive and economically prodigal becoming."

There is an increasing disagreement between the state and the powers (*poder*) that were typical of it in the times when it fully exercised national sovereignty, among them political legitimacy actualized and refounded in each crisis. In consequence, political and institutional capacities *fail* to regulate economic, informational, and demographic flows. This incapacity of the state to hold the dominant position in relation to economic flows removes from the system of domination one of its classic pillars: that of political hegemony supported by welfare achievements. A *return* to the Hobbesian state of nature takes place without mediations, but without any intention to pacify it, that is to say, to refound a transcendent power capable of politically organizing domination.

Following these premises, Matellanes discards the possibility of a *remake* of "the invention of the social" that the French state accomplished after the revolution of 1848 in the face of the impossibility of carrying out one of its fundamental demands—"jobs for all"—and the rupture of the "illusion of rights" that this impossibility made manifest. "The social," explains Jacques Donzelot, [10] was invented by the capitalist state as an interface between this unveiled rupture between the politics and the economics of capitalism. This same exercise was practiced more than once; the Welfare State was the last of those projects. Matellanes thus radicalizes the thesis of Polanyi: it is no longer a question of recreating types of state intervention that limit, humanize, or socialize the self-regulated market. The political regime ceases to be the key of social becomings. In this sense, from the state perspective there now opens a process of *de-socialization* (disarticulation of the socialization that was deduced from the operation of national states). Nothing guarantees the bonds of citizenship any longer. The disarticulation of this type of bond leads immediately to fragmentation at the same time that it opens the question of alternative forms of sociability.

This passage from a (so-called) national, Fordist, inclusive or Keynesian capitalism to a capitalism regarded as post-Fordist, neoliberal, exclusionary or competitive speaks to us of something more than techno-productive and economic changes. It is about the alteration of the fundamental conditions and points of reference of an entire form of sociability that prevailed until a few years ago. Under the new conditions, we see modifications of the parameters that made possible certain more stable forms of sociability, forms less crossed by uncertainty. The very idea of nation—and its meanings—is currently placed in contention.

Even the violence that always accompanied capitalism acquires new forms. The fragmented and disconnected ground of institutions, practices, discourses, and representations, and the emergence of the fundamental division between the supposedly *included* and *excluded*, removes from violence the politically subversive component that it used to have, in the time when the national state appeared as the organizing nucleus of societies. Thus, in its "irrationality," this dispersed violence is no longer directly married to forms of subversion of the social foundations but rather emerges as a direct—and unquestioned—consequence of the norms of the market. Matellanes' thesis returns to the first *great transformation*—the total autonomization of the economic sphere from social existence itself—in order to corroborate the impossibility of the agreement of human substance with the self-regulation of the market. The character of the present ruptures makes manifest the urgency of the invention and production of the social bond.

3. POWER AND SUBJECTIVITY (MICHEL FOUCAULT)

Understanding the transformation of the mechanisms of power constitutes an internal exigency of the processes of resistance. No subjectification is unconditioned. Michel Foucault wrote about the passage from a *disciplinary society*[11] to a society in which economics and technology deploy their control over existence. This transition implies a change in the forms of power, in the modalities of domination. Disciplinary societies were marked by the existence of institutions whose fundamental task was to produce a type of person adapted to the dominant productivist norm, and to educate and correct the deviances that turned that person opaque, unproductive, and deformed. Schools, prisons, universities, hospitals, and the military, among others, formed a network of institutions that functioned—and function—as sites in which the subjectivity of the individual was enclosed and disciplined. A fundamental coherence, supported by the national state, secured the interaction among these disciplinary institutions in order to produce a civil subjectivity founded on the adequacy of the body for production and on consciousness as a space to be molded through ideological discourse. Foucault reveals these micropowers as concrete supports of the capitalist system. In his last works, he provides us with the concepts that permit us to think through the transition from the *disciplinary* society to the society of *control*.[12] In the center of this passage we can find the emergence of a new technology of domination: *biopower*, namely the capacity to regulate the life of populations.[13]

Foucault shows us a concept of power that is not reduced to its negative character: power as repression, as limit. The *positive* dimension of power consists in producing meanings, mandates, and significations for the action of people starting from a complex dispositif of networks. Starting from these developments, we can project an analysis over the functioning of power with a foundation in *biopolitics*: a new modality of domination founded in the capacities of self-regulation and domination of the economy, the biological sciences, and technology.[14] An entire tradition of political philosophy has continued Foucault's final intuitions. From Antonio Negri to Giorgio Agamben,[15] the theorists of biopower work on the emergence of a *supra*-state power that has taken charge of the life of humanity. But what are the forms of resistance, the ethical forms[16] acquired by the struggles that unfold under conditions of biopower?

THE NEW SOCIAL PROTAGONISM: AN ETHICAL OPERATION

IN THE PRESENT market conditions—in the absence of a center that totalizes the sense[17] of each social practice—the macroeconomic flows take charge of the production of the dominant subjectivity. *Market subjectivity* is constituted by the habits of consumption and the operations of thought that help us pass through the present neoliberal society; by the forms of sociability and the values that *spontaneously* emerge from the new conditions and by the modes of *adequation* to an unstable and fluid terrain, to economic and political uncertainty and unpredictability. "Market," "postmodern," or "post-Fordist" are some of the adjectives used to name these subjective forms. They bring together knowledge of the strategies of survival, production, circulation, exchange, and consumption that spontaneously emerge within our contemporary societies.

The present mechanisms of control function through dispositifs of biopower that operate producing the figure of the *excluded* and the *included*. The *included*, far from being a figure of satisfaction, lives disciplined under anguished threat of exclusion. The excluded have been thrown into a no man's land. They do not participate in consumer society, they are not clients; the life of the excluded is invisible to the market.

The overcoming of disciplinary society, then, is no cause for celebration. By itself, it does not herald any liberation, as certain postmodern optimism proclaims. But, at the same time, the fact that domination persists does not mean that all the forms of resistance practiced until now retain their efficacy. Rather, the contrary is the case. A new form of domination does not necessarily negate the previous dispositifs, but rather tends to articulate them in a new oppressive modality. Thus, the repressive and ideological apparatuses of the state continue operating, but their production lacks its prior efficacy. These transformations imply great challenges for present resistances.

If the (state-centered) *political subjectivity*[18] that dominated disciplinary society produced certain forms of inhabiting the nation and, at the same time, certain subversive projects in its interior, today these formulas have been displaced. Or, at least, their use no longer produces the same effects. It is not simply a question of "trying to do it again," wishing that this time luck will be on our side. To give an account of the effects of a rupture—as we attempt to do here—does not imply disregarding the historicity of the phenomenon but rather, on the contrary, it supposes that all thought is posited inside the folds of history as a multiplicity of temporalities only unified by synchronic cuts or conjunctures that confer to this multiplicity a relative unity or consistency, just as Althusser wrote in *Reading Capital.*

The *new protagonism* shares, as modality of intervention, a common ground with postmodernism—namely, the market conditions— but rejects the postmodern conclusion: that the omnipotence of the market does not leave any room for struggles for liberation. The new protagonism is linked with the rebellious spirit of the 1970s, from which it is separated by the heterogeneity of its theoretical premises and practices. The new social protagonism is not, however, a "new subject." It never reaches such consistency. Its multiple and situated being tells us about its *eccentric* character.

The question is to understand this present ethical passage that goes from the *dispersed* to the *multiple*, as a movement between two radically different figures of subjectivities organized upon the same splintered ground of present capitalism. If there is something that differentiates the radical subjectivities from the subjectivities of the market, it is the impossibility for the latter to operate upon the basis of concrete thought.

Ethical action is always restricted. This restriction, which delimits the space of the situation,[19] is an indispensable condition for the operation of subtraction of the new protagonism with respect to the biopolitical networks. But situational does not simply mean *local*. The situation consists in the practical affirmation that the whole does not exist separated *from* the part, but rather exists *in* the part.[20] On the contrary, particularisms, localisms, and fragments are categories of a globalized subjectivity: there is no meaning, task, or practice that is not lived as a "part" of the global phenomenon.[21] They continue as a thinking of the part and the whole in which there is never truth in the part itself, while the whole, as bearer of the final coherence, is always more abstract and inaccessible.

NOTES

1. See Baruch Spinoza, *Ethics* (in *Complete Works*, vol. 1, edited and translated by Edwin Curley. Princeton: Princeton University Press, 1985) and Alain Badiou, *Ethics: An Essay on the Understanding of Evil*. London: Verso, 2001.

2. Karl Polanyi. *The Great Transformation: The Political and Economic Origins of Our Time*. Boston: Beacon Press, 1944.

3. And founds, at the same time, the figure of the—good or selfish—savage that *naturally* lives from barter, which Polanyi rejects as a caricature of mercantile psychology.

4. This *reading* also forgets that the law of economic determinism is only valid in a market economy. In earlier societies, markets were no more than an accessory to economic life. According to the anthropological studies upon which Polanyi's is based, the usual incentives for human activity were reciprocity, competency, the joy of accomplishment, and social approval. It was not, in any way, a question of a natural inclination towards profit as motor of the activity, as the *liberal utopia* foretold.

5. For an exposition on the nonseparation between the economic and the political, see John Holloway in *Contrapoder, una introduccion* (Buenos Aires: De mano en mano, 2001).

6. Polanyi calls "liberal utopia" the institution of a self-regulated market. The *utopian* in such a project is that, if it spread, the logic of the self-regulated market would entirely destroy human substance and nature. The passage to this type of mercantile social organization has been defined in various manners: the contract substituted for status (Maine), society replaced community (Tonnies) or, in the words of Polanyi, instead of adding the economic system to social relations, the latter come to be enfolded into the economic system.

7. Only under this profound change can the possibility of starving to death be installed. In primitive (premodern) societies, the principle of starvation did not exist as a threat. No one could die of hunger; the only way of running this risk was as a community; that is to say, in the case that the entire community suffered a catastrophe (by loss of harvests, fires, etc).

8. Polanyi, a communist militant contemporary with the German Nazi regime, carried out a series of very subtle considerations of the latter, regarding Hitler as "the gravedigger of economic liberalism": the end of the gold standard is in the cause of the *fascist solution*, he argues, as symptom of the impossibility of a self-regulated market.

9. Marcelo Matellanes, "Capitalismo siglo XXI. La impostergable alternativa: imperio hobbesiano o multitud spinozista," in Marcelo Matellanes (ed.) *Del Maltrato Social: Conceptos Son Afectos*. Buenos Aires: Ediciones Cooperativas, 2003. See also "Límite de la crítica, potencia de la alternativa"; mimeo.

10. Jacques Donzelot. *L'invention du social: essay sur le déclin du passions politiques*. Paris: Seuil, 1994.

11. Michel Foucault. *Society Must Be Defended: Lectures at the College de France 1975–76*. New York: Picador USA, 2003.

12. "Foucault generally refers to the ancien régime and the classical age of French civilization to illustrate the emergence of disciplinarity, but more generally we could say that the entire first phase of capitalist accumulation (in Europe and elsewhere) was conducted under this paradigm of power. We should understand the society of control, in contrast, as that society (which develops at the far edge of modernity and opens toward the postmodern) in which mechanisms of command become ever more "democratic," ever more immanent to the social field, distributed throughout the brains and bodies of the citizens. The behaviors of social integration and exclusion proper to rule are thus increasingly interiorized within the subjects themselves." (Michael Hardt and Antonio Negri. *Empire*, Cambridge: Harvard University Press, 2000 23).

13. "It seems to me that one of the basic phenomena of the nineteenth century was what might be called power's hold over life. What I mean is the acquisition of power over man insofar as man is a living being, that the biological came under State control, that there was at least a certain tendency that leads to what might be termed State control of the biological" (Foucault, *Society Must Be Defended* 239–40). According to Foucault, the emergence of the nature of the exercise of sovereignty is itself transformed: "This is the right, or rather precisely the opposite right. It is the power to "make" live and 'let die. The right of sovereignty was the right to take life or let live. And then this new right is established: the right to make live and to let die (241)."

14. "When power becomes entirely biopolitical, the whole social body is comprised by power's machine and developed in its virtuality. This relationship is open, qualitative, and affective" (Hardt and Negri, *Empire* 24).

15. Biopower, according to Antonio Negri, is the power of the empire over the territories that it takes charge of. This would be the ultimate truth of the process of globalization that is underway. For Giorgio Agamben, by contrast, biopower is rooted in the structure of every form of sovereignty. Thus, all domination aspires to something more than the threat of death: it seeks to control life. According to Agamben, beginning with Nazism, the alliance of medical and biological sciences and the economy constitute the framework of present biopolitics. Nowadays, an ethic, a libertarian politics, demands going beyond state forms, which are biopolitical.

16. An ethics in various senses. This has been theorized in many ways: in general, ethics was thought as a property—or essence—of the subject. Antonio Negri and the Italian autonomists believe in the ethics of exodus and—like Gilles Deleuze—of minorities. John Holloway wagers on an ethics of radical negativity and insubordination. Radicality implies subsuming politics in an ethics. Many are the philosophies that converge on this point. We think that an ethics has, as it were, two parts: a) subtraction with respect to the given conditions and b) affirmation in the situation that transforms the determination into condition.

17. See Mariana Cantarelli and Ignacio Lewkowicz. *Del fragmento a la situación*, Buenos Aires: Grupo doce, 2001.

18. See chapter six of this book: "Expression and Representation."

19. Moreover, the situation is closed and self-sufficient. This idea comes from philosophy and the so-called "hard sciences." From these last we adopt the notion of *autopoiesis*: the living organism is morphologically closed and open to information (see Humberto Maturana and Francisco Varela. *Autopoiesis and Cognition: The Realization of the Living*. London: D. Reidel Publishing Company, 1980). From philosophy we can retain the idea of the monad from Leibnitz.

20. The situation can be thought, then, as a "concrete universal." This thesis affirms that it is possible to know and intervene on the universal only through a subjective operation of interiorization starting from which it is possible to discover the world as a concrete element of the situation. Any other form of thinking the world—as exterior to the situation—condemns us to an abstract perception and practical impotence.

21. Thus, even the alternative retains categories and forms of thought proper to the global when somebody says "*think globally, act locally.*" The perception of a global environment as final producer of subjectivity is the origin of the abstract ideas and subjected subjectivities that predominate in our times.

CHAPTER 2

DECEMBER 19TH AND 20TH, 2001: A NEW TYPE OF INSURRECTION

INSURRECTION WITHOUT A SUBJECT

THE INSURRECTION OF DECEMBER 19TH AND 20TH DID NOT HAVE AN author. There are no political or sociological theories available to understand, in their full scope, the logics activated during those more than thirty uninterrupted hours. The difficulty of this task resides in the number of personal and group stories, the shifting moments, and the breakdown of the representations that in other conditions might have organized the meaning of these events. It becomes impossible to intellectually encompass the intensity and plurality connected by the pots and pans on the 19th, and by open confrontation on the 20th. The most common avenues of interpretation collapsed one by one: the political conspiracy, the hidden hand of obscure interests, and—because of that all-powerful conjunction—the crisis of capitalism.

In the streets it was not easy to understand what was happening. What had awakened those long-benumbed energies from their dream? What might all the people gathered there want? Did they want the same that we, who were also there, wanted? How to know? Did knowing it matter?

First in the neighborhoods of Buenos Aires, and then in the Plaza de Mayo, all sorts of things could be heard. "Whoever does not jump is an Englishman." "Whoever does not jump is from the military." "Execute those who sold the nation." "Cavallo motherfucker." "Argentina, Argentina." And the most celebrated, from the night of the 19th: "stick the state of siege up your asses." And, then, the first articulation of "all of them must go, not a single one should remain." The mixture of slogans made the struggles of the past reappear in the present: against the dictatorship, the Malvinas/Falklands war, the impunity of the perpetrators of the genocide, the privatization of public companies, and others. The chants did not overlap, nor was it possible to identify previously existing groups among the crowd gathered there. All, as a single body, chanted the slogans one by one. At the same time, the contemporary piquetero methods of barricading, burning, and blocking urban arteries appeared in all the streets.

Words were superfluous during the most intense moments of those days. Not because the bodies in movement were silent. They were not. But because words circulated following unusual patterns of signification. Words functioned in another way. They sounded along with pots and pans, but did not substitute for them. They accompanied them. They did not refer to a specific demand. They did not transmit a constituted meaning. Words did not mean, they just sounded. A reading of those words could not be done until this new and specific function they acquired was understood: they expressed the acoustic resources of those who were there, as a collective confirmation of the possibilities of constructing a consistency from the fragments that were beginning to recognize each other in a unanimous and indeterminate will.

The fiesta—because Wednesday 19th was a fiesta—gradually expanded. It was the end of the terrorizing effects of the dictatorship and the open challenge to the state of siege imposed by the government and, at the same time, it was a celebration of the surprise of being protagonists of an historical action. It was also the surprise of doing so without being able to explain to each other everyone else's particular reasons. The sequence was the same all over the city: from fear and anger, to the balcony, to the rooftop, to the corner and, once there, through a transformation of social relationships. It was Wednesday. 10:30pm for some, 10pm for others. And in the patios and the streets a novel situation was taking place. Thousands of people were simultaneously living a social transmutation: "being taken" by an unexpected collective process. People also celebrated the possibility of a still possible fiesta, as well as the discovery of potent social desires, capable of altering thousands of singular destinies.

Nobody tried to deny the dramatic character of the background. Joy did not negate anyone's reasons for concern and struggle. It was the tense irruption of all those elements at once. People resorted to archaic forms of ritualism, to a simulation of exorcism whose sense— an anthropologist would say—seemed to be the reencounter with the capacities of the multitudinous, the collective, the neighborly. Each had to resolve in a matter of minutes decisions that are usually difficult to make: moving away from the television set; talking to oneself, and to others; asking what was really going on; resisting for a few seconds the intense impulse to go out to the streets with the pots and pans; approaching rather prudently; and, then, letting oneself be driven in unforeseen directions.

Once in the streets, the barricades and the fire united the neighbors. And from there they moved on swiftly to see what was happening on other corners nearby. Then it was necessary to decide where to go: Plaza de Mayo, Plaza de los Dos Congresos and, in each neighborhood, to start finding targets more at hand: Videla's house, or Cavallo's. The multitude divided itself, in each neighborhood, and dealt with all the "targets" at once. The most radical spontaneity found support in collectively organized memory. Thousands and thousands of people acted with clear and precise goals, enacting a collective intelligence.

At dawn another scene began to be played. While some were going to sleep—some at 3 in the morning, some others at 5:30—discussions began about what had happened and what would come next. Many continued organizing themselves with the objective of not allowing Plaza de Mayo to be occupied by repressive forces since, formally, the state of siege was still in place.

By then the confrontation, which had not yet been unleashed in all its magnitude, began to be prefigured. On the 20th things looked different. The plaza was the center of the fight. What took place there, right after midday, was a true battle. It is not easy to say what happened. It was not easy to remember other opportunities in which such an air was breathed in the surroundings of the plaza. The violence of the confrontations contrasted the apparent absence of sense among the participants.

Young people openly confronted the police, while the older ones were holding on and helping from behind. Roles and tasks were spontaneously structured. Plaza de Mayo revalidated its condition as a privileged stage for community actions with the greatest symbolic power. Except that this time the representations that accompanied so many other multitudes that believed in the power of that massive pink building, so jealously and inefficiently defended by the police, did not materialize. There were detainees, injured, and many dead from the brutal police repression. Officially they said thirty in the whole country, but we all know there were more.

The city of Buenos Aires was redrawn. The financial center was destroyed. Or, maybe, reconstructed by new human flows, new forms of inhabiting and understanding the meaning of store windows and banks. The energies unleashed were extraordinary, and, as could be anticipated, they did not deactivate. The events of the 19th and 20th were followed, in the city of Buenos Aires, by a feverish activity of escraches, assemblies, and marches. In the rest of the country, the reaction was uneven. But in every province the repercussion of the events combined with previous forms of unrest: roadblocks, looting, protests, and uprisings.

WORDS AND SILENCES: FROM INTERPRETATION TO THE UNREPRESENTABLE

WITH SILENCE AND quietude, words recovered their customary usages. The first interpretations began circulating. Those who sought the fastest political readings of the events faced enormous difficulties. It is evident that no power (*poder*) could be behind them. Not because those powers do not exist, but because the events surpassed any mechanism of control that anyone could have sought to mount. The questions about power will remain unanswered: Who was behind this? Who led the masses?

These are ideological questions. They interpellate ghosts. What is the subject looking for who believes it sees powers (*poderes*) behind life? How to conceive the existence of this questioning and conspiratorial subjectivity that believes that the only possible sense of the events is the interplay of already constituted powers? If these questions had any value in other situations, they were never as insipid as in the 19th and 20th. The separation between the bodies and their movements and the imaginary plans organized by the established powers became tangible like never before in our history. Moreover, these powers had to show all their impotence: not only were they unable to provide a logic to the situation, but even afterwards they hardly managed to do anything but to adapt themselves to these events. Thus, all the preexisting interpretative molds, overturned and caricatured, were activated to dominate the assemblies that supported the movement of the 19th and 20th.

The diagnoses were many: "socialist revolution," "revolutionary crisis," "antidemocratic fascism," "reactionary market anti-politics," "the second national independence," "a crazy and irrational social outburst," "a citizens' hurricane for a new democracy," "a *mani pulite* from below,"* or the Deluge itself. All these interpretations, heterogeneous in their contents, operate in a very similar way: faced with a major event, they cast their old nets, seeking much less to *establish* what escapes through them than to verify the possibilities of consolidating and capturing a diverse movement.

The movement of the 19th and 20th dispensed with all kinds of centralized organization. It was not present in the call to assemble nor was it in the organization of the events. Nor was there any at a later moment, at the time of interpreting them. This condition, which in other times would have been lived as a lack, manifested itself as an achievement precisely because this absence was not *spontaneous*. There was a multitudinous and sustained rejection of every organization that intended to represent, symbolize, and hegemonize street activity. In all these senses, the popular intellect overcame the intellectual previsions and political strategies.

Moreover, not even the state was the central organization behind the movement.[1] In fact, the state of siege was not so much confronted as *routed*. If confrontation organizes two opposing symmetric consistencies, routing highlights an *asymmetry*. The multitude disorganized the efficacy of the repression that the government had announced with the explicit goal of controlling the national territory. The neutralization of the powers (*potencias*) of the state on the part of a multiple reaction was possible precisely because there was not a central call to assemble and a central organization.

Some intellectuals—very comfortable with the consistency of their role—feel also disavowed by an acting multiplicity that destabilizes all solidity upon which to think.

But perhaps we can get even closer to some hard novelties of the movement of the 19th and 20th.

The presence of so many people, who usually do not participate in the public sphere unless it is in the capacity of limited individuals and objects of representation by either the communicational or the political

---

* Mani pulite, literally 'clean hands' in Italian, was a national investigation on government corruption in Italy during the 1990s. Because the campaign took place at the same time when Argentinean newspapers were unveiling one corruption scandal after the other, the expression was quickly adopted by journalists and politicians. (Tr.)

apparatuses, destituted all central situations. There were no individual protagonists: every representational situation was destituted. A practical and effective destitution, animated by the presence of a multitude of bodies of men and women, and extended later in the *"all of them must go, not a single one should remain."*

In this way, without either speeches or flags, without words unifying into a single logic, the insurrection of the 19th and 20th was becoming potent in the same proportion as it resisted every facile and immediate meaning. The movement of the 19th and 20th blew up a series of knowledges (*saberes*) that weighted negatively on the capacity of resistance of the men and women who unexpectedly gathered there. Unlike past insurrections, the movement did not organize under the illusion of a promise. These demonstrations had abandoned certainties with respect to a promising future. The presence of the multitude in the streets did not extend the spirit of the 1970s. These were not insurgent masses conquering their future under the socialist promise of a better life.

The movement of the 19th and 20th does not draw its sense from the future but from the present: its affirmation cannot be read in terms of programs and proposals about what the Argentina of the future ought to be like. Of course there are shared wishes. But they did not let themselves be apprehended into single "models" of thought, action, and organization. Multiplicity was one of the keys of the efficacy of the movement: it gained experience about the strength possessed by an intelligent diversity of demonstrations, gathering points, different groups, and a whole plurality of forms of organization, initiatives, and solidarities. This active variety permitted the simultaneous reproduction of the same elaboration in each group, without the need of an explicit coordination. And this was, at the same time, the most effective antidote against any obstruction of the action.

Consequently, there was not a senseless dispersion, but an experience of the multiple, an opening towards new and active becomings. In sum, the insurrection could not be defined by any of the lacks that are attributed to it. Its plenitude consisted in the conviction with which the social body unfolded as a multiple, and the symbolic world constructing its own history.

RUPTURE OF THE CHAIN OF TERROR
BY LEÓN ROZITCHNER

What the genocide accomplished was the destruction of the social fabric in order to impose, by terror, only one form of sociability. As long as it was not possible to act without putting one's life at risk, the only thing that could appear on the debris of this terror was neoliberal market economics, which requires the dispersion of the subjects and reduces human bonds to the categories of buyer and seller.

But the (terrorized) subjectivity of Argentine society was scattered, separated, and annihilated by its own acceptance. Power, it must be said, required the subject to carry out the operation by means of which it produced itself as a terrorized and complicit subject in order to avoid danger. "There must be a reason,"* people said to justify themselves, because subjectively they endorsed such a reality and rejoiced in it. Above all when, with Menemism, they began to benefit from such atomization, fulfilling their desires through the solitary rite of consumption. Even though the country was going towards the abyss.

It seems, however, as if that which kept us separate was broken after the 19th and 20th. Suddenly, something different happened: breaking the crust, going out, encountering others, recognizing ourselves in the common suffering, and thus being able to activate the powers of our bodies to the extent that we began to feel that we could build a common powerful body. Collective encounters are, precisely, moments in which the corporeal presence of the other gives me the necessary strength so that I can break the mark that terror left in me, at the same time that I help the other to do so with my presence. We are

---

* The phrase was "Por algo será." Another similar remark heard in those days among the middle-class was "Algo habrá hecho," (He or she must have done something). The "something" made reference to political activism. (Tr.)

witnessing how the expression of a rupture of an unconscious and subterranean process that previously limited us become visible and emerge in social reality.

In this sense something has begun: the recognition that we have the power to influence forces that seemed impregnable. For the first time there was a cut that transforms submissive subjectivity and begins to recognize its own power when it is inserted in a collective unified by the same objectives. What emerged was the possibility of defeating that subjective terror and, thus, the recreation of the possibility of a renewed social power.

This does not mean that everything changed. Let's not fancy that we already did it. This is a process that requires time because the fears and coercions we have to overcome are very deep and the reality of repressive threat is very intense. The challenge is to be able to exercise a strategy that peacefully and democratically brings us to multiply our capacity to resist, after having discovered the power of large collective conglomerates of citizens.

This extended counterpower runs the risk of gradually restricting itself if its movement is linked to a certain velocity and acceleration demanded by some impatient sectors of the left. There is no subjectivity if there is not a collective producing and transforming it in a time span whose duration we can only determine through experience.

We have to say the following: let's be careful with the instantaneous, abstract, purely voluntaristic categories of the left. The phenomenon of social creativity has a much deeper complexity than that which their theoretical formulae assign to it.

The left must learn from the fact that it could not do what others spontaneously did by creating previously unthought forms of organization. For it is evident that

what happened on the 19th and 20th is not a product of
the left, but a converging experience of people formerly
separated and distant in their proposals. The question is
not to ask the left to step aside, but to accompany and
start learning anew in the school of facts, breaking with
schematisms frozen in the past.

There are thoughts, for instance, that attempt to explain
the new subjectivities of resistance as an unchanged continuity of the political strategy of the seventies. But what
happens today is, as a strategy, radically different from
what was attempted in the past. We have to learn that
things have changed, and consequently we have to continue to elaborate critically their past in our present. The
only way to make them present is to understand that
what they did was heroic in character, but because it
failed, it at the same time defines the boundaries of a
political strategy that today has to be modified.

DESTITUENT INSURRECTION

IF THE 19TH and 20th produced a mark upon the fragmented social
body,[2] the mark remains there, visible and inspiring anything that can
be done with it. The *politics* that derives from those days is not immediately readable. It requires an elaboration. It is not a question of knowing
just what it was we did on the 19th and 20th so that we can see how to
continue it. Nor is it about finding the truth hidden in the events in
order to decipher a mandate to unfold. The task is even more complex.
The question is: *what do we do with what we did?*

The events participate in a common heritage, present in each interpretation that is made of them, but at the same time resistant to
any attempt to appropriate them exclusively. Several practices that
transform sociability inspired by that mark have been appearing. This
exercise of militant research seeks not to claim ownership of a truth
regarding the events, but rather to try out forms of navigating the
opening of that space.

But this opening is not spontaneous. There are no becomings without elaboration, precisely because those becomings imply abandoning
the whole set of certainties about politics in order to venture into an

unknown time and space: those opened by the events of the19th and 20th. There are no assurances beforehand to carry this project through. Nor is it easy for each of us to take on the risks of a trip towards indeterminacy.

If we talk about insurrection, then, we do not do so in the same way in which we have talked about other insurrections. This one, the one of the 19th and 20th, takes place by opening spaces that go beyond the knowledges about other insurrections such as they existed in the entire Marxist-Leninist discourse on revolution. Indeed, it was an insurrection to the extent that we witnessed the disruption of an order that claimed to be sovereign over the multitude.

If we retain the notion of insurrection to name the mixture of bodies, ideas, trajectories, and languages that were present on the 19th and 20th, we do so aware of every resistance to inscribing the singularity of this event in a lineage of knowledges about history prescribed by an allegedly "scientific" subjectivity. In fact, the movement of the 19th and 20th was more a *destituting* action than a classical *instituting* movement. Or, in other words, the sovereign and instituting powers (*potencias*) were the ones that became rebellious without *instituting* pretensions—as a doctrine of political sovereignty would expect—while exercising their *destituting* powers on the constituted powers. This seems to be the *paradox* of the 19th and 20th. An assemblage of instituting powers disposed in such way that, far from founding a new sovereign order, operates by delegitimizing the politics executed in its name. It constituted neither a step toward a strategy of power (*poder*) nor the end of an accumulation process.

Unlike political revolutions, this *destituent insurrection* did not produce a "situation of situations," a center replacing the centrality of the state it questioned. This was an experience of self-affirmation (*autoafirmación*). In it there was a re-discovery of popular powers (*potencias*). In some way, this raises the following question: how could a national state function based upon the legitimate agents of sovereignty which, in fact, destitutes all representativity?

Destitution, therefore, seems to be a major signifying operation: if the politics carried out in terms of sovereign institution finds the point of its existence in the constitution of the social from the state, de-instituing action seems to postulate another path for practicing politics and enunciating social change. Such destitution does not imply an *a-politics*: to renounce support to a representative (sovereign) politics is the condition—and the premise—of situational thinking and of a series of practices whose meanings are no longer demanded from the state.

We call *aperture* the combination of the action of destitution, which expands the field of the thinkable, and the exercise of protagonism that does not limit itself to the instituting functions of sovereignty. In this line, it is not by chance that political organizations and unions were marginalized in the events of December. They lose relative weight in front of the presence of a multitude that destitutes representations. The encounter between organized militants and the multitude is not easy. It is as if the central character of a *Western* appeared by mistake in the plot of an Italian neorealist film. Each of the protagonists has a plot that does not meet the others at any point. Even when they seem to understand each other, it is nothing but an illusion, a transitory passage in which dialogue simulates agreement. Then, the neorealistic characters will explain to the *sheriff* that he does not rule in Rome, and that what is better for him is to choose between accepting the plot of the new movie or returning to the West. The worst the *sheriff* can do is to attempt to convince everyone of the authority of his role and demand obedience. This is the way militants from political organizations and unions act when they resist accepting the emergence of a new protagonism, which they could well accompany, but not foolishly oppose. The only thing these militants achieve is becoming the real "stones" that obstruct the elaboration of new paths.[3]

PROBLEMS AND CHALLENGES
BY HORACIO GONZÁLEZ

The events of the 19th and 20th can be seen from the angle of a visible absence of the familiar political banners. It seems to me that, for the first time in many years, there was a popular expression which, unlike what happened in the last few decades, did not need a visible chain of previously constituted allusions. Rather, one could argue that it was composed in those days and for that occasion. Of course, the discussion on spontaneity and determination could help us here to calibrate the portions of each thing. But I am afraid that this is the debate in which the left of the twentieth century ran aground, even though spirits as complex, diverse, and imaginative as those of Rosa Luxemburg or Antonio Gramsci left strong marks in this discussion.

Leaving aside this debate, in whose field we could barely fit one more tile, we say "absence of political banners" in order to start thinking from a subtraction, from what is subtracted, and what is reappearing as we thread the pieces of what appears. That is why the idea of the multitude seems significant, insofar as it refers to the constitution of a form of social thought that reclaims its bodies, their mobilization, their knowledge of the city. But how does it do this? Precisely by subtraction. The multitude, I think, is buried in the site of an already existing thought to which it subtracts consistency and stability.

In this sense the multitude and the people can be thought in order to remove from the latter the layers of stability it had, and not in order to contrast the multitude as a space of anti-state immediacy. The multitude would then be a mode of thinking a collective action in the present that reactivates the popular, or more precisely, a category of action in the present.

The night of the 20th I walked fifteen blocks down to Plaza de Mayo from my house and saw how levels of consciousness became more visible the closer I got. The description is very important because it was a very innovative day, with a great deal of originality, given by the fact that all the events pointed toward the horizon of consciousness: what can I do now, how far can I go? And all that was dramatized in the territory. The idea of the multitude as subtraction from something crystallized and that has to be reactivated allows us to use significant and important parts of a theory of consciousness that for moments seemed to have lost credit.

The inexistence of banners that night should not be considered a lack. On the contrary, it formed part of an interesting discovery: that it was possible to take up issues that belonged to the parties of the left and the social mobilization of the last years, while filling the plaza at dawn, in circumstances that were exceptional because of the hour and the state of siege. But those issues were there in a state of subtraction. They had been subtracted from the more fixed and stable formations of politics and were now available to ordinary people. And the themes involved that ended in the chant "Argentina, Argentina" meant the existence of collective thinking in common, not the reintroduction of an exclusionary conception of politics of a nationalist sort.

The pots and pans are a confusing and ambiguous element, like the very name Argentina. It looked to me as an invitation to think all those issues without downsizing or circumscribing them to the political thoughts that had been unfolding. It remains to be seen to what point will the left accept being considered "cacerolera,"* since that implies taking charge of the petty saver (ahorrista), of the "I want my dollars." This is a debate on the framework of interests that are admitted as valid at a moment of transformation. Are interests always particularistic? Are the interests that go beyond the individual horizon the valid ones? Are the crudest personal interests changeable into something else? Do interests present themselves in an immediate mode and must they be overcome by universalist interests? Or is it that each individualistic interest already contains the key to its own negation?

The debate has to do with the fact that for a sector of the left, the 19th and 20th was a sign of what was going to happen in Argentina. If one takes a look at the demonstration of the 19th, which ends with tear gas, as a moment that will give way to a higher step of consciousness, then what happened on the 20th, with its martyrs, cannot be inferior. But is the 19th handicapped with respect to the 20th? My impression is that the two days show advanced forms of consciousness, and the day of

---

* In the language of those days, "pot and pan banger." (Tr.)

the violent confrontation does not necessarily have a more advanced level than the previous one. I don't know if these are two complementary movements in which one is situated as the enlightening and advantaged part of the rest or, without being different, they are two moments that exhibit equal rights to present themselves as legitimate forms of consciousness acquired by the collective in revolt.

The 19th was a very interesting situation, of enormous violence and force, but was not necessarily that of the kid breaking bank windows. For example, Casa Rosada* was dark and nobody sneaked out from there. The only thing missing was an orthodox Peronist** crying "when will we see the General," or at least the minister, but nobody sneaked out, nor could they: that was the original and very serious situation. But that seriousness was the most interesting aspect, because it was a call to a self-understanding of the multitude. Instead of that agglutinating voice, which on the other hand nobody was asking for, there was the chant "Argentina, Argentina," which resembled those from football stadiums when the national

---

*   The Casa Rosada or The Pink House is the presidential palace of Argentina in the Plaza de Mayo of Buenos Aires.

** Peronism is the name given to the movement founded by Juan Domingo Perón in the late 1940s. During its complex history, the features of Peronism that have remained constant have been its populism, pragmatism, and dependence on strong leaders. After the expulsion of De la Rúa by the revolt of December 2001, Partido Justicialista, Peronism's official party structure, was almost unanimously supported by the political establishment as the most secure means to reestablish institutional continuity. Peronist senator Eduardo Duhalde was appointed provisional president in January 2002 after three members of his party failed to form a sustainable government. During the 1990s, when he was the governor of Buenos Aires, Duhalde consolidated a powerful network of support in that province whose visible side includes the exchange of votes for assistance plans and political favors. Journalistic investigations have revealed that these networks also include connections with organized crime and the provincial police of Buenos Aires. Duhalde openly put this political machine (or what was left of it after the downfall of representative politics) to work for Nestor Kirchner's electoral campaign. (Tr.)

team plays (indeed, there were many people wearing the team's T-shirt). The other question was: when was that going to finish? How long should one remain there? The tear gas came because the feeling was that there was no way to end it. For the Argentine Federal Police this turn of events—that people remained there at two or three in the morning, without doing anything, without a way out—was too much violence. Thus, it was a moment of political tension that contained an enormous violence. The gas came to break that inspiring nothingness, where the only thing that was visible was a kid climbing the tall pole of the plaza with a flag between his teeth, as in those competitions of the soapy pole, making the crowd concerned, who asked him to get down from there. The gas came after the kid, who attracted the attention of the whole plaza, descended.

Clearly, the fact that there were no banners gave it an unsettling aspect. It was a formidable night. Never before did I live a night like that, because there was nothing that could contain the expansion of the multitude, except for the Casa Rosada, the police, the Argentina chant. That is, abstractions that were in the place that made up for what the multitude still needed, namely, to outline the words that would project it in time, beyond the refusal of the present situation. All that was needed for that refusal was the originality of sticking together and the obviousness of the claim of its generic condition: Argentinean.

That night I met acquaintances that were not acquaintances any more, because nobody knew how they had gotten there. Even I was not entirely an acquaintance to myself. I had a pot, but I felt a little ashamed about banging it, because, for me, as for so many others, that was the reminder of Chile. The pot was associated with the fall of Allende, and, while it was a little difficult, for some reason I picked it up. It is as if I had said: "well, it seems to me that this is worth it." Walking toward Plaza de Mayo there were some open businesses that were closing their shutters. We had to tell them: "look, this is not a looting, you should come along." But in reality what was going on was in dialogue with looting. It had the force of looting, but it had not yet found the secret of its creative impulse. It was like putting the force of looting in different terms. It was not the opposite of looting, but rather placing it in a different space of the city-turned-into-polis, that is, into a collective promise of democracy in action.

I remember that I later heard a description by television journalist Gustavo Silvestre, certainly not the most adequate political commentator, because he has a rare ability to capture the obviousness of the moment and say it as a personal summary that empties knowledge in its admissible point. But he did say something interesting because he made a sort of phenomenology. People were invited to the sidewalk of their houses to see what happened and they stayed there for a long time. They then went on to the corner, where they again remained for a while. Finally, they went to the plaza. In other words, in that narrative there was recognition of a new terrain, and I saw that. Not only did I see it; it was my own case. For the first time a trivial television political analyst perfectly reported my case. I went to the sidewalk, I was there for a while and I did not know what to do, there were many of us already. I went to the corner. There were many more of us already and we went to the plaza. Those were steps or planes of consciousness measured in meters of street.

Nobody could say "I started this," and days later, in the Británico bar, people were discussing: "I saw you and then I started." It was a chain almost without origin. Somebody told me that she had left the television on at her house because she thought she was going down to the street for a while and coming back soon. Hours later, when she returned, the television was still on, impatiently waiting for its owner. That was also my case. All these elements of microdomestic everydayness seemed very interesting to me. That is, spontaneity is interesting because it has these supports, not because it is some sort of great current whose expression could never be detected. What is interesting are these little breaks in relation to a routine that could have been otherwise. The spontaneous did not appear as the opposite of the articulate, but as something that had always been there but needed a differentiated instance of visibility. Hence a phenomenology of the way in which the present manifests itself does not seem useless or anachronistic.

Plaza de Mayo is a place with a constant feature that has to be analyzed. So have the attempts to burn the Cabildo* in successive cacerolazos. It is true that they were not militants. Rather, they were some sort of 'bad pupils' that were responding to a boring lesson on May 25th. But those who were on the top of the Cabildo in the middle of flames coming from the pavement were asked by people to get down, with which the latter ended up becoming a sort of voice of collective responsibility. It may be called a post- and pre-Foucauldian Plaza de Mayo, which still postulates a momentary collective thought but with great capacity to operate over the events. Because, in some way, when we talk about Plaza de Mayo, people, or nation, we talk about a discourse that has been broken as a space of reception of large demonstrations. These are stagings about power that restitute the idea of a visible unity of power but turn these symbols into a disciplinary question to be deciphered. That is why I say that they are before and after Foucault, to the extent that we must ask ourselves what new texts better serve all that happened.

The neighborhoods, the hours of arrival, the use of the night, are all new elements that force us to get back to our theme of thinking Argentina on the basis of that experience of everyday life organized upon routine icons of the city. It is necessary to think new concepts

---

* The Cabildo is another public building in the Plaza de Mayo of Buenos Aires that was formerly housed government activity but is currently a museum.

because the superposition of the everyday to the extra-everyday of the way in which the day, the night and symbols interpenetrate each other presupposes a strong originality and the promise of a new condensation of these elements. Perhaps there is not an experience of the Argentine people to which we can go back so that, as we pose questions to it, it resolves the current dilemma. In this sense, I think that what today "is" is what remains to be said about what we did. My feeling is that, by appealing to this idea of collective practice, we did not imagine that the demonstration was going to necessarily end there, nor that a form of violence that is not the traditional insurrection was going to emerge.

I see that this evokes some textbooks, and that it also has to be useful to interrogate them, because without them we do not go anywhere. I also see that there are works of Argentine history that can be dehistoricized, charging them with new meaning, fitting them in a new way in what is going on. Even from the point of view of the efficacy of the marches, the Argentine textbooks are very interesting. The unanimous screams are school children screams. One can say that they are lower levels of consciousness; maybe, but they are the strongest. They are the screams that can be heard in football stadiums. The unanimous screams are in relation to property and the nation, and adopt a conservative form. It is the established thought, a strong thought of identity, in relation to both the bank and my educational capital, my school capital, which is a capital called "Argentinean" precisely because it has apparently been there since the beginning, and resists any critical interrogation. It is like having gone to the bank and not depositing anything, but having deposits done to you. And all the school vignettes are there: Plaza de Mayo, the Pirámide, and the Cathedral. Those school vignettes are our shared "capital" and it is logical that in the demonstration they appear in their pure state, which does not exempt this from being the necessary step for their critical re-elaboration.

"All of them must go" is another dilemma, because the great importance of that statement is that it does not have an object. It is as drastic as it can be and nobody can lay claim to it. It is strictly a collective creation; the problem is whether it merits that we take it literally. Perhaps this should not happen, because if it does, the political discussion that would take place would be less interesting than the state of historical balance in which this slogan puts us. I did not dare to say "all of them must go," because of the Argentinean prudence, having seen other subsequent chapters of Argentinean history when those strong moments unfold in all their splendor. But I was shocked by the literality. I should have accepted its state of allegory to embrace it. Conversely, there are people who chant it having in mind its real conclusion, and so they imagine an immediatist revolutionary solution that might be fundamental, but its price is that it ruptures the level of collective caesura and inspiration of the all of them must go. Now, when it is pronounced in front of the Supreme Court it does seem to acquire an object: the members of the Court should definitively go. It seems to me that that is a deeply democratic demand that certainly opens new issues.

But this cannot be confused with a naive obstinacy as in the case of some members of the popular assemblies who say "all of them must go, we stay." It is then when it loses the drastic, anguishing, and abysmal form it has. Because if there are only a few assemblies that stay, what they are doing is removing the enormous allegorical force the slogan has. Sartre would say: it is fundamental, but abstract. It needs a singularity. It does have it with the court, but I understand that the "all of them must go" contains an enormous foundational project, because we are all forced to unceasingly seek objects. Paradoxically, to fill it with immediacy consists in taking away its effectiveness. Because it is valid not just as a form of watching the entire scene, positing on it a new force, and retaining its resolution. To me it is interesting this way: all of them must go, but there is still a government, in other words, we are all watching them. And not just from forms of control and surveillance, but from heralding new forms of history.

The power (*potencia*) retained from this slogan does not need a Left making the facile remark "all of them must go, the assembly stays." Hence, another government would finally be instituted. One that the generalized effects of the "all of them must go" would not reach. But what kind of government would it be that it would not be reached by the general effects of that law? It would pay a hard price for its literality as it becomes the earner of the same critique it upholds. This again raises the question about the origin of politics and political force. That is why we should not disregard any of the issues that have come up, because the big issues of politics need grand texts, which start up by being street screams or forms of displacement of people through the geography of the city. At the same time, we have to have some courage to discuss with insufficient or routine forms of resolution of the singular potentiality that these fundamental forces have, which remain in a state of sign, of insinuation, and which some times, instead of asking us to pass toward a literal organicity or to be "concrete," as sometimes a certain Left rushes to consider, it demands us to think that the most effective thing to do might be to remain in a state of creative allegory, of active disposition through symbols that the collective constantly reelaborates.

THE POSITIVE "NO"

THE EVENTS OF the 19th and 20th hardly let themselves be captured by a literal reading of their slogans. Here we are faced with a paradox: in order to be grasped, the statement "all of them must go, not a single one should remain" requires a labor of understanding capable of finding the *positivity* even under its *negative* form. Here the breakdown of representations inhibits any straightforward interpretation: one speaks in order to absolutely renounce "programmatic" discourse.

The scream of December implied the entry of the—thus far—*spectators* into the play. But this entry, as traumatic as it is for the actors (who cease to be so at that very moment), becomes more serious in the face of the interruption of the script that the invasion of the scene produces. In fact, this entry *disrupts* all the internal possibilities of the play. The new protagonism refuses to sustain the conditions that make representation possible.

Those who enjoy theater are left with three options. The first one is the most immediate. The audience might reject this unpredictable act that visibly annihilates all theatrical possibilities. If every work has as an essential condition the scission between actors and audience, and if that separation gives theater its specific space and dynamics, then the audience may disavow the facts and demand that each go back to their seat, to continue enjoying and pretend that nothing happened. In this way, theater would be a production with two authors. One, the explicit one, the one responsible for the play and the scenes such as they appear in front of us; the other, invisible, the one who assigns pertinent roles: some to the seats, others to the stage.

Second option: to lament the failure of representation. The verification that the game is eventually ruined, that there is not a way of keeping the audience fastened to their seats, tells us about the failure of the invisible author, who does not know how to consider theater without the characteristic separation.

There is a third position. It is possible to wreck the plans of the authors of the work, and force the indistinguishability between audience and actors, without destroying the possibility of a theatrical meaning (without an author). But now there will no longer be *one* work and *one* author, in other words, history will not be reduced to a theater, but every one will have to find a meaning to their own drama, their own tragedy, their own comedy. Unlike the traditional position, sense will no longer derive from an *a priori* coherence given by the author, but will open as a becoming to go through.

Nevertheless, the simultaneity of acting and interpreting is complex and condemns us to not finding a permanent meaning to events, even those in which we are involved. The indistinguishability between stage and seats institutes a unique, but infinitely diverse spatiality.

It turns out that sometimes, whole dialogues only find their consistency from an apparently disconnected event. This is how the circumstances of the events of 19th and 20th seem to have occurred. For many of those who went out with their pots and pans what they were doing there was not clear at all. Many others believed they understood it, until an unpredictable intervention showed them that the movie in their head did not form a harmonic composition with the events. From a more traditional position the participants of that insurrection are accused of lacking feasible proposals, of not making a reasonable use of their demands. In the end, we are apparently dealing with an *incomplete* event. The balance is hurried: excess of disorder and violence, shortage of words and proposals.

Nevertheless, a perspective focused on finding sense in these events might ask what it is that connected so many people in the same intense and concentrated time. The hypothesis could be enunciated in this way: the positivity of the negation lies as much in the destitution of the existing political forms, both representative and institutional, as in the becomings it opens.

In other words, the power (*potencia*) of the 19th and 20th consists in the possibility of constituting a single plane of action, which disavows the hierarchies that organize institutional and political interaction.

It is the fall not just of a government but also of every transcendent level to the plane of immanence[4] founded by the multitude. Of course, the forces of the market accomplished the destitution of the state as a metastructure. But what happened on the 19th and 20th occurred at the level of the elaboration of forms of resistance, of their internal hypotheses. It was an experiment on effective forms and also on those already useless. The popular verification of the impotence of the classical political forms does not become a foundation of hopelessness, but of power (*potencia*): it exhausts a period of illusions and waiting, it activates creative and inquiring mechanisms on the most effective forms of struggle.

There is here a deferred and subtle affirmation of the instituting powers (*potencias*). The verification of blocked paths does not close a sequence of struggles but opens it. This deferred institution does not operate according to the familiar forms of popular sovereignty. It acts affirming the conditions to experiment with new forms of counterpower. Indeed, the social atmosphere was reorganized by the onrush of an unexpected force that lacked a predictable direction.

The mass media apply their own logic: they attribute a "minimal" rationality to an un-channeled stream of energies. And that minimal rationality points towards the reconstruction of the terms of a traditional theatrical work: to renew the representatives so that the relation of representation does not fade. Only in this way is it possible to understand that on a television show, for instance, a group of well-intentioned journalists got enthusiastic about doing a *casting* of new political leaders among the members of the assemblies of Buenos Aires.

But the *no* of the *pueblada** was an affirmation in a deeper sense: there is a possibility inscribed in the very form the insurrectional negation taken on. The fact that the multitude has acted as the single author means that the power (*potencia*) of the *no* lies, precisely, in that it does not become state power: it does not need to *legitimate* itself by means of proposals, nor does it respond to the communicative norm that requires seductive discourses and attractive images. The energies of the movement are, in their way, *constituent*. Their effects will not be passing. Against all the attempts to limit, channel or institutionalize it, its productive effects are already unleashed, and their forms of re-elaboration will be able to unfold at a situational level.

In a more decisive plane, this is an important challenge to the dialectical tradition of thought that conceived negation as a previous and necessary moment with respect to affirmation. Negation, dialectically understood, was formulated by Hegel as the preceding moment of a superior affirmation. Only in this sense does it possess an indirect "positivity." The negation we talk about does not allow itself to be captured so easily. It does not unfold in a linear time, but in a multiple one, and, as a negation, it is itself a multiple opening.

We are not talking about a negative moment in history that could become positive towards the end of the process, but a pure, unilinear negativity, a mere sign of crisis and decomposition. The *dialectical now* allows itself to be grasped as "it is still no, but it will be yes." It is a lacking *no*, a necessary moment but which must be overcome.[5] This philosophical consideration is not capricious. An entire cycle of insurrections was analyzed by the dominant revolutionary political theory under this sign. In this way, the rebellion of the oppressed was conceived as a necessary moment. It was itself derived from an unjust, negative condition. Revolution, at the same time, was understood as the movement to negate that negation, in an organic becoming towards the reconciliation of the social and historical totality with itself. The old contradictions were, finally, overcome. The revolt, as negation, affirmed "the new," socialism.

The negation of the negation was the key moment. Lenin theorized this moment of the "revolutionary situation," which becomes crisis and then affirmation of the proletarian forces. Its condition was that those below do not let anybody govern them and that those above can no

---

* In Argentina *pueblada* has been used to refer to uprisings in cities and smaller towns since late 1960s. *Pueblada* means both uprising of the village and uprising of the people. (Tr.)

longer govern. The political vanguard operates as the carrier of historical reason, the positivity that navigates the oceans of negativities, waiting for its realization.

This ocean is the image in which economic and political structures of domination are diluted: the change in the political relations of social classes confronted with each other. It is the moment in which the relations of exploitation are either secured or inverted. In the first case, societies would overcome the capitalist condition, i.e. the source of every oppression. In the second, the dialectic fails and the cycle would start again—to infinity—in ever more degraded conditions.

This was the dominant historical philosophy of contemporary revolutions. Both success and failure were thought about from an unquestioned hypothesis: societies either transform themselves or preserve their invariants from above. We cannot continue considering historical events from this philosophy. Social structures are not *moldable*. The determinist conception, according to which we live in a linear and homogeneous temporality in which we are all capable of manipulating and producing causes and phenomena and in which the challenges of the present are thought about and "administered" from an ideal image of the future society, is not suitable today to interpret the events of the 19th and 20th.

The Argentinean insurrectional experience insists in going beyond the *failures* of modern revolutionary experiences and their forms of thinking history. It tells us about radical change under new modalities that neither overlooks nor submits themselves to inherited images of the revolution. Like in the Zapatista "Ya basta," affirmation does not take the form of a promise. It starts with the rejection of the present state of affairs. But, when we look at it closely, that rejection is not a merely reactive negation, but a gesture of self-affirmation that permits the exercise of negation. That power (*potencia*) is not announced. It is not described. It is not a threat. Rather, it erupts as the corporeal presence of men and women who, without many words, alter the everydayness inside the nation-state or the fast flows of the market.

In the movement they appear as a single body of experiments without prior bonds. It is a complex phenomenon of multiple *connections* between different situations that does not give rise to only one situation. Its methods of confrontation and its fugacious leaders were radically situational. One of the most important insurrections of Argentinean contemporary history and the first great insubordination of the post-dictatorship era was incubated without bosses, without models, without promises, and without programs.

IRREVERSIBILITY

> *"The possibility that we go back to be what we were is*
> *not in question. Nor is it that we become others."*
> *— Subcomandante Marcos*

How to think of the causes of the revolt? The deterministic form of causality is not neutral. It is the idea of a homogeneous and reversible temporality, a spatialized time in which the subject observes, ponders, and, therefore, knows. If every event is caused by another, and if it is possible to establish a legality of the interplay of causes and effects, the events could be explained (and foreseen) easily. The prospects of manipulating, controlling, and directing natural and social processes would be well grounded.

But that is not the case. The separation of subject and object, the reduction of all rationality to the analytically foreseeable and the simple forms of causality, function only as an anachronistic ideology. They are valid only inside a determinate set of premises, but they no longer tolerate their operation as the foundation of being in the world.

Nor does the postmodern position stand up. The announced end of history, revolutions, struggles, and ideas was radically refuted these past years by a true popular counteroffensive that, under new conditions, has given birth to unthought forms of resistance.

It is not mechanical causes but *fusion* that explains the 19th and 20th. Althusser would say *overdetermination*. Neither fundamental contradiction, nor pure inconsistency. Its emergence is not reversible. Neither were the effects of the insurrections of October 17th* and the Cordobazo.** It is the same but very different. In other words, its effects

---

* As Colonel, head of the Department of Labor, Vice President, and Secretary of War from 1943 to 1945, Juan Perón gained support from prominent socialist labor unions like the Confederación General del Trabajo de la República Argentina (CGT). Because conservative opponents within the military forced Perón's resignation and imprisonment in 1945, workers took to the streets to demand his release on the now famous day of October 17, 1945.

** During the legendary Cordobazo uprising of May 29–30, 1969 in the

are as instituent as those of the previous ones, although its efficacy is not direct but paradoxical. Its condition of effectiveness is the destitution of the representative forms in effect up until then. From this comes the astonishment, the impossibility of reducing what happened to pre-existing structural logics.

The constitutive forces of the insurrectional movement are not deduced from trajectories of classes or individuals. Without negating such trajectories, they produce a *beyond* that reinterprets them and exceeds any conscious plan.[6]

The new protagonism does not operate from choice but from *decision*. As Miguel Benasayag affirms, we need to make this distinction.[7] Choice is characteristic of the *rational subject*, the author of history. Its coherence is such that it allows the subject to confront the dilemmas offered by the world without significantly altering its own consistency. *Decision*, on the contrary, does not depend on the available information. It does not suppose a sufficient and transhistorical subject (individual or group). *Decision* tells us about the ephemeral and the temporal, about an intersection, a fusion of previous elements, and a multiplicity that constitutes itself as collective body. The situation simply emerges.

The insurrection of the 19th and 20th belongs to this paradoxical logic of fusions, emergences, and non-absolute unforeseeabilities. When it comes to talking about causes, about history, a reflection appears, at the same time, about the structure of this history that is usually supposed to be linear. Indeed, fusion is the mixture and eruption of a series of local resistances, old defeats, irredeemable injustices, and frustrated illusions of several generations expressed under the exigency of fidelity imposed by the times. It is the existence of struggles and generations that had decided not to get used to the violent "social exclusion" amalgamated to an exaggeratedly "absent" state (or what can be technically called "Argentinean style neoliberalism").

Can this undefined magma be called a "cause"? We do not know. In any case it was not an "accumulation" in the mechanical and deterministic sense, according to which, after arriving at certain point, a straw—say, the state of siege—breaks the camel's back. Taken separately, none of these dissimilar memories can be understood as a cause, for they only act as such once they have entered under the dynamic that actualizes them.[8]

The point of fusion, at which all the elements that converge lose the

---

northern province of Córdoba, automobile workers who held a series of strikes in the prior weeks were met with violent police repression. The population of Córdoba then occupied the city with riots.

solid state in order to mix with each other giving way to a new consistency, occurred, indeed, around the state of siege. But just as temperature measures the boiling point while heat is what causes it, the state of siege was not cause but trigger, measurement, point of irreversibility of the process of fusion.

The immediate effects of the insurrection were evident for its protagonists. It left the present indeterminate. In the "cause," then, there is a complex mesh of dimensions and temporalities. The present turned on itself, opening unexpected becomings from an explosion of layers of knowledges and resistances that actualized past defeats. Suddenly the past appeared, revealing that it had not been neatly closed, that it had extended over all these years. Time elapses in overlapping dimensions, and the hegemony of its spatial representations does not exhaust the possibilities.

What has burst is time. Hence the irreversibility. The effects of the 19th and 20th are not exhausted in the appearance of a new political conjuncture. On the contrary, the value of the current situation is given more by the ways in which it can situationally produce the effects of this mark, of this opening, than by the immediate capacity to obtain "political achievements" in the way they are traditionally conceived.

Irreversibility[9] does not allude to an eventual irremediably progressive character of the effects of the event, but to the alteration of this temporality. In the new political scene there are neither guarantees, nor definitive novelty, nor closed discoveries. Everything remains to be done; it is being done. Even if the energies declined, if the movement was dispersed or, even worse, more or less institutionalized, the mark of these events and subsequent experiments that sought to develop it will remain.

What has emerged, then, is the possibility of carrying out an ethical movement, a passage: of enduring the imperatives of a time and a space, the capacity to create them. From being overburdened by an alienating everydayness, to the question concerning the possibilities of organizing this passage in a different way.

INSURRECTIONAL VIOLENCE

AMONG MANY OTHER merits, the insurrection attained a perspective from which to appreciate in all their magnitude the myriad of subjectifying practices that exist in our country. This visibility was not evident before December. It was imperceptible. The hypothesis is that that visibility does not come separate from another practical discovery: the multitude made an effective verification of the nature of the changes in the structure of power.

Indeed, since the end of the dictatorship—after the struggles of the 1970s—a task remained unfinished: the readjustment of ideas, conceptions, and tactics of struggle after the transformations that had taken place both in the political-economic structures and in the popular perceptions of them. This is the mechanism that the revolts, roadblocks, factory occupations, assemblies and the banging of pots and pans set in motion.

The state of siege crystallized two simultaneous processes: the realization that state rule—without having necessarily lost repressive capacity—no longer functioned in the same way as in the 1970s, and the process of creation of multitudinous and non-centralized forms of struggle.

The state of siege was decreed in much of the national territory in response to looting, just as the political opposition had demanded it, the governing alliance, and the main corporations based in the country. It failed not because of a certain degree of political weakness, but because of the determination of the popular resistance, which made it impossible in such political and institutional circumstances to carry out the repression. A state that had been deserting from every popular demand was unable to react when all the demands were presented together. It became entangled in its own incompetence.

Everybody knows that the Argentinean state can no longer guarantee the order desired by investors and politicians throughout the territory. What is new is that popular resistance has proven that it knows how to play with this new element. The point is not to attack power but to disorganize it. The starting point of confrontation is the capacity to neutralize and disperse repressive forces. Hence the importance of not confronting them from a central organization.

Of course, none of this supports the thesis of a hypothetical "decomposition" of capitalism. It has existed in many ways, and, contrary to what many "anticapitalists" think, its disappearance will not happen as a result of one of its "cyclical crises."

Behind the relative incompetence of the Argentine state there is a complex process of uninterrupted reconversion. Indeed, the decade of

Menem distorted the process of "transformation" of the federal state into a postmodern agent. As present-day neoliberals say, the Menem administration successfully accomplished the phase of destruction of the capacities of intervention of the federal state, but it did not manage to build a *competitive state* in its place. It was Cavallo who most radically denounced this situation when he argued that the state—adequately privatized—had been handed over to "mafias." In Argentina the neoliberals have not managed to carry out the second part of their program—which coincides with the second generation of reforms or second Washington consensus. Rather, they become entangled in the arrangement of fast deals and lack any capacity to articulate a stable political hegemony. This becomes evident with the downfall of the Alliance that opposed the Justicialista party. Its ostensible failure clearly tells us about this political impotence to carry out even the political program of neoliberalism.[10]

The state of siege did not impress anybody. Supposedly, the measure would be backed by the middle classes terrified by the looting episodes, as happened after the lootings of 1989. It was a disastrous calculation.

This seems to be the complexity of the situation: in the face of the extreme weakness of the national state it seems that very different expectations have emerged. On one hand, the extreme neoliberal position considers that this can only be fixed with more businesses. Businesses and repressive capacity against those who pose obstacles to the logic of profit. The traditional statist political position clings to the remains of the nation-state and believes in a reconstruction: it is concerned with the defense of constitutional institutions by the country's most important political parties. There is also a position that insists in building a state of new type, capable of establishing rules for ensuring businesses, a minimum of predictability, and a legal authority ruling economic and political conducts. There is, also, a classical revolutionary position that sustains the Marxist-Leninist theses of taking power and the dictatorship of the proletariat.

Of course there are nuances between these positions. Nevertheless, what matters is not to depict each of them properly, but to insist in the emergence of a new position, generic and diffuse, which considers that social change does not operate on the basis of these different political programs. This is the position that has gained strength on the 19th and 20th. It is an active, constituent force that has realized the conditions in which it has to operate.

Even when the confrontation is open, as was the case with the battle of December 20th in the surroundings of Plaza de Mayo, the terms are no longer those familiar to us for the past three decades. In fact, the violence of the 20th does not resemble the forms of confrontation of the 1970s in the least. This was mass violence, without organizations, with a level of intensity in the clashes between forces that finds its precedents in football stadiums and neighborhood rock 'n' roll concerts. These are new, absolutely unruly forms of violence, which have been coming to include more and more spaces that have become, in the past few years, true "no man's lands." These are forms of violence that count on neither "explicit rules" nor mediations, and which are regulated by codes that are unintelligible for any external agent.

The topology of postmodern capitalism operates by dividing territories of inclusion and exclusion. The former exist as true *fortresses*, the latter as true *no man's lands*, where a Hobbesian state of nature rules. The 19th and 20th can also be understood as the moment in which the resistances that developed during the last years in the *excluded* territories erupted in the public square, the place of support of national political representations. Nevertheless, popular violence cannot be reduced to gang violence or looting.

The precedent of the piquetero struggle is relevant in this regard. The pickets instituted forms of violence with characteristics of a legitimate and effective self-defense. Right in the middle of no man's land, piquetero[11] groups act resisting the lack of rules of the game to found social, political, and cultural consistencies. On the basis of these consistencies they open an organizational capacity that is both democratic and militant.[12] On the 19th, these elements articulated with each other until they originated a very particular form of violence: forcing all the foreseeable forms of social mobilization and overflowing, in this way, every repressive capacity.

The legitimacy of these acts of violence possesses characteristics that are likewise novel: legitimacy is self-conferred. It does not depend on the recognition by any other actor. It is not a classical war game in which an enemy seeks the formal declaration of war as the necessary recognition to give consistency to its own violent act. In this way, the struggles constitute by themselves—beyond the very fact of confrontation—their own criteria and values of justice. The defensive and self-affirmative character of violence operates as foundation of this fundamental *asymmetry*.

These differences could be perceived during the events of the 19th and 20th. The violence disseminated by power operated in two fundamental ways. On the one hand, using its firepower against the multitude and murdering at least thirty people, as well as many others that have not been recognized. On the other hand, instituting a psychosis, functional to the *ideology of security*, which intended to reanimate in everyone their own individuality, retracted and fearful of others. The intelligence and "psychological war" operations, particularly in the neighborhoods of the province of Buenos Aires, were destined to reinforce this power mechanism.[13]

The effects of *popular self-defense* are opposed to those of isolation and retraction of the *unruly violence* applied by and against disorganized individuals. Precisely, while the former is founded in the composition of supra-individual bonds, promoting the constitution of a common, cooperative and amplifying force, which potentiates and continues individual forces and desires at collective scales, the second reinforces the separation of individual and operates intensifying the fear "of others"— allowing the manipulation from power and the loss of all autonomy.

After the December insurrection and the events that followed, violence cannot be thought about abstractly. The new protagonism affirms its own ways of understanding and intervention by developing concrete practices of self-affirmation. They do not appeal to intangible unities that justify offensive and centralized violence in the name of transcendental[14] values, but, on the contrary, they are the popular experience of this asymmetry made by opposing to the action exerted by power through a series of representations, an ethics of physical presence founded in motives and knowledges that are both potent and radically legitimate.

IN THE STREETS
BY LA ESCENA CONTEMPORÁNEA

Much has been said and written about the events of December 19th and 20th. Nevertheless, it does not seem reckless to suppose that there will be many more opinions, hypotheses, and interpretations referred to events that not only seem to have become a local milestone, but which have also been taken as a case by European and North American thinkers, who laboriously seek to verify their hypotheses about the transformations of capitalism and the consequent strategies of rebellion that might—and should—be put into practice now. These interventions also produced heated responses from local militants and intellectuals who, without ignoring the effects of the mutations that have taken place at the world level, sought to re-situate these struggles within the framework of a singular history, which is that of Argentina as a nation.

We, the members of the editorial collective of *La Escena Contemporánea*, would like to venture a few reflections on these events and their effects inside the Argentinean society. We do not try to elaborate sociological theses on the 19th and 20th, nor do we seek to turn the events into one more milestone among the rituals of the leftist or populist traditions, and, even less, to consider what happened as a confirmation of what we had always maintained. On the contrary, we prefer to think and intervene from inside the experiments and recognize ourselves in the uncertainty—that oscillation between happiness and anguish—that also caused the mobilization of December.

To begin with, we could say that the events of December 19th and 20th were, like October 17th or May 29th were for other generations, a moment of condensation and collective corroboration of intuitions that were dispersed up until then. First, the intuition that political parties are exhausted as active organizers of social transformation, but also that of their crisis as stabilizing agents of order. Second, the intuition that the dictatorship had finished: nobody felt that the institutional order had to be defended from a possible coup and, in consequence, military terror no longer was a threat standing in the way of street action. Third, the intuition that Argentina was not the desert in which to lament the absence of an organized left wing party, but a field with a different kind of grass. And fourth, the intuition that socio-economic position is not an impediment to the organization and production of new vital forms of sociability: the movements of the unemployed and middle class neighborhood assemblies destroyed classist and structuralist prejudices.

These were at least some of the intuitions that had encouraged and animated our experience as a magazine. However, the mood in which this collective condensation occurred turned out to be absolutely unexpected. Everybody knows it: events always escape (or exceed) the rationalizing and anticipatory plans, but then they open to the encounter with the meanings we confer to them. Walking some of the most significant avenues in the political memory of this country, the multitude created an unprecedented path. This connection between a path that is inscribed in the historical experiences of Argentina and new modes and contents of that avenue is one of the distinctive signs of those events. The occupation of streets and public spaces was done with symbols, memories, and words of the Argentine traditions. The robes, as Marx would have said, were those of the nation, but they were also the festive imagery of the murga* and the militant energy of football stadiums and rock concerts. The wrapping of bodies in flags places us before an obvious datum: it is the work of symbolic appropriation and confrontation that activates and endows with new sense the national memory, and not the latter that drives the struggles.

Let's recall an old image used to refer to another unexpected eruption that condensed experiences, yearnings, and intuitions: the rebellious subsoil of the nation. A geological metaphor that, in its compact form, referred to the laborious, resistant, and subterraneous existence, on the one hand, of an oppressed people and, on the other, of a national horizon in which to intervene in order to end that oppression. If we wanted to be faithful both to that powerful image and to our reality, we would need to say that we are now faced with the rebellion of the remains of that nation. Could these fragments be connected to a renewed nation? Should they be so? Or are they embryos of another type of collective experiences that no longer have the nation and the national State as a possibility, even though they have them as an

---

*   Murga refers to both a genre of popular music and the clubs of dancers, musicians, and jugglers that perform it. Its origins date back to the culture of African slaves brought to the River Plate region in the times of the Spanish colony. (Tr.)

aspiration? Because it is evident that as desire and as horizon, the nation continues to tinge the demonstrations; yet it is difficult to consider it a significant dimension of the existing conflicts. These struggles, we believe, place new subjects in front of us. Or place us in the presence of new practices and experiments that indicate to us that the quest of the traditional subjects is not only in vain, but also reactive.

These experiments can be innovative for two reasons. First, because what has radically changed are the social, economic, political, and cultural conditions under which subjects constitute themselves and on whose conflictive points social struggles, resistances, and critiques of the prevailing order are spun. The other reason is not in the plane of external causality or that of the structure, but in the quest itself and in the creation of more effective forms of struggle put in practice by those groups that have decided, more or less consciously, to create new forms of life. These are not contradictory reasons; rather, they converge. Because if it is true that the roadblock is to the society of 20 percent unemployment what the strike is to that of full employment, it is also true that neither the strike nor the roadblock are mere techniques to make demands, but signs of cooperation and creation whose effects are deeper than what is obtained in the work stoppage or the roadblock. The incipient attempts at community construction, which we usually call resistances, are not just mechanical and defensive reactions in front of the destruction of social bonds. Sometimes they also imply dimensions and practices that are lines of flight, creations that go beyond the designated terrain.

Sometimes in the neighborhood assemblies there is more going on than "making virtue out of necessity." They also experiment with bonds and possibilities on the ground of an unexpected encounter with others that raise the possibility of creating new living conditions. The neighborhood bonds have reorganized: it is easy to corroborate that if a few months ago the neighbors found themselves organizing repressive measures or making resounding requests for security, today the encounter happens upon a different ground. That is not too little.

That it is not too little also has to do with that which the events of December 19th and 20th produced with regard to the collective understanding of the possibilities of the streets or, rather, the streets' understanding of the collective possibilities. And that comprehension or intuition was the one that transformed its protagonists into subjects of a larger fabric: that of the forms of resistance, insurgency, and creation that, beginning with those events have become undeniable evidence. Before that moment, there were numerous vital experiments that rebelled against the dominant values, groups that resisted the commodification of existence, organizations that struggled for narrow issues but that also, in their own becoming, allowed for people to come together under other principles. The piquetero movement was perhaps the largest emergent among these new resistances. Over the years, however, these experiments were evaluated in ways that were, at least, small-minded: either they did not belong to the appropriate class, or their claims were exhausted in the state subsidy, or their struggles did not have a national projection. All that these analyses discarded, and today discover with astonishment, is the creation or foundation of forms of sociability and cooperation reluctant to accept commodification and mass mediatization, even though they did have some of the latter.

The usual blinders prevented an understanding of this, but also, for a wide social spectrum, the greatest obstacle was the decision—conscious or unconscious, who cares—not to understand. Although, from a discursive point of view, the political culture of Menemism underwent harsh critiques, its fundamental core remained safe while convertibility* lasted: because it remained as a culture of consumption and extravagance, as the subordination of the community

---

* *Convertibilidad* or convertibility is the popular name given to the law introduced by Menem in 1991 that pegged the peso to the U.S. dollar. (Tr.)

to market logic and individual accumulation.

Menemism—and we do not believe we are being original by saying this—was nothing more than the culmination of a reconversion—which had started during the last dictatorship—of Argentinean society in terms of the market and, with it, the primacy, in the definition of life, in terms of user, customer, consumer, or spectator. For this reason, beyond any moral or political critique, Menemism was such a booming success in practice.

The destruction of the associative and political forms that had unfolded since the seventies, operated not just by state terror but also by deep economic and cultural transformations, was a condition of possibility for the abolition of politics as an instituting activity. Over the last twenty years, voluntaristic simulacra were easier to find than collective creations. Under those conditions, resistances were strongly limited to a question of individual ethics, giving the illusion of a possible personal salvation. Only when economic processes and governmental measures knocked down the possibilities of reproduction of those living conditions, that is, when they turned that practical decision into nostalgic illusion, did the existence of collective experiences become socially understandable and it was possible to glimpse at their value beyond their organizing around demands or issues that were most of the time narrow in scope. That does not mean that, to say it rapidly, the corralito* triggered a middle class insurrection. This is not the type of interpretation that would allow us to explain anything today.

What we do want to say is that, if by the 19th and 20th the exhaustion of established forms of life—the crisis— was evident, it was the experience of collective mobilization that permitted new perceptions—about the crises, about resistances—found continuities and kinships with what existed, but also gave birth to other realms of

---

* The *corralito* was the seizing of bank accounts to limit withdrawals out of fear for capital flight after the failed Menem devaluation. (Tr.)

encounter, dialogue, and cooperation. And from there, open quests for articulation or learning. The slogan "piquete and cacerola: there is only one struggle" resolves the question with too much simplicity: not all the quests operate in the same way, and the questions about the subtle threads that link some experiments with others are also part of this same path, and not an excuse to apply a recipe, a knowledge or a theory that allows us to interpret and compose them from their exteriority. For that reason, we do not believe that in the face of the crisis and in the face of these experiences we can embrace protective certainties that shelter us and resolve for us what to do as intellectuals, as militants, and as members of a community that knows it is in a state of dissolution.

NOTES

1. Here we use *movement* in the neutral sense of "things that happen," precisely in order to respect what was unrepresentable about it. In several chapters we also use the idea of movement as multiple or as movement of movements.

2. The opening brought about by the events of December implies a rupture and, at the same time, the crystallization of latent social processes. The reasons why it is possible for us to date these events mysterious. It is not a question of magnitude or spectacularity of the events, but of the practices they make possible.

3. Struggles, as Karl Marx said, have neither a utopia ready to implement nor ideals to carry through; they just need to affirm the elements of a new society present in their reality.

4. In order to exist as such, this plane of immanence must account for the "issue of the media." In this respect, the absence of an in-depth debate on the power of the mass media and the society of the spectacle is as evident as the fact that the relation with the media is intelligently used by radical experiments. This is a generalized phenomenon: the movement knows how to separate what "happens on television" from what "happens in reality." We consider this an opening towards a new way of "seeing" what television shows, to be suspicious about it, to "use it." In Avenida de Mayo—in downtown Buenos Aires—there is a graffito that reads "turn off the TV set and go out to the street." The movement does not abandon its relation with the media, but it does administer that relation, revealing an active, thoughtful, and critical position in relation to the media. In a recent television show two renowned journalists attempted to broadcast from the place where an assembly was taking place. But the people meeting there frustrated the show. This is not an affirmation that the movement has elaborated a consistent and radical theoretical critique that, without a doubt, does not exist, but that it does not let itself to be openly manipulated. In fact the media have taken the abused ahorristas as the symbol of the pots and pans, which entails a total failure, since it is evident that the movement of the assemblies cannot in any way be reduced to the movement of the ahorristas.

5. The dialectic can be thought about as a philosophy of the subject and the state. It operates from the notions of contradiction and diversity from the perspective of a synthetic unity. However, the dialectical tradition recognizes heterogeneous approaches. John Holloway has recently articulated a reading of Marx, Bloch, Lukács, and the Frankfurt School tradition of negative dialectics and proposes to think resistance as a "scream that says NO," as an experience of "insubordination" and a passage made possible by a practice of non-subordination. In this regard, see his articles "Doce Tesis sobre el Antipoder," and "Por un Enfoque Negativo, Dialéctico, Anti-Ontológico," in *Contrapoder, una introducción*; op. cit. ["Doce Tesis" is available in English online at http://www.commoner.org.

uk/04holloway2.pdf (Tr.)]

6. For Alain Badiou this is a classical enigma of state rationality. Any time a "real event" takes place, the state "tells" what happens as a pair: on the one hand, the site where it occurs, the prior situation with all its elements as they have been thus far represented, and, on the other hand, the event as such, the insurrection. What it cannot manage to fix is the rationality of the bond between both. In general, the state accuses the "infiltrated," the illegal agent, with the sole purpose of giving some name to the un-namable: the cause of the event. In market conditions, in which the state of the situation is destituted, the possibility of finding a meaning of the event is dispersed. Causes and effects vanish, making it impossible to fix meanings. Hence the importance of producing spaces and above all tem-poralities that can knit a subjectifying sense and provide meanings.

7. Miguel Benasayag. *Pensar la libertad: la decisión, el azar y la situación* (Buenos Aires: Nueva Visón, 1996).

8. This combination alters the linearity of each individual path, canceling any possibility to analytically calculate a predictable point for interven-tion. Walter Benjamin put it this way: "He who gropes in the past with examples and analogies, as if in a junk warehouse, does not have yet the bare notion of how much it depends, in a given instant, to bring that past to the present" ("Apuntes sobre el concepto de historia," in *La dialéctica en suspenso: fragmentos sobre la historia*, Santiago de Chile: LOM-ARCIS, 1996).

9. One of the most important discoveries in the rupture of the determinist paradigm has been the logic of irreversibility. It is the theme of, for in-stance, the book *The End of Certainty: Time, Chaos, and the Laws of Nature* (Free Press, 1997), by Illya Prigogine. He points out: "[T]ime-reversible processes are described by equations of motion, which are invariant with respect to time inversion ... For irreversible processes, however, we need a description that breaks temporal symmetry" (18). Prigogine explains that irreversible processes—the majority of natural phenomena—can explain chaotic transformations because they consist precisely of the recognition of the spontaneous appearance of "time arrows" in the most diverse levels of matter and, therefore, in the discovery of "self-organization." It is not a question of transferring (abstracting) concepts emanated from specific mechanisms of thought, but of realizing how the problems of an epoch express themselves in all the dimensions of thought.

10. Thus, the "Argentinean case" can be understood through these three char-acteristic tendencies: 1) a unique efficacy of the dominant block to dis-articulate one of the most integrated national states of Latin America in just two decades; 2) an incapacity to build a political hegemony capable of producing an efficient postmodern state; and 3) an increase of popular struggles.

11. MTD of Solano explains the significance of the use of violence in their ex-perience as follows: "In addition, we began to use violence as self-defense:

we do not throw sticks or stones to attack but to defend ourselves. But it is also essential to highlight that the road blocks are just one factor in our struggle, and not the fundamental one." And later they point out: "For this system, the roadblocks are a crime, are illegal, but for us they are legitimate. That is the fundamental change that we experienced as organization." From *Conversación con el MTD de Solano, Cuaderno de Situaciones 4*. Buenos Aires: De mano en mano, December 2001.

12. See chapter 4: "Multiplicity and counterpower in the piquetero experience."

13. See chapter 5: "Looting, social bond, and the ethics of the militant-teacher."

14. This element of the new forms of popular violence appears very clearly in the Zapatista conception of war. In the article "The Fourth World War," published by the Mexican newspaper *La Jornada* on October 21st, 2001, Marcos argues: "And the Indians don't speak Spanish, don't want to use credit cards, don't produce, they grow corn, beans, chilies, coffee, and happen to like to dance with marimba without using a computer. They are neither producers nor consumers. They are superfluous. And everyone who is superfluous can be eliminated. But they don't want to leave and they don't want to stop being Indians. Moreover, their struggle is not for taking power. Their struggle is for their recognition as indigenous people, for the recognition that they have the right to exist, without becoming others."

CHAPTER 3

SITUATIONAL THOUGHT IN MARKET CONDITIONS

WE NEED TO REFLECT IN THE FACE OF THE EVENTS OF THE DAYS OF THE 19th and 20th. What happened? How to go on *being the same* in the face of the power (*potencia*) of those events that we still don't fully understand? How to approach the space of a not yet deciphered signification, that invites us—under the promise of being relevant—to work through its possible meanings? How to dare ourselves to suspend the corpus of knowledges available to us on the social and the political, the certainties referring to "the middle classes," "the excluded," and "the politicians"? How to travel through our contemporaneity under the inevitable (insofar as it is present) condition of the instability of meanings, of the versatility of facts, and the game of evasions that *truth* maintains with us?

These are questions that thought cannot evade, if it seeks to constitute itself as a productive dimension inside the process opened by the new social protagonism.

THOUGHT AND CONSCIOUSNESS

To THINK IS not to know. One and the other—thinking and knowing—constitute two different moments. We could assimilate a generic idea of thinking to the capacity to resolve problems. Thus, we think when confronted with obstacles. To think is an activity, a labor. A power (*potencia*) of the soul, said Spinoza. Thinking is something we all, and not only people, do. Life itself thinks, and is forced to do so time and again, since life itself depends, in order to continue being such, on constantly facing up, taking on, and resolving problems.

Thinking, in this sense, does not necessarily imply an activity of "consciousness." According to Gilles Deleuze, if there is something in common in the materialist philosophies of immanence, such as those of Spinoza and Nietzsche, it is the distinction between "thought" and "consciousness." Thinking is what the soul does, says Spinoza, but also what the body does. Plants and animals think. Consciousness, on the other hand, the central character of modern politics and final threshold of the individual, is nothing more than a human capacity for retaining—as separate—certain ideas, sensations and knowledges.

In the terms in which he has been interpreted, Spinoza would be saying to us something that, centuries later, has been fully adopted: beyond consciousness there is thought. And if this unconscious exists, we should add, we can no longer resist admitting that the "ego" that usually speaks, "does not know"—entirely—what he or she says.

There is thought in excess. Consciousness does not know all that it would like to know about what it says, about what it wants nor about why it "wants" what it "wants." There is more thought in it than it would have imagined. Thus, perplexed and resigned, consciousness discovers that it thinks when it sleeps. It thinks with the body. Something, of which consciousness is a part, goes beyond what it can control.

Nietzsche said that this little "ego" that believes itself to be consistent and undivided, sovereign and self-sufficient, is nothing more than a small part of the "self." This "self," the body, is the one who desires, fears, feels, and thinks. The little "ego," ignorant of the ocean on which it is standing, convinced of its powers (*potencias*), believes it is controlling everything when it tries to make the pleasure it suddenly feels last, or when it tries to evade the pain and anguish that suddenly flood it.

Consciousness is not prepared for taking charge of life. This "ego" so sure of itself, is not in a condition to "dominate." Its powers (*poderes*) are scarce, and the problems that life should resolve in order to *continue living*, are complex.

That is why, when consciousness seeks to extend itself beyond its powers (*poderes*), it ends up paralyzing the living body to which it belongs. It is as if a body that let consciousness—which wants everything, but can do almost nothing—subjugate it, was condemned—defenseless, sick—to paralysis. We can verify this daily. Any pianist, football player, or professor—including professors of philosophy—can corroborate daily the curious fact that their activities could not unfold if consciousness were to take possession of them entirely in the moments in which the concert, the game, or the lecture began. How to calculate consciously the succession of keys, of notes that have to sound in the next thousandth of a second? How to calculate consciously the infinity of movements, equilibriums, and distances at stake in a subtle and definitive pass that enables the scoring of a goal? How to take charge of expounding complex metaphysical theses while seeking not to betray the texts being explicated, to be at the same time clear and pedagogical and keep a certain control over the interest of the public and the pace of the exposition, whose limits were already set and that it is necessary to respect?

In all these situations, consciousness has to step aside if we do not want to be paralyzed, slow down our movements to the point of ridicule, and, finally, be seriously reprimanded by those that believed in our talents. And yet, thought acts permanently and beyond consciousness. It almost does not require consciousness. Thus, the great artists, athletes, and professors require *concentration*, that is to say, they need to remove this "ego" that believes it controls the situation but that strictly speaking should remain in suspense—between parentheses—while the task for which it has been summoned lasts. Later, of course, with the applause it comes back at full speed to receive all types of congratulations, and to corroborate its infallibility, in order to seduce, in order to make that happiness that floods it *last* as much as possible.

The myth of the power (*poder*) of consciousness comes from far back. Reason, as the pretension of dominating the world—internal and external—expressed in the equation *I think therefore I am*, is at the origin of the rationalism upon which western modernity was founded. The conscious "ego," theoretical reason, as object of critiques and apologies, constituted itself in the subject of a history that it sought to understand and control. To think, thus, was the labor of a consistent, autonomous, and privileged entity—man—whose destiny was marked by its powers (*poderes*) of understanding and domination.

Interests given by the immediate appetites shape the liberty to which the rational individual aspires and desires.[1] From the control of this "interior" the "ego" extracts a certain knowledge of "itself." This knowledge, always imperfect, is the result of an operation of domination of consciousness over thought, over the body.

It all happens as if consciousness, as rational consistent unity, was our very essence. As if it were the ultimate foundation of our identity.

To be free implies, then, a labor of "conquest" and "colonization" of one's own body (of the "passions," classical rationalist philosophy would say). A "physical education," a discipline. Thus, the healthy, normalized body acts "controlled" by consciousness, obeying.

Herein we have the knowledges about the body and sexuality that Foucault describes in his history of sexuality: from the practice, the discipline and the self-control of the body and desire arise knowledges, stories, rites, practices, and discourses.

But this liberty idealized by the modern rationalist is not affected on a purely individual level. It requires now "to go out to conquer the world." And consciousness goes out to make its experience, to confront the resistances that nature and other people offer. Hegel thought this moment of the "experience of consciousness" in his *Phenomenology of Spirit.*[2]

To be free is to escape being "determined." To be free is, more precisely, our capacity for self-determination without being determined from outside. The subject, says Hegel, is consciousness in the act of conquering without being conquered. The subject is such with respect to itself, but also with respect to nature. That is why, while being nature ourselves—"negated nature," "negation of nature"—we are called to work on it, to adjust it to our projects.

The concept organizes the world, transforms it, and appropriates it for itself. And the same happens with respect to "other men." Liberty is the contrary of being a slave. Liberty exists as the other of being "dependent."

The works of Kant, critic of "pure theoretical reason" (and main theorist of a transcendental subject), in which the autonomy of reason is identified with economic autonomy, are well noted. One of the features of the "autonomous use of reason," Kant tells us, is to be an "owner." The liberty of the bourgeois individual is thus characterized by the myth of a sovereign reason, of immediate interests, and of power (*poder*) over the self, nature, and the rest of humanity, which would permit enjoying "the world." Far from bringing us toward freedom, these three myths considered together, bring us to barbarism.

The sovereignty of conscious reason reduces all thought to that which is analytically predictable. The material multiplicity of life and things are nothing but an obstacle that makes all prediction fail. There is always something—of the order of the real—that alters the plans.

The resistance of the real to the powers (*poderes*) of consciousness—the theoretical reason of the transcendental subject—is a repeated and permanent warning that humanity cannot live as mere negation of nature. In fact, this resistance of the real operates as a warning that must be heard, even by consciousness. Thus, immediate individual interests, as true essence of capitalist humanity—as Karl Marx got tired of explaining—are "Robinsonades." These full individuals could never exist without their very possibilities of existence being questioned by the mere fact of disowning their bonds with the world.

The individual, as such, exists always bound. It always exists in situation. It always exists incarnated in nature and *with* "other" people.

These resistances of the real, of the body, of nature, of "other people," of "the situation," are what time and again ruin so rationally planned plans. They show us, and we can experience, that thought circulates by and through these resistances, and that liberty—as "consciousness of necessity"—resides in this fact of accepting the world, the real, and the situational character of our being.

KNOWING AND THINKING

KNOWING IS NOT thinking, we said. One thinks beyond knowledge, says Alain Badiou, following other words: those of Lacan.

Thinking implies, if we follow Badiou in this: making holes in the existent knowledges in-and-about a situation. Here, to make holes means a double operation of *destitution* and *going beyond*. Destitution, insofar as those knowledges begin to saturate the possibilities of realizing an affirmation whose necessity does not derive from the knowledges available in-and-about this situation.

Destitution is not "praise to novelty" for its own sake, but rather an epistemological premise that informs us that there are not sufficient knowledges capable of totally embracing the real. "Going beyond" implies, thus, the affirmation of an opening in the situation, which permits us to investigate and produce new knowledges, which will in turn also be destituted.

A situation saturated by a dispositif of knowledges that weighs on it is incapacitated to be able to think this "beyond" (which is not simply a new knowledge, but rather an affirmation that opens new possibilities to knowledge and thought that are deduced neither from the premises that constitute the situation nor from the knowledges that represent the elements of that situation).

Thinking, said Althusser, is a "productive process." It demands raw materials, labor power, appropriate instruments, and capacity to operate, with this power and those instruments, upon the raw materials offered by history. Thinking is a practice. It is an activity of elaboration. Thinking is how we produce the world, the situation, and sense. Thinking is how ideas, knowledges, projects, practices, and becomings are produced. But thinking is a practice, we said. Thought itself is practical. Thought is practical and situational. Intellectual thought is only one form of thinking. A book is a support of thought. But there are others. One thinks before each problem. Each activity is, already, thought.

Thinking and knowing encounter one another. Both refer to something: one knows "about something," one thinks "about something." Knowledge (*saber*) manages the acquisitions of thought. To know (*conocer*), to discover, is to retain one operation of thought. It implies fixing a moment of the fluid process that thinking is about. But knowledge is not simply a residual fragment of thinking. As such, it has its own ontological weight. Knowledge, says Miguel Bensayag, has more or less power (*potencia*). It has an efficacy inside a system of premises that produce sense and inside which it acquires its own operating principles.

Thus, knowledges are neither fictional nor universal, but rather they acquire value from two great systems of references: on one hand, by responding to a particular system of premises—situation—and, on the other, by their practical capacity to give an account—through the production of "useful" hypotheses—of the real that we want to know, to theorize.

The knowledges produced by thought have a situational value that consists in a specific capacity to give an account of a certain efficacy that we would call ontological. Each theory, or consistent hypotheses, acquires a relative value that no longer entirely depends on its internal coherence—as with mathematical models—but rather, in addition, each of these models is at the same time a hypothesis to corroborate once and again, in accordance with the becomings of being. Knowledges, then, are situational as well. They are coherent systems that measure aspects of the real and, as such, their instrumental value is neither universal nor eternal.

Finally, a materialist—immanentist—epistemology organizes knowledges, practices, and ideas starting from the values granted by its situational meaning.

QUESTIONS OF VISIBILITY

THE INVISIBILITY OF alternative experiments in public discourse for more than a decade was not the work of an innocent blindness. If a certain kind of formal statements about democracy and traditional forms of social intervention gained support against all evidence, it was because the gaze of those who maintained—until quite recently—these "certainties" itself was slanted by a very particular form of historical perception: *political subjectivity*, that is to say, a form of organizing thought that gives to *politics* the last word.

A whole series of affirmations that qualify what is "central" and what is "peripheral," "important" and "superfluous," "serious" and "irrelevant," organizes itself according to this way of "being in the world." Thus, in its complexity, reality comes to be understood through the value that "politics" gives to each fact, each phenomenon, and each experiment. Politics operates as practical meaning-giving dispositif with respect to the entirety of existent practices.

The final assumption of *political subjectivity* says that at bottom society is a thick, opaque, and chaotic entity that must be turned—by means of categories of analysis and political actions—into something malleable enough so that it can be transformed. Any "disfunctionality," any "deviation," any "opacity" of the social is assumed by politics under its responsibility. Politics is that which must keep watch over the good order and health of the social body. Political subjectivity, indeed, takes charge of the pruning of the excesses, the adjustment of the pathological, and the formatting of the multiple character of the social. Politics is the activity of "directing" or "conducting" the destinies of a society toward a predetermined end, always ensuring that such possibilities of leadership are actualized and made concrete in the control of the state apparatus.

Politics thus implies the separation between those who form part of a "social" that, in its heavy being, might not have the capacity for self-determination unless it is by means of the action—representation—by elites that, once in charge of the central apparatus of administration, would accomplish the final truths to which societies aspire. The central apparatus of administration comes to organize a true "situation of situations": a center that distributes roles and meanings capable, in theory, of organizing the specific form of an entire multiplicity of experiences that develop on the national soil. This sense-giving operation depends at the same time on a classificatory capacity: the state operates reinforcing a structure of roles. Its action is therefore classificatory and hierarchizing.

Antonio Gramsci theorized the powers (*potencias*) that the state develops in order to protect the invariants of this structure: each subaltern class, each social group or individual occupies a place in the structure of roles and the state provides to each one—according to the state's capacity for producing consensuses and cooptations—a meaning that permits it to assume its role. To that purpose, the state expands through civil society disseminating these meanings. But when people actively resist assuming their place, well, they have to confront the other face of the state, the open repression that operates as violent reassurance of domination.

Throughout the twentieth century—time of "socialist revolutions"—the dominant idea of social change, of transformation, was conceived as subversion of the social foundation through the control of the political and military apparatus of the state. The social groups, the classes, struggled over the dominant position. All the political theory of this century—revolutionary, reformist, and reactionary—coincided in this central point: politics is a "zero sum" game in which the dominant organizes its power (*poder*) from the state, and whoever challenges its power (*poder*) has to be conscious of the major import of this position.

Political parties constitute themselves as the representatives of social, economic, and cultural tendencies of the grassroots and starting from there their tactics unfold inside the political game, which consists in their capacity to organize all the participants by the primacy of their own interests. Then, inevitably, the "part" that aspires to dominate the "political totality" will have to "totalize" itself until it loses its specificity—postponing its specific interests—in a quest to articulate the rest of the parts to its hegemonic domination. This is the way in which consensuses and the hegemonies constitute specifically political mechanisms by means of which a more or less broad social group mediates its interests in the whole, thus organizing domination from the center of state power, the nucleus that permits the block of leading social groups to organize themselves as such and to fully dominate over the social whole.

The word "politics" was overcharged to such a point that nothing escaped its capacity to signify. The whole illusion of an era was encompassed by the pleasure implicit in the idea of controlling history, society, and human destiny. All this filled the sound of the word politics with eroticism.

As a way of thinking, *political subjectivity* consisted in the articulation of struggles for justice and for the highest social values with the modern notion according to which those changes acquire practical relevance by their inscription in the realm of the state. Of course, this "illusion" was not whimsical. It corresponded to a specific configuration of power (*poder*) that Foucault has called "disciplinary society" and in which state institutions took charge of the constitution of the subjectivity of the citizen.[3]

Today we are witnessing the exhaustion of the disciplinary functioning of power (*poder*), and the establishment of biopolitical mechanisms.[4] Indeed, it is our feeling that current relations of domination do not constitute themselves on the basis of the principle of state sovereignty nor do disciplinary institutions on the basis of persons and social groups that inhabit the national territory, but, rather, they result from a destitution[5] of that sovereign power (*poder*).[6]

Today the principle of domination is the autonomization of the market, capital flows, and the (macro)economy with respect to the institutions charged—until now—with regulating them. Thus, neoliberalism constitutes a displacement of the proper political terrain of domination and a substitution of this principle.

We have seen the economy humiliating politics, ridiculing it, sanctioning its total impotence, and expelling it from the reign of effective and desirable practices. Not so long ago, while the electoral campaign was in full swing,* a billboard for the brand All Star proposed the following text to the reader: "Behind this poster there's a politician smiling. You are welcome."

In many senses this poster turns out to be highly symbolic. On one hand, because it demonstrates the extent to which the market is capable of building with the consumer a much more solid common sense than that which the citizen maintains with the state. In fact, a citizen disgusted with "the politicians" becomes, in an instant, an ironic consumer who shakes hands with the "most prestigious" brands in order to remove from the streets highly archaic forms of the social bond. But, at the same time, this action not only has the symbolic value of showing, as a truth about the social bond, something that is already happening. Covering a campaigning politician, or substituting in reality, *factually*, a fundamental dispositif of state domination (such as the electoral campaigns), and proposing in their place a specifically distinct type of bond—brand/consumer—amounts to exercising directly, without political mediations, very active forms of the production of a market subjectivity.

---

* The authors refer to the elections of October 14th, 2001. (Tr.)

We are confronted, thus, with a paradoxical situation: if, on one hand, the relations of domination are no longer "political" but rather "economic," on the other hand, from the side of the rebellious struggles there is an ongoing insistence in articulating liberatory responses from a *political subjectivity* that, anachronistically, supposes that it can still aspire to control, humanize or subordinate the economic flows that have become independent from it.[7] This precarious resurgence of *political subjectivity*, however, unfolds in conditions that are very different from those in which it came to establish its domination. Its anachronism consists in its incapacity to understand the disappearance of the conditions from which it extracted its own consistency: *the political centrality of state sovereignty over the national territory.*[8]

At the same time, experiments multiply that are capable of carrying out social transformations without starting from the state as the dominant position—even when those accomplishments remain inscribed in the political sphere of the state.

The immense prestige of struggles like those of Zapatismo in Mexico and the MST in Brazil—as well as those currently taking place in our country—has its origin, precisely, in their capacity to actively acknowledge the transformations operated in the terrain of domination, at the same time that they rebel when faced with them, inaugurating a new cycle of struggles characterized by a multiple subjectivity that cannot be mistaken for the political subjectivity of the previous cycle of struggles.

This is the profound *historicity* of a rising *new protagonism.* This protagonism not only tries to verify the reasons for the failure of the resistance strategies founded on *political subjectivity*, but it also constitutes an exercise of corroboration of the transformations operated in postmodern subjectivity and in the present configurations of power (*poder*), experimenting with forms of production of a non-capitalist sociability. There is, therefore, a dense history that precedes and accompanies these movements. The *national memory* of each of these experiences turns out to be—in this sense—undeniable. The past operates over these groups less as an obstacle that prevents them from experimenting with new forms of thought and struggle than as that which they can appropriate for an ongoing experimentation. Thus, the national memory of these struggles is inevitably a fundamental aspect: not only is it invoked and recreated, but also this encounter is produced by a wearisome labor of resignification whose key resides in the affirmation of a situational sovereignty to, from there, exercise this memory intelligently.

This new protagonism does not come into being, then, as reconstruction of national state sovereignty. On the contrary, it arises as corroboration of the sovereignty of the forces of the market. Its efficacy is rooted in the decision to sustain an ethic on a radically transformed terrain.

The new protagonism unfolds from a fractured sovereignty. Or, in the terms of Horacio González—an interpretation of his words that perhaps he himself would not support—it operates against the background of some "pampean remains," upon which it disintegrates the configuration of political subjectivity, which does not find a foundation upon the fragmentation under way.

The thesis, then, is that the new social protagonism works against the background of the market—market society, says Polanyi—at the height of *neoliberalism*, producing an ethics capable of inhabiting and producing the world beyond the strategies inherited from the previous political subjectivity. And that in its operation it constitutes other forms of the political, that no longer consist in a passage, "a qualitative leap," from the fragmentary to the centralized (state) but rather in a subjective affirmation that transforms dispersion into multiplicity.

In turn, this ethics no longer functions according to the parameters of *political subjectivity* but rather, as Nietzsche used to affirm, according to the capacity to produce *novel sense*—in new contexts—from the power (*potencia*) of the practices of the new *protagonism* in order to create the *values* of a sociability alternative to the dominant one.

The issue of the control of the state apparatus as it is organized in the perception of the new protagonism is very different: it would just be the central organ that administers the always finite resources of a society and with respect to which it is necessary to adopt certain *positions*. Thus, the central administration is perceived more as a site coordinating and representing different tendencies rather than as the sphere of production of sense for practices; more as a place of management of finite resources, than as one of production of the social bond. Gradually "politics" separates itself from the "affairs of the state" and, between both matters, which in the past were mixed up, new forms of confrontation, friction, and bonding take over. But this separation is not absolute. The state still tends to be an inevitable presence in every situation.

If what characterizes the new protagonism resides in that it effects a spatial-temporal cut within which it exercises a restricted action that produces sense as the origin and foundation of its sovereign affirmation, this self-affirmation establishes, at the same time, new possibilities with relation to the state.[9]

NOTES

1. Spinoza tells us that the consciousness of appetite is called *desire*. However, contrary to what the "ego" expects, it is not possible for us to know why "it wants what it wants."

2. In his celebrated dialectic of the master and the slave, Hegel describes how, when striving for liberty, consciousnesses (self-consciousnesses in formation) confront each other and are reduced to being one of the sides of the master-slave relationship. Here we are not interested in the resolution of this dialectic, but rather in pointing out that the motive of the struggle is given by the decision of both consciousnesses to no longer exist as biological, natural life.

3. In the same sense we can read the functioning of the *ideological state apparatuses* theorized by Louis Althusser ("Ideology and Ideological State Apparatuses," in *Lenin and Philosophy and Other Essays*. London: NLB, 1971).

4. See Michel Foucault, *Las redes del poder* (Buenos Aires: Almagesto, 1991) and *Society Must Be Defended*; op. cit. See also Gilles Deleuze; *Conversaciones (1972 - 1990)* (Valencia: Pre-Textos, 1999) and Giorgio Agamben; *Homo Sacer: Sovereign Power and Bare Life* (Stanford: Stanford University Press, 1998).

5. See Mariana Cantarelli and Ignacio Lewkowicz; op. cit.

6. For more perspectives on the transformation of sovereignty, see *Globalizacion capital y estado*, by Joachim Hirsch (Mexico: UAM, 1996) and the already cited work by Michael Hardt and Antonio Negri.

7. See Miguel Bensayag; "Metaeconomía" in *Contrapoder, una introducción*, op. cit.

8. All the research we have consulted coincides in affirming that the sovereignty of the national state and its classical functions do not disappear under the conditions of market domination, but rather that they are resignified under the effects of this new dominance. In fact, state institutions, thus reorganized, have their place in the constitution of the globalization of the market and a supranational biopower. The larger transformation, then, resides in that the institutions that previously regulated the economy are today refounded and oriented by the market.

9. We come back to this problem in chapter six, "Expression and Representation."

CHAPTER 4

MULTIPLICITY AND COUNTERPOWER IN THE PIQUETERO EXPERIENCE

THE ROADBLOCK AS PRECEDENT[1]

THE PIQUETERO STRUGGLE WAS BORN OUTSIDE TRADITIONAL POLITICAL and social institutions. Its autonomy and novelty relates to the disrepute of traditional political organizations, after they showed their incapacity to either reformulate their understanding of the conditions of domination of so-called late capitalism or produce changes tending to improve the conditions of existence for large strata of the population.

The roadblocks* are a modality of struggle that brings together those who were expelled from the factories: unemployed workers seeking to solve problems connected to their own existence, reorganizing themselves on a territorial basis in extended zones in which the hardest battle is against the dissolution of the social bond. From a structural viewpoint, the roadblocks are the consequence of the decomposition of the industrial base of the country.

Currently piqueteros recapture many elements and knowledges from the experiences of struggles of the working class of previous

---

* The word "piquete," used to refer to roadblocks, comes from the English word picket. We are going to translate "piquete" as "roadblock" and leave "piqueteros" in the original, since their identity has become much more than that of "road blockers" or of workers in a picket line. (Tr.)

decades—the "picket" itself was borrowed from "factory pickets." This methodological extension was not incorporated mechanically, but rather transformed under the new condition of "joblessness." This precise point is the elaboration of the legacy rather than the passive acceptance of the inheritance. Here the subjective powers (*potencias*) of the roadblock are staked in the capacity to invent forms of struggle by restoring a situational sovereignty.

Indeed, this is the elaboration that allows the roadblock to think from a *singular place*. From there, the piquetero operation consists in establishing a complex relation to the state apparatus and recreating new modalities of inhabiting the territory—the neighborhood—reformulating in novel ways its relation to the working class and unionist tradition with which it doubtlessly has points of contact.[2] Among those points there is one that cannot be overlooked: both unionists and piqueteros have had to invent forms of struggles capable of altering the normality of things; they have had to elaborate concrete forms of making themselves heard. If workers count on the capacity to interrupt the productive cycle by means of a strike, the piquete assumes its fundamentally territorial condition by obstructing the circulation of commodities through a direct, simple, and bold action: the blocking of roads.[3]

Horizontally organized, the piqueteros adopted as their modality of work and decision-making the permanent state of assembly. Their origin is recent. They appeared in the middle of the decade of the 1990s in the interior of the country and generalized in less than a year. The adoption of the roadblock dynamized the participation of the unemployed in struggles all over the country in a movement that went from the interior toward the province of Buenos Aires. The speed at which the roadblock was socialized exceeded all forms of cooptation and state repression.

The media christened them as "piqueteros" and produced a stereotype. Afterwards, diverse interpretations came into play, creating, along the way, the figure of the "piquetero." In its dominant version it is a description shaped by the place they occupy in the social structure: "excluded," "jobless," "victim." This "piquetero position" arises from linking neglect to a single methodology: the roadblock.

But, as the "piqueteros" began to speak out, it became possible to see the extent to which "piqueterismo" was grouping a multiple and heterogeneous variety of social practices. At the same time there were also attempts to unite the entire, essentially multiple, movement under a homogenizing and institutionalizing pretense. All these attempts have failed.

The piquetero movement is a true *movement of movements*. As such it has produced an authentic revolution in the collective perception about the popular capacities to create new forms of social and political intervention.

THE CONJUNCTURE AND
THE OPTIONS OF THOUGHT

THE SO-CALLED NATIONAL Piquetero Congress that took place in the first half of 2001 was a key moment in the constitution of the movement. In it nearly all the piquetero experiments in the country came together. The goal—partially accomplished—was to give birth to a national coordinating body. The proposal was to link the piquetero heterogeneity on the basis of the relative community of demands and forms of struggles. A plan of action that was immediately approved had a double effect: it showed the vigor of the piquetero struggle, the justice of its demands, and the high level of organization they had reached. Moreover, for the first time the very different ways of conceiving the struggle became visible.

Two different positions subsist within the movement. On one hand, the more structured organizations—mainly the Land and Housing Federation (FTV), connected to the Argentine Workers' Center (CTA), the Combative Class Current (CCC), the Workers' Pole (PO), and the Teresa Rodríguez Movement (MTR)*—whose thought derives its premises from terms such as "globality," "socio-economic structure," and "conjuncture." Their way of thinking is constructed in terms of "inclusion/exclusion." Their positions are not homogeneous. They are crossed by the traditional axis of "reform or revolution." On the other hand, in the less structured organizations the landscape is no less heterogeneous. Among the latter are the Aníbal Verón Coordinating Body of Unemployed Workers (CTD Anibal Verón) and the Unemployed Workers Movement of Solano, in the municipality of Quilmes (MTD

---

* The names in Spanish of these organizations are, respectively, Federación Tierra y Vivienda, Central de Trabajadores Argentinos, Corriente Clasista y Combativa, Polo Obrero, and Movimiento Teresa Rodríguez. CCC is linked to the Maoist Partido Comunista Revolucionario or PCR (Revolutionary Communist Party) and Polo Obrero is linked to the Trotskyist Partido Obrero (Workers Party). (Tr.)

of Solano).* In their thinking, these social practices assume, as both condition and term of their elaboration, the bonds that constitute the materiality of their experience. In this way they subtract themselves from the classical terms of the debate between reform and revolution. The characteristic of this operation is self-affirmation and practices of counterpower. With the generalization of the piquetero phenomenon the political organizations set up their apparatuses to face the emergency—either to coopt or to fight, depending on which case. Traditional or left parties, churches and unions—they all noticed the appearance of this movement and reached out with the intention of capturing its power (*potencia*).

The media have contributed to making the movement accessible to the public. They show the piquetero struggle subordinated to the coordinates of the "political and economic conjuncture." The struggle of the roadblocks lost all singularity and became an element of an "other" more important, more general situation: the *national situation*. The piquetero struggle ceases to be, in itself, a situation to which one commits oneself, to become an actor, a part, and an element of the *general situation*.

But to accept the inevitability of the *general* standpoint implies in turn to subordinate any other situation as mere portion or segment of an always already constituted subjectivity. This way of thinking constitutes a subjectivity that separates itself physically and affectively from the situation, taking it as an object and linking itself to it in a purely analytical fashion. This rationality indicates how careful each of us has to be when choosing their options, because it is no longer about the piqueteros, which were turned into "a part of the whole," but precisely about the well-being of that "whole" that is "the country," "the common good," etc. When we abandon concrete responsibilities, we abstractly assume responsibility for the fate of governments.

---

* The Spanish names of these groups are Coordinadora de Trabajadores Desocupados Anibal Verón and Movimiento de Trabajadores Desocupados Anibal Verón. Anibal Verón was a piquetero murdered by the police in the northwestern province of Salta, a crime never recognized by the government, who blamed the piqueteros for it. After a schism at the end of 2002, the CTD Anibal Verón adopted the name MTD Anibal Verón. In turn, MTD Solano, along with two other MTDs, split from the MTD Anibal Verón at the end of 2003. Solano is a region within the municipality of Quilmes, located in a highly (de)industrialized area in the southern suburbs of Greater Buenos Aires). (Tr.)

The concrete operations of thought distribute positions within the piquetero movement itself. From where do we begin to think our own situation? From the situational concreteness we inhabit or from a hypothetical—and not always effective—national situation? From where are we to begin the elaboration of the *sense* of experience?

If we accept the premise of a thought that abstracts the concrete conditions of its intervention and draws its sense from a general situation, we arrive at a subjectivity governed by the times and requirements of *political conjunctures*. Piqueteros that follow this path find themselves required to derive the rationale of their struggle from the senses available inside the totality in which they operate, assuming a rationality conditioned by the socially instituted forms of legitimacy.

In this way a meaning for the struggle is configured: either *inclusion* or *revolution*. The first argument goes like this: the struggle is legitimate because there are no claims of rights other than those that arise from the fact of being part of the whole—citizens, workers, human beings. The struggle for *inclusion* is a struggle for recognition. It is a question of being admitted as a part that legitimately—and legally—belongs to the nation-state totality. This form of obtaining legitimacy presupposes an undeniable premise: that the nation-state preserves its capacity for integration and that political struggle consists in the passage from *exclusion* to *inclusion*.[4] Once this reading is assumed, the piqueteros who adopt such a perspective abandon all pretension to *impose* their terms upon the rest of those who constitute the society in which they intend to include themselves—the non-piquetero population. A contest of tensions and consensus to define the terms of democratic inclusion begins. Therefore, the premise is formulated as the existence of a democratic state capable of exercising its integrative powers (*potencias*) from consensual and representative principles.

The second argument, the *revolutionary* position, states the need for social alliances to conquer state power. The roadblocks that adopt such position regard themselves as the *revolutionary vanguard of the Argentinean people*. The social totality will be transformed after taking control of the state apparatus and thus forcing a change in the principle of social organization. The expectation is focused on the possibility that the parts of the social whole recognize the roadblock as a true representation of that social totality reconciled with itself: the piqueteros as the new proletarian subject of history. This position shares a premise with the previous one: social classes acquire meaning through their economic being and aspire to social change through the powers (*poderes*) of the state.

Situational thinking acts from different premises. Of course, classes do exist. But their economic existence is not enough to give rise to social change. In order to bring about social change, that is, to activate the production of values of a new non-capitalist sociability, it is necessary, above all, to affirm situational *sense*. Thus, the thought of counterpower subtracts itself from the general term as purveyor of meaning in order to affirm a radical and irreducible stance. The situation is not perceived as a part of the whole but as a concrete totality that does not subordinate itself passively to any abstract totality. This subtraction opens the doors to an ethical process, of subjectification, of reencounter with power (*potencia*). In this way, clearly, the traditional polarization between "reform and revolution" is secondary.

REPRESENTATION

IN THIS POLEMIC the question of "political representation" played a central role. The call to unify the piquetero movements brought about the discussion. The position from which the call was made proposed a complex operation: to make a representable unit out of the multiplicity of the movement as such. To be representable the One must constitute itself as such. Multiplicity was perceived more as an obstacle than as a potentiality. Or, in any case, as a potentiality to control. This affirmation acted as an answer to the questions about how to make that power (*potencia*) a determining factor in the general situation, or how to transform that power (*potencia*) into a "socio-political" force capable of directly influencing the national situation.

These questions tell us about a hegemonic will that has started to experience multiplicity as a dispersion of forces. Suddenly, what was admittedly a potentiality becomes the main obstacle. How to build a finished representation of the multiple? How to build a leadership, a leader, and a single discourse on a basis that was not conductive to such operations?

To be sure, the leaders of the movements that insisted on this path entered a difficult terrain: their decisions began to be each time more mediated by the complexity of the conjuncture, their aspirations, and the needs to sustain their movement. In this way the links to the grassroots of their movements was transformed.

Political representation condemns those who put forward this operation to an irremediable exteriority with respect to the forces that express themselves at the grassroots of the movement. This exteriority arises from the role as *administrator* of those energies.

In the specific case of the National Piquetero Congress, the highlights and shading of this position made themselves present: on the one hand, the strengthening of the capacities of a structured movement leans toward obtaining concrete achievements related to common demands to the national government. But, on the other hand, this operation by which a handful of leaders take on the representation and leadership in the name of the movement weakens the piquetero movement itself in two senses: it annihilates multiplicity and grants the leaders a disciplinary faculty within the movement. This faculty consists in the power to discern who is and is not a piquetero, what is the right way of acting, etc.

This complex mechanism was set in motion during the first day of the program of protests organized by the First National Piquetero Congress. In his first public appearance the main leader accused those who opted for radicalizing the forms of struggle of "not belonging to the movement." Once this transformation of the irrepresentable multiple into the represented one was affected, the piquetero phenomenon was made transparent: it is only an actor of the political conjuncture. Its rationality is given by its economic interests. Its efficacy is thus reduced: from the power (*potencia*) of a multiple struggle to the capacity of its leaders to act as "valid spokespersons." The original multiplicity becomes a predictable "actor of the conjuncture." The success of this operation will now depend on new factors such as "containing" from within the action of piqueteros according to the goals the movement sets for itself. Two different logics appear. The leaders think at one level, the grassroots at another. And the fate of the whole, we are told, depends on the adaptation of the movement to the perception of the leaders. Those goals on which the success of the movement depends come to be played at a purely superstructural order of action. Assemblies and demonstrations continue to take place. But they will be resignified by a logic that escapes the members of the movement and that only the leaders fully understand.

The political importance of this operation is sometimes underestimated. But the effects are very concrete. When the movement takes the image of its leader, the latter ceases to be a spokesperson, a face among faces, and begins to act in the name of a "general piquetero will" that he interprets. And this happens regardless of who such a representative is. The exercise of representation disempowers (*despotencia*) the represented. It divides into two: the represented and the representative. In order to do his job, the representative calls the represented to order. The represented, if they are docile, if they do not want the relation of representation to fail, must "let themselves be represented." In this way, the representative administers the relation. It is the active part. He knows when it is convenient to demonstrate and when it is better to stay quiet. The representative tends to expropriate sovereignty from the represented. He forgets the mandate. The mandate begins to bother him. It becomes an obstacle to his cunningness.

After all, the representative feels he is the one who has to act in a place that the represented does not know: *political power*. The representative has, indeed, a *vision of power*. He goes on knowing and learning. For the well being of everyone, he becomes the master of the represented. He explains to them what they can and cannot do. He acquires particular skills and begins to obtain support for his own points of view from the represented. The representative can thus construct his own mandate by taking into account the part that the represented have to interpret: to be *his* grassroots support. When this happens, too often the struggle loses its radicality. The representative becomes rational, but the rationality is incomprehensible to those who share with him the experience of struggle: *their thought is no longer constructed collectively*. The represented no longer thinks like him. The assembly ceases to be an organ of thought and becomes a place for the legitimation and reproduction of the relations of representation. The representative constructs a *dispositif* of control over the assembly. The latter becomes a plebiscitary place. People vote for options, but these come already presented beforehand.

None of this means that representation could be avoided, or that representation necessarily separates itself as a dominant element. The delegate with a revocable, rotative mandate, *who thinks in and with the assembly*, does not have a reason to separate herself from the whole. Or, in any case, if she separates herself, she does not put the organization at risk, since nothing has been delegated in her but a punctual mandate. The key to this question is to prevent representation from becoming independent, which is what happens when one thinks in the terms of power, when one separates oneself from the situation of concrete thought, from the enterprise that gives rise to it.

A thought that extracts its own premises from the conjuncture determines an overstretched form of existence of representation. Only when this operation is carried out successfully do the conditions open up for negotiation, for the *inclusion* of piqueteros to the institutional dialogue that is opened through cunning and maneuvers, in the end, to the consensual play of the political system. All this development is linked to a politics of *integration*.

THE INCLUSION OF THE EXCLUDED ... AS EXCLUDED

IN ORDER FOR this operation of representation to be possible a prior recognition of a shared feature of the represented is necessary, a determination that makes it possible to speak about them as well as speak in their name in recognizable, *legitimate* forms. Thus, the interlocution and the dialogue constructed by the representative requires, as a condition, the pre-existence of a social group defined by some shared characteristics: workers or unemployed, students, excluded, or whatever it may be. It's the complex problem of *identity*.

Identity can be deduced from a structural problem of the existing whole, that is, from a more or less sociological category, such as the unemployed; or it can also arise from the creation of a new term, not deducible from already constituted identities. This is what happens with the identities of rebels and insurrectionists. Identity is produced by means of a name that is associated to a subjectifying act.

In the first case, the name, the identity, the representations that surround the whole, saturate and objectify it. Sociological categories condemn these subjective forms to act out—as in a theatrical play—the script imposed by the structure of roles. How to really *be* an unemployed, an excluded, a piquetero? Which is the adequate appearance? How does a jobless person speak?

The category of the unemployed does not manage to capture the radicality of the piquetero practices. This representative path reduces the totality of the experiential multiplicity of the struggle. Because of this modality, the entire situational richness is subjected to a process of losing intensities that belong to the real and the living. The movement is reduced to a passive place. It must adapt itself to an image that exists to it: an unemployed is someone who, above all, is looking for and desires a job. She wants to work, *not to question the society of wage labor*. She lacks something to be a full human being: she is an *excluded*. Her complaint is transparent: she cannot enter the regime of work.

In contrast, the *name* piqueteros expresses something different. *Piqueteros* tells us about a subjective operation. It is not a synonym for *unemployed*. The unemployed is a subject determined by need, defined by a lack. The piquetero is someone conditioned by need, but not determined by it. The difference is a major one: the piquetero has managed to produce a subjective operation on a socially precarious background. She cannot deny her condition, but neither does she submit herself to it. And in this subjectifying *act* she appropriates her possibilities of action.

Nevertheless, "piquetero" has frequently been just another name for the unemployed. These readings do not capture the subjective potential of the roadblock. They are external gazes, even if they are assumed by the unemployed themselves. They define the roadblock as an act of desperation carried out by the "victims" who do it in order to survive. When that happens the roadblock is turned into an automatic reaction. It is depoliticized. This view does not recognize the very experience of piquetero organizations. It denies their insubordination and their elaboration of an alternative sociability. Just as the worker whose wage is lowered automatically goes to the union, the unemployed, a step lower, goes to the roadblock. Since she cannot strike, she invents the roadblock. That is all there is: social automatisms.

This is how the representation of the paradoxical figure of the *excluded* is constructed. Because the *excluded* is not really so. *Exclusion* is the place that our biopolitical societies produce in order to be able to include people, groups, and social classes in a subordinate way. In the words of Giorgio Agamben, *the excluded is the name of the included as excluded.*[5]

Contemporary political thought is constituted on the basis of notions of *excluded* and *included*. The former participate in the social body under the miserable modality of being only subjects of needs—economic, educational, medical, etc. Their action is so mechanical that it cannot be considered to an action. More than an action, every activity is nothing but an illusion. The real activity is that of cause and effect: want provides the causes and desperation the effects. Thus, any action of the excluded has an a priori interpretation: it is about demands for goods and services that any observer would be able to deduce immediately. An excluded is a being of lacks that by nature demands inclusion. There is nothing more.

The politics of integration is founded on this distinction between *inclusion* and *exclusion*. It enunciates its prescriptions by assuming the premises of such distinction. The point is, then, to threaten the regime on the basis of the desire for *inclusion* of millions of *excluded*. This pressure is paradoxical. Because once we understand that *inclusion* and *exclusion* are places that belong to the same society, we admit that exclusion is the concrete and historical form in which a group of people is included in this society, and that, by no means, they are people who are outside.

Nevertheless, the illusion of inclusion, it is believed, can exert enough pressure to yield benefits one way or another—either because society deploys integrative social policies of larger scope (minimalist version), or because it forces the crisis of a society that constitutes itself on the basis of this operator of places (maximalist version).

The former case does nothing but strengthen the positions of *inclusion* and *exclusion*. In the latter, however, the operation is very different: there is a demand for *inclusion* precisely in moments when such *inclusion* is impossible, in such way that it would expose the lie of an integrative discourse that conceals the biopolitical separation of the social body. They argue that to demand inclusion—be it economic, political or social—is to ask for the impossible, at least under neoliberal conditions. In this way, they believe themselves to be carrying out a subtle operation in which a politics of radical transformation underlies a universally acceptable demand. The power (*potencia*) of such politics is rooted in the legitimacy it achieves. Its advantages would arise from three aspects. On one hand, they would be carrying out a politics of rupture under the form of an inclusive politics, that is, they would be going beyond inclusion. On the other hand, this going beyond would take advantage of the legitimacy of the discourse of inclusion itself. Finally, this politics offers valid intermediaries to power in times of chaos, which always gives them the possibility of getting resources.

There is, however, one objection that perhaps challenges a good deal of this argument. It may turn out that there is an anachronistic supposition in the reasoning we just reviewed. Exclusion is not part of a hegemonic politics. There is no promise whatsoever for the excluded. By choosing inclusion what is strengthened is the position of exclusion and there is not even the smallest weakening of the *dispositif* that separates the ideological positions "inside" and "outside."

Inside and *outside* are, therefore, not objective places within a formal structure but an ideological spatiality useful to process the current forms of domination, distributing people in separate sites. Thus, within the included there is a ferocious competition. Not only against others but also, and above all, against ourselves. The point is, above all, to resemble more and more what the norm of inclusion prescribes. Exclusion, on the other hand, is nothing but the "low" form of inclusion. The logic that organizes this topological structure, however, is not dual but *fractal*. As in the yin and yang symbol, both poles live in the space of the other: there are peripheries in the centers and centers in the periphery.

The risk lays, therefore, in the politics that, pretending to rupture this spatiality, reproduce it. While pretending to make exclusion disappear, in reality they affirm the place of the excluded, contributing to produce the figure of the poor. The concrete risks of the politics that think in terms of inclusion are rooted in the confirmation of the pair "inside" and "outside," at the same time that they forget that the excluded is but a subordinated inclusion of the excluded as subjects that affirm want. Hence the loss of radicality of the movements whose politics is structured by the ideology of integration.

PIQUETEROS AS A POLITICAL ILLUSION

IF THE POLITICS of inclusion implies accepting one of the main premises of the current modality of power, the politics of rupture carried out by the groups that sustain the party line of taking central power reveals how a *political illusion* operates inside the piquetero groups. These currents affirm themselves in a classic revolutionary position.[6] They put forward more radical methods of struggle and enunciate an unmediated confrontation with power and security forces.

We claim that this current shares with the "inclusionist" one a tendency to think in terms of political conjunctures. This methodology has three fundamental components: the class, the program, and the strategy to take power.

Particularly after the events of the 19th and 20th, this tendency assumes that we are living a situation of social agitation of the masses and a profound crisis of the power bloc, what has traditionally been called a "revolutionary situation." From this reading of the conjuncture and of their own conception of social change these currents consider that the time has come to constitute a revolutionary political vanguard with the goal of providing orientation to the struggles. This operation consists in attaching to the most militant piquetero groups a representation of radical struggles. This current considers that there exists a capacity and an opportunity for a leap "in quality" allowing the passage from dispersion to the synthesis of popular struggles under their leadership.

This *political illusion* is not a delirious reading of reality. It is rather an option of thought that consists as much in drawing concrete lines of work from general readings as in a will to force a political program incapable of problematizing the concept of revolution. Indeed, the illusion of arriving into power in order to change things from there produces immediate consequences in everyday practices. The "political" timing of an accelerated conjuncture forces and disorganizes the timing of the situated constructions. The militant efforts begin to have abstract goals. Discussions that hierarchize priorities are regulated according to increasingly general criteria. Social practices oriented to produce new social relations get disregarded and the entire movement is recentered in the name of "serious" tasks.

The impossibility of subtracting from the timing and exigencies of these conjunctures weaken the work at the grassroots. Finding spaces for open reflection becomes increasingly difficult. In this way confrontation ceases to be a requirement posed by the struggle to become the latter's "highest moment." Organizational hierarchies are justified either by the very requirements of the political conjuncture or because people arrive at the conclusion that, as a well known piquetero leader is supposed to have said, "only the grass grows from below." This is also the way in which a distance between the leaders and the collectives that produced them appears.

Grassroots work is regarded as something transitory, a basic experience but one that lacks political density. Political construction proceeds through "levels" with advantages for the professionals of conspiracy. The strength of the apparatuses most of the time substitutes the social movement and all the faith is put in the advent of a political supplement. All militant agitation is arranged in waiting for the messianic "leap" that would launch the movement towards the final struggle for power.

FROM MULTIPLICITY TO COUNTERPOWER

THE MOST DIFFICULT discussion at the National Piquetero Congress was around the issues of *unity* and *organization*. From the beginning, the radical movements working at the grassroots level have taken organizational forms as a central discussion topic. With a preeminence of assemblies, committees, plenaries, and horizontal forms of decision-making, the multiplicity of the movement is by no means a synonym for disorganization. On the contrary, it is characteristic of the combination of its multiple being and high levels of organization. This configuration is not exclusive of each of the group's experiences within the movement but also, at the regional and national levels, there are, moreover, coordinating bodies that honor high levels of organization without neglecting the heterogeneity of the movement. And the same happens in terms of their leaders. To think the roadblock from its specific powers (*potencias*) implies understanding its singularity. The piquetero leaders are more effective when they act inside the assembly and the coordinating body than when they separate themselves from those mechanisms in order to win public opinion. In fact, their leadership consists in their capacity to contribute to sustaining situations of thought along with their comrades, collaborating in the development of the power (*potencia*) of the group experience. Outside that concrete situation leaders are of no interest for the piquetero struggle.

The force of the roadblock does not lie in the demand for inclusion. As the members of the MTD of Solano explain, the point is no longer to "enter back." They know that there is not a desirable "inside." On the contrary, to regard oneself as "desiring to enter" is to enlarge the bunch of those who configure their subjectivity because there is a spot for them in sociological studies, in the discourse of power, in the archives of the ministry of welfare, in the plans of political groups or NGOs.

The power (*potencia*) of the roadblock, according to our hypothesis, is based in a capacity of the movement to become subject that exceeds their character as excluded, poor or unemployed. Its singularity tells us about the dignity of insubordination and about the exercise of resistance as creation of sociability.

THINKING THE RADICALITY OF STRUGGLE

SUBCOMANDANTE MARCOS SAID that what is peculiar to the *revolutionary* is struggle for power with an idea of a future society in his head, while the *social rebel*—the Zapatista—nurtures rebellion on a daily basis in her own circumstances, from below, and without holding that power is the natural destination of leaders. For the Zapatistas it is clear that any situational action subtracts itself from the traditional polarization between "reformists and revolutionaries." At the same time, this reveals to what degree such positions conceal the same image of *power* and *politics*. Both pass over the power (*potencia*) of popular struggles and offer the same difficulties at the time of working in immanence to the situation.

Marcos' social rebel thinks not in terms of globality but of *singularity*. A strategy of thought that affirms its capacities by putting *globality* between brackets. This is the philosophical difference between an abstract universal and a concrete universal.

There is no naivety: the point is not to negate conjunctures, but to think them as internal elements of situated thinking. This capacity is what radical groups, such as the MTD of Solano, call *autonomy*: to think independently and according to the concrete situation. This implies knowing how to ignore the *extraneous urgencies* projected by media circuits and militant microclimates in order to reencounter themselves with their own capacities to understand and intervene.

Radicality, then, does not consist in the infantile negation of reality, as the *realist* critics of counterpower contend. On the contrary, it is about thinking in terms of *concrete actions* by *concrete comrades*. In these excessively simple formulae there is already a fight against the *quantification* and *instrumentalization* of experiences and struggles. Radicality is the effective capacity to revolutionize sociability by producing values that overcome the society of the individual. This option, in the case of the MTD of Solano, implies also an investigation into the forms of organization of the movement, the possibilities of practicing an alternative economy, the development of training programs, the type of relationship with the state administration, etcetera.

This modality is, moreover, especially apt to understand the ways in which the issue of violence appears in the piquetero movement. It appears in at least two levels. The more evident is the blockage of roads. But there is also the violence of those who have decided to begin a resistance against present forms of domination. These levels of violence do not hold much relation with the traditional forms of political confrontation. They do not conceive piquetero violence as a political strategy tending toward taking power. Their violence is not a tactic planned to generate an impact on public opinion but a secondary and inevitable derivation of a form of resistance.

Thus, the roadblocks assume violence as an element of the struggle that neither is nor becomes the fundamental event. It is one more element of the multiple, when it is conceived as *decentralized practice* and a legitimate form of *self-defense*.

THE CASE OF THE MTDS
(UNEMPLOYED WORKERS' MOVEMENT)

JUST AS WE have read in the Argentine Workers' Center-Federation for Land and Housing (CTA-FTV) and the Piquetero Bloc a way thinking and doing, we take the experience of the MTD of Solano, as a distinct modality of practice and thought.[7] The movement originated at the chapel of Solano, Quilmes. From there, they were evicted by bishop Jorge Novak. Later, they began to organize the MTD Teresa Rodríguez,[8] in collaboration with their peers from the district of Florencio Varela. The force of the movement began to intensify when they managed to collectively administer their own unemployment subsidies—*Planes Trabajar*.* Very soon they founded committees and workshops on political education (*formación*), bakery, blacksmithing, trade apprenticeship, popular education, and a pharmacy for the movement, among other areas. Their roadblocks were quickly noticed because of several characteristics: the social representativeness in the neighborhoods where they work, the mobilization, the use of balaclavas, and the particularity of their blockades.

The comrades of the MTD of Solano participated in the First National Piquetero Congress. They did so convinced of the importance of the national coordination of the struggle and the need not to isolate themselves in the face of the repressive apparatus. On the occasion of the repression of the piqueteros from Mosconi, province of Salta, by the Gendarmería Nacional,** the MTD of Solano had a noticeable presence in the blockage of the access roads of the city of Buenos Aires carried out in solidarity with their comrades in moments when the repression was still taking place. However, they attended the Congress without excessive enthusiasm. They already knew the differences between their approach and those of the three forces that were then calling it (CTA,

---

* In the late 1990s, Argentina's federal government created monthly subsidies for unemployed workers specially designed to appease the rising wave of roadblocks and uprisings of single-company towns such as Cutral-có, Tartagal, Mosconi, and Ledesma. These subsidies became known as "Planes Trabajar" (Work Plans) and are administered in different ways by piquetero organizations. During the Duhalde administration, the subsidies changed name to "Planes Jefes y Jefas de Hogar" (Head of Household Plans). The subsidies have also been extensively used by the networks of clientelism of political apparatuses. (Tr.)

** Gendarmería Nacional is a militarized police force whose mandate is to patrol the borders. Since the early 1990s, Gendarmería has increasingly been used in crowd control at demonstrations and has participated in the repression of numerous roadblocks. (Tr.)

CCC, and PO). They felt very excited by both the power the delegates from the interior of the country had at the Congress and, more generally, the prevailing militant climate. During the first day of struggle they watched how the forces of the majority attempted to format the movement. An episode from those days shows the positions that were at stake: in the first day of the plan of action—August 2001—the MTR took control of a bank demanding payments that were late. This action had not been agreed upon by the coordinating body and immediately became a dilemma for each of the movements that were in attendance.

The MTD of Solano decided to withdraw from the coordination with the MTR because of their unagreed upon actions, but, at the same time, stayed there to cover their rearguard. While they were there, however, they found themselves surprised at the reactions of the rest of the movement. While all the forces that belonged to the coordinating body were leaving the scene denouncing the MTR, the top leaders of the piquetero movement made accusations on television and the newspapers against those who wore balaclavas. Three days later two leaders of the MTR were detained after they seized another facility, this time it was the ministry of labor of the Province of Buenos Aires. At that point, the MTD of Solano decided not to participate in the demonstration to Plaza de Mayo and they marched instead to La Plata to demand for the liberation of the prisoners. During the third day they stayed in their neighborhoods resisting the audits the government sent to detect "irregularities" that would allow them to suspend the unemployment subsidies.

In their later assemblies, the members of the MTD of Solano discussed these issues. Their strength, they thought, did not lie in positioning themselves in the conjuncture to compete with the other piquetero movements but in prioritizing the construction of a counterpower, from below and according to their possibilities. Thus, they decided to dedicate themselves to strengthening each workshop, each committee, each work, each activity in the neighborhoods. Their position is neither a *localism* nor a lack of vision of what happens in the country, or in the world: during the repression in Salta, as we saw, they immediately went out to the streets. And they did it without reserve. Nor is it a useless isolationism. It is rather a necessary *disengagement* from the logic of globality.

The same methodology guides the way in which the MTD of Solano assumes its relation with the governments—national, provincial and municipal. They manage the unemployment subsidies granted by the government without this meaning by any means capitulating. They simply understand that a process of situational affirmation implies a complex relation to the state. And in this process they elaborate their own knowl-edges on social change and revolution. One of those knowledges is the acknowledgement of the complexity involved in receiving funding from the governments while establishing very high levels of confrontation with them. Agreements and confrontations, however, do not exhaust the bonds between the MTD and the state. There is also the autonomy of thought and action that leads them to organize an alternative economy in order to sustain the movement when the subsidies eventually run out.

Social change, therefore, knows these three tactics or forms of relation-ship with the state. Each of them corresponds, at the same time, with the very nature of today's state. On one hand, it is a disarticulated nation-state that no longer has the monopoly of political legitimacy over the national territory. On the other hand, it is a state that has been coopted by the forces of the market, which frequently leads them to violent clashes. Finally, it is the representation of capitalist hegemony that exists at the level of the popular grassroots, which results in autonomy being the only guarantee to develop non-capitalist tendencies in the political conjuncture.

Meanwhile, they are candid about the repressive functions of the state, building within the movement a character of autonomy ready for the confrontations to come. In line with this, the autonomous popular organizations—not just the piquetero ones—learn increasingly effec-tive forms of popular self-defense. The permanent search for ways of not isolating themselves when confronted with repression is another way in that situational groups reckon with the conjuncture: always in terms of their own needs and circumstances.

The lines of development of the MTD extend in the labor of the coordinating bodies. At the present time, the MTD of Solano operates inside the Anibal Verón Coordinating Body of Unemployed Workers (Coordinadora de Trabajadores Desocupados Anibal Verón).* They are meeting places in which the territorial movements do not dissolve themselves but empower (*potencian*) resources, knowledges, and mobi-lization capacities according to the circumstances.

---

* At the end of 2002 the Coordinadora split into two. The group of move-ments that maintained the same politics and system of alliances took the name of MTD Anibal Verón. One year later, the MTD of Solano, along with three other MTDs, separated itself from the MTD Anibal Verón. (Tr.)

IDENTITY AS CREATION

WE HAVE SEEN how two ways of thinking have different consequences. There are no practices without thought. Thought materializes itself in practices to the extent that it becomes impossible to find differences—other than formal ones—between thought and practice. The first politics highlights the existing structure of society, such as it is represented in the analysis of the conjuncture and the discourse of power. The identities of worker, unemployed, poor, emerge mechanically from the social structure, productive or distributive. Each worker is subjected to its capacity—its role—as worker and each unemployed is reminded that she is a "jobless" person. Multiplicity is lost and with it goes the force that identities have in struggles. As we were saying above, this is not the only way of thinking things, even if it is the dominant one and, for that reason, the one that appears to be natural.

In fact, the identities that are constructed in struggles operate in precisely the opposite way: instead of expressing in the conjuncture those who form part of the same slot in the battered social structure, they de-structure the structure itself. We refer to nominations that designate a multiplicity and not to a property that produces an alienated subjectivity. Thus, the identity of the insubordinate always implies a recreation, a resignification. Workers normally struggle—with all justice—for higher wages, or they oppose them being cut. But *workers* as radical category struggle against the *wage relation itself*. The unemployed struggle for employment, for jobs, for entering the productive structure. When this does not happen, then they struggle for an unemployment subsidy. But the *unemployed* we have been talking about, the *piqueteros*, struggle against the society of alienated labor, individualism, and competitiveness.

The construction of the piquetero movement is still in full swing. It is a movement of insubordination but also of construction of new social bonds, of counterpower. The consistency of the figure of the piquetero as an insubordinate or social rebel, however, is *fragile*. This fragility is not the product of its youth, but of the fact that it depends on a fragile libertarian spirit from the moment that it is not developed from any site of power. It is the inherent *fragility* of counterpower, which pursues the line of power (*potencia*) through research, thought, affect, and the production of the new knowledges of the emerging social protagonism.

THE 19TH AND 20TH
BY THE MTD OF SOLANO[9]

On Monday, December 17th we had started carrying out a plan of action against the coming repression:
for more subsidies, for regular payments, and for food
and health benefits. We had decided, in the space of
the Coordinadora, to do something forceful against the
private sector. That is why that Monday we surrounded
eight supermarkets in the Quilmes area, clamoring for
our demands and proposals. It lasted the whole day,
and at least the Federal and Provincial* governments
acknowledged these actions hurt them. At one point we
crossed the line: the comrades hung on to the fence because the managers didn't give a shit about us. They
communicated with the government and put pressure on
it so that it would give us an answer. The supermarkets
only gave us four hundred kilos of yerba maté. But they
passed the ball on to the state. "We are doing badly,"
the manager from the supermarket told us.

The roadblock at a supermarket was not limited only to
the problem of getting food, but went way beyond. The
organization of all that allowed us to think and go deeper into what it means for us to strike at a multinational,
and not go out just like that, in a reckless way, without
even understanding the difference between looting a supermarket and looting the neighborhood mom-and-pop
grocery store. Before and after posing a demand like
this, we need to reflect more deeply with the comrades
on the meaning it has: why is this action about much more
than food. It helps us to think how we are sustaining our
struggle.

The week of the 19th and 20th, then, caught us in the
middle of a plan of action. We had a promise of payment on time and food assistance, but nothing in concrete. We had decided to attend on Tuesday a round
of talks with the Federal and Provincial governments for

---

* The government of the province of Buenos Aires. (Tr.)

a follow-up. On Tuesday, December 18th we signed the agreements and therefore stayed in the neighborhood. That night the looting began in San Miguel, Moreno, in the province of Entre Ríos, and it was clear that it was on the rise. We had been promised the goods for Saturday and they sent them to us on Thursday the 20th, causing a big mayhem to us because it happened in the middle of the convulsion of the looting episodes. On the evening of Wednesday the 19th a state of agitation began in the neighborhood. The rumors of looting, that somebody was about to hit the stores, set in. When the comrades came to the neighbors to pick up the goods the cops got nasty and began to shoot with bullets. Already the previous day had become heavy with the declaration of the state of siege: threats, in some cases rubber bullets, people imprisoned, and surveillance.

On Wednesday the 19th we went to the plaza with a group of comrades. The state of siege generated a lot of contradictions among us, it caught us in the middle of a plan of action and we were beginning to prepare ourselves to face a serious situation. At that moment we thought that the state of siege had been conceived to crush the organized groups like us. In fact, today we evaluate that if that demonstration of the middle-class had not taken place, going through all of this would have been much worse for us. When we saw what was going on in downtown, some comrades decided to head that way. We arrived at the Congress in the middle of a repression. There were some wounded already. We must have arrived at 1:30 and people had already dispersed. Then, we decided to go to Olivos,* because on the media we could hear that something interesting was happening there, and when we arrived nothing was going on. Finally, we came back, we began to discuss what was going on and the assemblies discussed doing something local, here in Solano, because the cops were harassing us.

---

*. Olivos is the neighborhood where the presidential mansion is located. (Tr.)

On Thursday the 20th we had to go to free the imprisoned comrades and it was evident that many groups of kids had fallen. That is, the repression hit not only organized people, but also the entire neighborhood. The idea was to scare the neighborhood, to stop people in the neighborhood, so that they wouldn't go out, so that they wouldn't go to the Plaza. After midday we began to notice the whole situation developing in Plaza de Mayo and at that point we changed the approach. We realized that the struggle in the neighborhoods was not as relevant as what was going on there. In the neighborhoods where we could we had assemblies, we argued that the situation was fairly complicated, and that those who participated had to do it knowing that this could get out of hand big time. Thus about seventy comrades went there with a bus we got. The cops were not letting anybody out, and when they saw groups of people walking they imprisoned them. We lost a lot of time trying to organize ourselves to find a way out. Comrades from other organizations called us telling us to be careful because they were stopping people at the bridges. We arrived cautiously, but as we got there it was all screwed up.

The closest we got to Plaza de Mayo was one block. Something funny happened as we arrived: when we got off the bus with balaclavas they quickly identified us as piqueteros, and the comrades that were fighting with the police felt more self-confident and started to throw stones at them like mad. For us it was a matter of setting foot and the repression, the horses, and the teargas came right away. We didn't have time to even think what to do. Then was the first retreat without organizing ourselves even in a barricade; it was sudden. So we needed about five blocks to regroup and organize ourselves. We resisted for a couple of hours.

By the time we confirmed that 9 de Julio Avenue had become very agitated, they started to shoot at us with lead bullets. They enclosed us, we took a bus and the driver tried to take us out. Other groups stayed and we later found each other here. We all came back all right.

We could not foresee that something like this was going to happen, and that day we were euphoric. Already the night before, when people began to go out to the streets, we began to gather a little more strength, we breathed fresh air. From the very first moment it seemed to us that we had to participate because we felt that something interesting was happening to the people. We were all restless, coming and going, meeting, discussing, calling each other on the phone. We remained all the time in the warehouses; the comrades did not stay home. All the time there were assemblies, bigger and smaller; and the debate mixed up a little with the looting and what was going on in Plaza de Mayo, with the goods they were sending us and the unemployment subsidies we were renewing. A mixture of things, but one could notice a great euphoria among the comrades. Above all because we were coming from a moment of anguish and knew that in the budget for this year there were going to be very tough cuts. We even discussed with the comrades, several times, that if the Argentinean people didn't play its card, we were going to lose the battle. It all seemed very complicated in front of Cavallo's advances and his economic policy, the new measures, the repression. We had that anguish and we saw as a very distant possibility a reaction of this kind to put an end to the economic model that was crushing us to pieces. So it was an explosion of adrenaline, of wanting to participate because we knew that in this way we could oust Cavallo.

But we also had the feeling that we were "one." When we arrived at the Plaza we feared, because things were screwed up and there were many young kids with us, for whom we felt responsible. We heard rumors about the dead, but we knew we were participating in something historic. And solidarity was very apparent; there we were not piqueteros, we were not middle class: we all had the feeling of being "one." From the balconies people threw us water to drink, they drenched us when we were very tear-gassed, and threw hot oil on the cops. The comrades that came running told us "don't go there because there is a police operation." There was a very strong unity, without banners, we were one. That is, flags were not necessary. I believe that the goal of all of us who were there was the same: enough of this fucking economy, and there was great hope for what that supposed as well. It was the end of something, and that is why the hope of something new was reborn, at least at that moment it was lived like that, with great intensity. With the announcement of the resignation of De la Rúa we decided to return to the neighborhood, because they had called us telling us that there were comrades that had been detained. We were very concerned about what might happen here in the neighborhood, because we had left the work unfinished. Thus we opted to come back and see how things were.

We analyzed who played in the different scenarios: who was there and rallied their forces on the side of the people, and who acted as allies of the government. We understand that many of those who up to that moment had walked in the popular camp, apparently, operated on the government side. We know they were in hiding in those days, and not because they were naive. Thus we began to see that certain things in the popular camp have become clearer, at least among the groups organized in struggle.

THE TIMES OF THE MOVEMENT

An important question arises with regard to the middle class and the cacerolazos. We ask ourselves where this is going, who leads it, how to coordinate it. At the beginning we didn't really understand how all that worked. Later, as we went along, we understood that it consisted in many spontaneous things. Later the assemblies began, the debates, but it all started as something spontaneous. It is something strong, at least for us. Inside the MTD this inspired reflections, debates, and nothing is the same after December 20th. History has changed.

We wondered about a few things. The assemblies, for instance, demand "all of them must go"; the parties and some organizations begin to say that it is time to overthrow this government. In this we are a little different; we understand that we have to go slowly, at our own pace. We are going to several assemblies, to Parque Centenario, and we are very involved in the assembly of Avellaneda.* We have marched together with them, we blocked roads together, but we do not go with banners. They know we are from the MTD, that we are piqueteros, but we understand that we should not put a banner to this struggle. We think it is necessary to unify the struggle, but that nobody should homogenize it. We all have to go out, strike together, but nobody owns that struggle. We contribute from where we belong and do not think, as some comrades understand, that we have privilege because the piqueteros started this struggle.

I believe that it is possible to perceive that there is something that did not finish in the 19th and 20th, but that there is continuity. It is taking a more definite expression that shows that there is an attempt to form something new, that by putting an end to the representativity of these politicians the seed of what we would like that society to be begins to emerge. A society without a house of deputies, without senators, but rather with assemblies that exercise the decisions without representation and its entire circus. There is also a bit of disappointment when we see that the banners of the parties begin to appear and we notice that the assemblies are also invaded by hidden "militants."

Today there is a great deal of discussion around politics. In our case the expectations come from outside and not so much from inside the movement. There were

---

* Parque Centenario is the park in the city of Buenos Aires where the Interbarrial (inter-neighborhood assembly), an assembly composed by all the assemblies, used to meet every Sunday between early January and late March, 2002. Avellaneda is an industrial municipal district south of Buenos Aires city, half way between Buenos Aires and Solano. (Tr.)

comrades who asked us about the national political calls made by some piquetero groups and parties of the Left. They wanted to know if we were going to be there, what were we going to do. And they questioned us because we did not go. At the Coordinadora* the question about whether or not to participate came up. There was only one group that stated that we had to do it and that we had to enter with a super column to show that we were the biggest space. The opinion of the great majority of us was that we didn't have to, that we are in a different time of construction. From Solano we think that the struggle is going to be long, we believe that repression will go deeper, and we do not think that there is going to be a revolutionary change in favor of the people. Of course it is very interesting that the struggle is generalizing and there is no doubt that it is necessary to be there, and not watching from outside. But we think that the process is longer than most people suppose, at least in the imaginary that is going around. We have to go slower so that we do not smash against the wall, because there is still a long way to go. It is necessary to consolidate concrete constructions. It would be a shame to lose the capacity to articulate and consolidate cool things with organizations such as APENOC,[10] MOCASE,[11] and, outside Argentina, with the MST, with the MTD of Brazil, with campesino groups in Paraguay, that is, with so many organizations where there are other proposals for construction. It would be a mistake not to give ourselves the opportunity to bring all of this to concretion, jumping over to "the other side," which we think is going to be truncated. For us it would be a loss; to recede in the terrain conquered by the people.

This question of radicalization is something that is very present. In fact, there are comrades who are questioning the latest plan of action. We have had to go out, on the defensive if you will, because the government has

---

* The reference is to the Coordinadora de Trabajadores Desocupados Anibal Verón, the coordinating body that MTD of Solano had with other autonomous MTDs of greater Buenos Aires and the province of Río Negro. (Tr.)

changed its policy as regards to popular organizations and their autonomy. There is a direct attack organized through the crisis committees and the municipality: hidden behind the allegation of transparency, democracy, and justice is a new return to the traditional model of control, not allowing organizations that are outside the apparatus to develop. However, we have not doubted that we have to hold a firm position in order to defend autonomy and all the things that one way or another we had conquered last year. But in other organizations we notice that the issue of the vanguard appears. They think that we are going through a moment of orphanhood in which the people does not find guidance, and that therefore the responsibility of the revolutionaries is to say which way things should go, and show that path. We don't share that. Moreover, when we hear "all of them must go," we also include the left-wing parties; and it seems that they do not take the hint. Because they are part of the old, and can get to destroy this experience. We are confident that the people who are fed up and sick of always the same thing have the capacity not to frustrate that experience in which we see seeds of something new: the assemblies, direct democracy, and the autonomy from unions and political representation. Then, when we say "all of them must go" we want the parties and all their worn out ways of understanding the process of struggle to step aside. We get very upset, even with comrades who we know are honest, devoted militants, but who cannot understand, cannot see beyond their schemas, and that is what can spoil this process. We hope that this develops and matures, even though there will be crisis.

We are delighted about this initiative, this genuine quest for democracy without representation, already with no trace of the old. And the discussion is going that way. For us there never was "work with the masses" and "political work": the point is not to develop the conditions of the unemployed in order that, at some point, they assume the political. We don't make that distinction, but many comrades do make it and argue: "well, until now we struggled for this; now it is time for politics." And that we don't share. In fact, we are going to continue making an effort in this day-to-day work, which has its grey areas, which is very heroic, even though for many comrades it is more heroic to be at the head of the vanguard, destroying everything. We are not going to give away the construction we do every day: that is our decision.

What we need is to go deeper into what we do. Since December we have had only a few moments of peace; we need to think. And not only in Solano but also with the rest of the comrades. The risk is to be devoured by "reality." We are very practical, and we are proud of it, but we run into the danger of superficiality. We have to find the times and spaces to deepen the reflection, because sometimes there are things that put us out of gear, that impact on us, things that are happening to society.

Now we have a new situation, because, after a significant recovery of economic power, the Justicialista Party is rebuilding an entire apparatus of social networks. Then, one of the challenges we face is to consolidate ourselves here, because we know now that the struggle is going to be hand-to-hand.* They are going to put in motion the entire apparatus and that has a meaning for us: repression, bullying, and making us compete with each other. They understand it this way, because we are not in a power dispute but we are defending our work. They, however, do all this in order to offset the autonomous organizations.

So, for us, that is one of the challenges, and we have talked about it a lot. There is much to grow, to mature, and we are preparing ourselves for the worst. The worst, hopefully, will not come, but it is damn hard not to be caught by surprise, unprepared for the attacks, which can be anything from rumors or defamations to sending thugs to disrupt an assembly. Those are the challenges:

---

* The expression used is *cuerpo a cuerpo*, which literally means "body to body." Elsewhere Colectivo Situaciones has highlighted the importance that the expression "putting the body" has for the MTD of Solano. (Tr.)

to redouble our efforts in popular education, territorial work, and unity with the neighbors beyond the movement. In that regard we follow the road opened by the comrades of Mosconi*: the reconstruction of the fabric of the community, premised on the common good, the environment, health, the kids, and other neighborhood problems that are yet to be resolved.

The fact that the system represented by this government cannot give an answer for problems as fundamental as unemployment, health and education plays in favor of the autonomous organizations. This generates for them a background of conflict that, somehow, they cannot hegemonize with the work of the local bosses, because they can give 100 unemployment subsidies to the bosses, but they leave a hundred thousand more waiting. We do not mean that worse is better. But we remember that in '96 or '97, faced with the smallest demand, Duhalde** gave immediate response. And today they cannot do that, they cannot respond to everything. Then, they can attack us but it is going to be difficult for them to destroy us. We sometimes say that they are going to destroy us when this society changes, because if they want to destroy us they will have to build a better society.

---

* The authors are referring to Unión de Trabajadores Desocupados de Mosconi (Union of Unemployed Workers of Mosconi), based in the city of Mosconi, in the oil producing region of the province of Salta. (Tr.)

** Eduardo Duhalde, the provisional president of Argentina at the time of this interview, was the governor of the province of Buenos Aires since the early 1990s until 1999. During his tenure as governor he built up a massive clientelistic network, particularly in the poor neighborhoods of Greater Buenos Aires, which belong to the provincial jurisdiction. (Tr.)

NOTES

1. This chapter has been elaborated on the basis of a previous text: "Borradores de investigación 3," published in *Cuaderno 4 de Situaciones*; op. cit. This version has been updated with recent interviews with the MTD of Solano.

2. The piqueteros do not emerge directly from unionism. Their irruption in Argentina's social struggles imposes the need to have open eyes and think the specificity of both their presence and the effects it produces. It is true that there are lines of continuity between one form of struggle and the other, but it is also evident that the conditions and procedures are very different in important points. In any case, the attempts by unionism to expand its control and its forms to the roadblocks have been sources of conflicts. In the roadblocks there are elements that cannot be reduced to any intention to subsume their singularity in systems of practice that are different.

   On the other hand, the deterioration of union structures is not absent from the perception from roadblock. Even though trade unionism originally consisted in a form of collective association tending to reinforce the cultural experience of the working class in its autonomy, the role of union apparatuses was later radically altered. The arrival of Fordism as a method of organization of production effected a profound change in the character of those organizations. The mechanization of labor and the institutionalization of the wage relation as specific mechanisms of domination brought the unions to become the conveyor belt of power vis-à-vis the working class, effecting its incorporation to the state and destroying its autonomy as experience. See Raúl Zibechi, *La Mirada Horizontal*; op. cit. Rather, the roadblock can be thought about in relation to early unionism, as a world of socialization in which knowledges and victories are shared while establishing communitarian social bonds.

3. The roadblocks did not inherit knowledges exclusively from working class struggles. They also constitute levels of elaboration of more recent struggles. In 1993 began a cycle of insurrections and urban revolts* in several provinces of the interior of the country. The roadblock appears as a higher level of the organization of the unemployed and contributes to channel those struggles. The roadblock is the weapon of those who do not have any other means than their capacity to control territories with their presence. In this sense it is the common heritage of the unemployed, indigenous peoples, evictees, and a broad conglomerate of people that neoliberalism calls "the excluded."

4. This position can be identified with the theses of the CTA and the FTV.

5. Giorgio Agamben, op. cit. and *Remnants of Auschwitz: the Witness and the Archive*. New York: Zone Books, 1999.

6. We can identify these positions with Bloque Piquetero, which recently emerged as an alliance that draws together different currents of the left

---

* The authors use the expression pueblada. See translators' footnote on Chapter 2. (Tr.)

within the movement. Grouped there are, among others, the already mentioned Workers Pole (Workers Party) and Teresa Rodríguez Movement (MTR), along with the Independent Movement of Retirees and Pensioners (MIJP), the Territorial Liberation Movement (MTL, Communist Party), and the Movement Without Jobs Teresa Lives (Socialist Workers' Movement).

7. For a development of the point of view of the MTD of Solano see Cuaderno Situaciones 4. See also *La Hipótesis 891: Más Allá de los Piquetes* (Buenos Aires: De mano en mano, 2002), co-written by Colectivo Situaciones and the MTD of Solano, published a few months after this book. (Tr.)

8. The MTD Teresa Rodríguez split in 2001 into the movements that continued to work as MTD and the already mentioned Teresa Rodríguez Movement, MTR. [MTR took the name from Teresa Rodríguez, a 24 years old woman who worked as a maid and was killed by police bullets on April 12th, 1997, in the town of Cutral Có, Neuquén, during the repression of an uprising.—Tr.]

9. The two sections with which this chapter comes to a close are transcriptions of recorded conversations between the MTD of Solano and Colectivo Situaciones. The interventions of Colectivo Situaciones have been deleted. Therefore the authorship of the two texts that follow belongs to the MTD of Solano.

10. Campesino movement of the north of the province of Córdoba.

11. Campesino Movement of Santiago del Estero. For more information see *Cuaderno Situaciones 3. Conversaciones con el MOCASE* (Buenos Aires: De mano en mano, September 2001).

CHAPTER 5

LOOTING, SOCIAL BOND, AND THE ETHIC OF THE TEACHER-MILITANT[1]

LIBERATION AND DEPENDENCY?

THE PASSAGE FROM CERTAIN FORMS OF DOMINATION—STATIST, DISCI-plinary—to others—neoliberalism, autonomization of the economy—has suggested to many people the naive fantasy of an immediate libera-tion. And so they celebrate the end of *classically* disciplinary institutions such as, for example, the school.

As a matter of fact, decades of resistance and struggles for freedom beginning in the 1960s and 1970s have lead to a questioning of nor-malizing institutions such as work, the family, the school, the univer-sity, and the armed forces, among many others. And although these institutions continue to exist, they no longer exist in the same way. Optional military service* and budget cuts seem to have put an end to the old forms of military domination. To this we have to add the discredit of the Argentinean military by the testimony organized by hu-man rights militants after the genocide. But, in addition, neoliberalism has smoothed the strategic tasks of the past. The military will continue to exist, but not as we have known it thus far.

---

* In Argentina, the draft was lifted in 1993, after the murder of the soldier Omar Carrasco by an officer was covered up by the army and exposed by investigative journalists and human rights activists working with the family of the victim. (Tr.)

A similar thing happens to politicians: neoliberalism perceives that political mediation is expensive and inefficient. Politicians will continue to exist, but their functions will no longer be exactly the same.

Universities, of course, will survive. But their economic crisis—the asset stripping of which public universities are subjected—determines a reduction of the specific weight of these institutions in society as a whole. Too "politicized," denounce the technocrats of the international credit organizations. Too "expensive" for the state, they add. Or excessively "theoretical." In other words: inadequate for neoliberal times.

Thus we could go on until we perceive the bankruptcy of each of the disciplinary institutions. But, at the same time, many of these institutions have altered their meanings with the advent of *free market society*.

Family, work, and school, to name three "basic cells" of society that have been questioned and even transformed, have become true shelters in the face of the torrent of fragmentation: shelters for illusions, possible spaces for socialization and for securing basic resources for subsistence.

What is left, then, of the old subversive ideas of those decades? Have we been reduced to the defense of the very institutions that had to be radically transformed, if not abolished, according to not so distant utopias?[2]

Neoliberal domination condemns many of these institutions. For the same reason that they no longer occupy a central place in the present relations of domination, they are left to their own devices, while the question of meaning is left in their hands. This is the context in which alternative projects of, for example, health and education, have come into being. And the question no longer is to simply substitute the state in the functions it vacates. It is not a problem of simple humanitarianism, nor is it about nostalgic actions destined to maintain the old promises of integration and progress of the nation-state, but about taking charge, under the current conditions, of a way of finding the meaning of existence, thought, and solidarity.

These are becomings that detach themselves from the norm by means of the most diverse procedures and propose the establishment of social bonds right where capitalism acts as a force of separation, sadness, and the formation of isolated individuals. These experiences are part of the emergent social protagonism and, as such, they find themselves in processes of inquiry about the forms of intervention that really produce the social bond in the midst of the present fragmentation.

The events of December 19th and 20th have reflected in concentrated form the dilemmas that these experiments face day by day, and demand from them more creativity and originality.

LOOTING

DURING THE 19ᵀᴴ and 20th the agitation spread through the city. The itinerary started from the pots and pans in every neighborhood and ended, at dawn, in Plaza de Mayo. This trajectory has been ritualized in the months that followed the uprising and each Friday, from dozens of points in the city, detachments of cacerolazos went out in the evening to occupy the plaza. At the moment when these lines are being written, each Friday the plaza is occupied. Only now—unlike the early morning of the 20th—those who make the calls to the plaza are the assemblies of neighbors from all the barrios of the city.

Like on December 19th, each Friday the festive climate is repeated, not in order to forget the massacre of the 20th, nor because people are unaware of the repressive apparatus, but because it is the original tone of the movement. However, in the province of Buenos Aires, the paths were very different. The piquetero struggle has altered the social climate for more than a year.

Each year, the misery, unemployment, and destructive effects of neo-liberalism over the social body, disintegrating and marginalizing entire regions of the country, grow exponentially. And the slum belts—which were once industrial belts—surrounding Buenos Aires City concentrate a good portion of the slum population.

In the province of Buenos Aires, December 19th and 20th was, above all, two days of looting, fear, confrontations, intelligence operations, and repressive threats.

Norma, a neighbor from Moreno*, tells in these words how she lived those days:

> "The hardest part of what I lived through was what happened on the 20th. I spent the whole time crying, seeing how [the police] beat people up, without being able to believe that with a democratically elected president they beat up people in that way and he did nothing. What I saw of the looting was people taking things, and my son saw someone carrying more than thirty boxes of oil in a shopping cart, and when he asked for one, the other person responded 'no.' Then I heard all the shootings around the Carrefour supermarket: people running on those streets and those who were swarming into that place. My son,

---

*   Moreno is a municipality located at about 50 km to the west of downtown Buenos Aires City. (Tr.)

who is 19 years old, went to a deli nearby. He told me that, as they walked, people carried away by excitement stopped trucks and destroyed the ones that were not carrying merchandise. They later got into a butcher shop and, he told me, the first thing some of them did was to rush to the cash register. Then he pushed them and threw the register to the ground, so that they did not steal the cash but only took the food they needed. That is when they started to fight and he left, but, before leaving, he took food for everybody and brought a piece of cheese.

"The small businesses of the neighborhood were prepared: they were armed, waiting to presumably shoot those who stole from them. On the 22nd they began to tell us that "trucks with people ready to steal" were coming and the neighbors began to make bonfires at the corners and to wait armed. Many of the warnings that came were rumors. They came from everywhere repeating the same thing: that "trucks were coming," that they were "attacking." As so many identical versions appeared, it seemed to us that it was no longer just a comment, so we came back because we were afraid. I went to sleep and my husband stayed at the corner. The police arrived at about half-past two in the morning saying that everyone should go to sleep, that nothing was happening, and that the neighborhood was quiet. In other words, they invented everything and, at the same time, dissolved it. Everybody was in a panic for about two days."

Oscar, who was at the center of the action, tells us his experience in this way:

"I learned about all this because I was coming back from work and saw that there were bonfires. It looked very strange to me; and when I reached the corner there was another, and another. This is something they told me, because in my neighborhood nobody mounted guard during the night. On the 19th I was at home having lunch, and heard blasts coming from the side of Carrefour. I live two blocks from there. Since my kid, who is 14, was out on the street I went to look for him. I found him at the corner looking at how people were throwing stones at the police while the police were shooting at them. I told him to go home, and I stayed. Then I tried to talk to people to tell them that the situation was going nowhere, because all the police were at Carrefour and throwing stones against rubber bullets, real bullets, and teargas was not going to lead us anywhere. But since, at the same time, I was conscious that in my neighborhood there are people with lots of needs, I proposed to go to the road, without violence, to stop trucks. The people who were throwing stones against Carrefour must have been more than one hundred. Then, in the surroundings there were four hundred more. I talked to many people I know from the neighborhood and we went to stop trucks. I talked to those we stopped, explaining to them that people were really in need, that the insurance was going to cover everything, and that nothing was going to happen either to them or to the trucks, but they had to give us the merchandise. Then, the driver would open the cover for us and we would distribute the merchandise. We did that with a truck loaded with oil, with two from La Serenísima (a yogurt and milk distributor), and with a meat truck. But later people with different intentions began to arrive. When we were with the oil truck, a pickup truck appeared with four or five persons, two-meters tall and with shoulders "this" broad, with broken beer bottles, who wanted all the oil that was left. They loaded the bottles into the pickup and left. We didn't know the guys; they were not from the neighborhood. Moreover, two or three who were with them stopped a car, threatened the driver with a bottle, loaded three or four boxes of oil and left. Later, when we stopped the truck from La Serenísima, we distributed four or five bottles of milk and a cheese to each one. I did it in solidarity, because there were people who were really doing very badly. But later it was distorted because they began to stop everything. They stopped, for instance, a mail truck, and we told them to let it go because it was not carrying merchandise. Then we diverted it to the service road. But there they caught it and emptied it completely (afterwards they were all wearing the Correo Argentino shirt). We let go a moving truck and further on some people caught it and took everything. People were leaving with beach umbrellas, hammocks, and couches. It was enough for me. The thing had been distorted, and a lot of people who were not from the neighborhood had arrived. At some point they also stopped a van, whose scared driver run away with the keys and they destroyed it completely. That had nothing to do with it, because the question was to get goods for the needy people from the neighborhood. Later, at Carrefour, we had a confrontation, but not because we wanted to take food. Women had lined up because the authorities had requested that women line up in order to receive goods. People were not at the access door but on its side. There were more than a hundred women. And at one moment they opened the door and let them in, almost taking them as hostages, and began to repress, there, inside. That outraged me, and, I tell you, I did not want to enter Carrefour to steal. I wanted to go in to burn it down, and kill all the police officers. So we got a cart, broke the sidewalks, gathered a lot of rocks, tore down a sign that was covering us, and began to stone the shit out of the police. At one point they ran out of bullets, and we got four or five of the Gendarmería and beat the shit out of them, just because we were enraged. There were several injured people there; I, for instance, got shot with a rubber bullet on my elbow and another on my back. But they were also shooting with real bullets. We later took a look at the signs that were behind us—during the confrontation—and they had huge holes, from lead bullets. It was tough. At one point, my indignation was such that I chased a police officer. The guy began to shoot. It was like in the movies, because I heard the bullets passing by my side. They buzzed. And of course, the police officer was surprised because he had not been able to hit me. Then he stopped and lowered the weapon and at that moment I threw a brick at him that broke his head. I went over to kill him. At that moment the Gendarmería arrived and they almost caught us.

"After that, the people from Vital, a food wholesaler across the street, gave us some goods. And it was all by chance, because when we backed off, we were about two hundred, all with slingshots, and the police officers were four. Then the police called the manager, and he said that he would give us food if we did not attack. We didn't even think about attacking, since we were backing off from the Gendarmería. They produced twenty shopping carts, which we took. Everything calmed down after that.

"Now, after January 1st there was an event that surprised me about the people from Vital. We used to go there every week with very needy people from the neighborhood to ask for food. The first day we were five, later ten, and then fifteen.

"One day, in early January, I was having lunch and my kid dropped by with a whole cheese. Where did you get it from?—I asked him. And he answered that there was a truck parked in front of Vital, with the doors open. I took the bicycle and went there. Indeed, there was a trailer in front of the doors of Vital with the doors open, and there were a lot of people watching and nobody dared to go in. Then I went in: it had about three thousand kilos of cheese. The rumors were that the truck had broken, and the driver had left the trailer in order to get another truck, and that a kid had found a set of keys under the truck, which belonged precisely to that lock. It was too much like in a movie.

"When people who were looking saw that I got in, they all got in. The pieces of cheese were in plastic baskets. It was then when my kid arrived with a couple of his friends and I brought home about fifty pieces of cheese. We later distributed them in the block.

"Carrefour hired the provincial police and the Gendarmería, and all of them in uniform. That is why I was talking to you about the difference: Vital had three officers from a security agency, and had hired three more officers from the Buenos Aires province police force. That is, they were six. While in Carrefour they numbered more than 150 between police officers and gendarmes. And Vital is larger; perhaps it has more merchandize than Carrefour, because it is a wholesaler.

"Last week I was working, doing some masonry repairs. And the guy who rents the house to the woman I work for told her: "is that guy with you a friend of yours?" She said yes, and the other guy said: "what friends you have! I saw that guy stealing trucks on television." And in the neighborhood there are a lot of people who no longer say hello to me. But I know why I did it and I am not ashamed of it at all. People are like that, they have needs but they don't get involved, and disapprove of others when they do.

AT SCHOOL

THE SCHOOL CRECIENDO Juntos* is located two blocks away from the Carrefour supermarket. While the looting episodes were taking place, the school was holding support classes.

Juan B., a math teacher, tells us his experience:

"I remember that I got home and there was an impressive movement of people. Although at Carrefour there were shootings all the time, the neighborhood was as it always is. There were no people on the streets, except here at the school, where there was a lot of movement. It was a very strange situation, because we were inside the classroom, with the kids (in the compensatory period), and we were trying to work. And we heard the shootings at Carrefour: the blasts could be heard from here. And we delivered the class with a spontaneity that would have seemed completely inconceivable if one had tried to imagine it in advance. I go back to that situation now and it is difficult for me to understand—up to the present moment—our position, which was as sincere as it can be, but, at the same time, at bottom, it was not possible for us to react in the face of the speed and magnitude of the things that happened, because it was really hard to believe.

"I remember that the kids walked by the window and said: 'we are going to Carrefour', and we had to stay here. To demand them that they should be in here because they were missing their studies was not our position. That was not the question; rather it was: 'that's all right, but be careful.'

"In the classroom, the children were talking to each other

---

* Creciendo Juntos translates as "growing together." (Tr.)

and it was impossible to order them to shut up. Imagine that we were hearing shots and some were thinking about going there later. Besides, although we were doing something different, we felt totally ridiculous, in the sense that we were working on something absolutely detached from what was happening. What was going on outside was of an impressive magnitude, and we were here trying to do something else, at least to avoid thinking or taking charge of what was happening outside, at least at an unconscious level."

Comunidad Educativa Creciendo Juntos is not just another school. There, for many years, parents, teachers, the kids, and the administration have been trying to build a different school.[3] The teachers are giving shape to the ethical figure of the "militant teacher."

The "militant teacher" exercises commitment inside and outside the school. It is here where we see the difference with the conventional militant instructor, who perhaps is an excellent militant of her group, but is not a militant while being a teacher. Militancy is not normative: it is related to a certain consistency between what one does and what one thinks. The *militant-teacher* seeks to suture that scission and integrate the action in the social, even in the private sphere, undoing the false distinction between public and private.

This ethic, they say, is not normative. It is not an "ought," but an attitude: "to be in a perpetual quest." And in that quest, the events of December 19th and 20th pose greater exigencies to the school. In fact, Creciendo Juntos, like any school, testifies to the general crisis of education. What distinguishes this experiment, in any case, is the fact that the radical positions are not sustained by one or two teachers, but by the community as a whole.

With the doors open to the community, the school questions the meaning of educating and learning when the big promises of the public school—progress, social mobility, and integration—have fallen to pieces.

How to sustain a school in moments when the feelings that derived from a—faded—project of nation have been broken? How to sustain a teaching practice on the basis of values that are now impracticable? Or can anybody affirm, in front of a group of kids who know very well what are the forms of gaining power in contemporary society, that school education makes people *free*, and not radically fail in the attempt? And the fact is that the school no longer "knows" anything about the world, the parents, the kids, not even the reason why it educates.

On December 19th and 20th, the looting episodes—that is the ac-
tualization of the destruction of the social bond—interpellated each
member of the Creciendo Juntos school directly. What can be done
with those children who, while the class was being delivered, were at
Carrefour and saw their parents come back with rubber bullets in their
bodies? How can anybody talk to them about the meaning of school
and education?

Juan B. says:

> "We are thinking about raising that issue again, be-
> cause we are now reuniting to organize the activities of
> the courses and also of the workshops we do, which this
> year are going to be on cinema. Then, one of the ideas is
> to reintroduce the issue of looting to try to materialize the
> vision the kids have about what happened in those days."

This work is all the more important if we take into account the radicality of the situation. Juan J., teacher of natural sciences, says:

> "It is interesting to narrate the experience of Silvina,
> a girl who lives in Las Cantonas. There is a split there
> between those who looted and those who didn't. The
> neighborhood of Las Cantonas is a complex of apartment
> blocks, twenty blocks away from here, from where some of
> the kids come to the school. This is the neighborhood that
> is blamed for anything that goes on. It is like the Fuerte
> Apache of Moreno.* And I am sure that those things are
> going to happen here, because we listen to the parents,
> who are already coming, and notice those divisions, those
> discussions. These are challenges faced by this school re-
> garding how to deal with that issue; and it will be neces-
> sary to listen to what they think, and, certainly, to formu-
> late the school's position.
>
> "I don't have an answer, I think the point is rather to
> elaborate one. That is the reason why parents here are all
> over: because we always wanted to build a school that
> is neither ahead of nor behind the community that sur-
> rounds it. We always thought about this project in this

---

* Fuerte Apache is an inner city slum in the district of Ciudadela, a suburb
  west of Buenos Aires City. (Tr.)

way. It is not possible to be ahead, because we are not il-
luminati, and things have to be built together. And what
happened that day was just that. Later we will probably sit
down to analyze it. One way or another we are going to
start doing monthly meetings again, with all the parents
or with those who want to come. We had finished the last
meeting about democracy, on the issue of who was making
the decisions at the school, and the issue turned into considering that what we had was not really a democracy, because it was apparent that we were making decisions that
did not represent all that was going on underneath, which
was something else. And that is what had come up here,
fifteen days before the looting. That shows that we have
to keep pace. I think it seemed neither right nor wrong
to us. But I think we have to think about it together, and
see how each of us lives it. I, for example, see it like him,
because I want to enter Carrefour and burn everything up,
because it is an ideology of penetration.

"If you ask me about our answer as an institution,
whether it is right or wrong, I will say that I don't have that
answer. Because the institution is the surrounding community, and so is the answer."

Oscar, who is part of the institution because he has his child at the
school, has an opinion about the response from the school:

"Even though the function of Juan B. and Juan J. is
to educate and teach, if the school has to give an opinion
from the standpoint of what the mass movement was able
to generate, to engage in looting for a reason as primordial
as hunger is, the school cannot have arguments against it.
You can teach math or natural sciences to a kid, but if the
kid is starving you cannot tell him that it is wrong to loot a
supermarket and oppose it. You cannot argue against that.
If you do, then you are talking nonsense."

There is a difference between this attitude and those foreseeable in the
traditional school, which could likely sustain that those who do not go
to school are *maladjusted*, or *do not meet the conditions* and that, therefore, other institutions should take care of them—they would hand

over the problem to institutions such as the municipal government, a psychiatric hospital, the police, a school for children with learning disabilities, or a children's eatery. The classical school operates by adjusting people to a norm. That is why when it finds resistances and serious obstacles it refers to them as "failures."

When the classical school is overcome because the kids persist in *abnormal* attitudes, it declares itself impotent and "hands over" the problem to other disciplinary institutions. That is what many schools would normally diagnose and do.

A very recent real story tells us how these situations are produced. At the end of February, the Counselorship for Minors of the Autonomous City of Buenos Aires was consulted by several high schools that foresaw a massive take-over of the institutions during this year by their respective students. Faced with the consultation, officers from the Counselorship went to the schools to talk to the principals and suggest to them, following politically progressive parameters, that they should not judicialize the solution of eventual take-overs. When they arrived at the meetings in question, the officials ran into a different landscape. Not only were the directing bodies of most schools inclined toward that solution—thus protecting themselves from legal responsibilities—but they also had another concern: they had received dozens of requests from neighborhood assemblies asking for the school facilities to meet in winter, a request many of these schools did not know how to answer.

And they did not know because the assembly is not an institution of disciplinary societies. It does not talk from institution to institution, but presupposes a different, neighborhood-based, communal bond; a dialogue in which the school cannot appear as the guarantor of the general knowledge of the world that assemblies appear to be questioning, at least in part. And the school is not always ready to assume these invitations.

In the end, the traditional vision of disciplinary institutions is to appeal to a range of other institutions of the state network in order to hand over the problem that escapes its immediate jurisdiction. Their duty is to "educate" kids who, within the foreseeable resistances, "let themselves be educated." If such a thing does not work, if any anomaly interrupts this process, the school then reaches out to other institutions for help.

In the case of take-overs, it will be the judge or the police. In the case of looting it is usually the family. That is what happened in most schools during the looting episodes of 1989. This means that the school presupposes a family capable of solving the situation and reaches to it.

Here we see two different problems. On one hand, there is the functioning of a school that takes kids—or assemblies—as objects of a disciplinary intervention. If the kids do not let themselves be "educated," the school declares itself impotent, announces its failure—which always falls on the student—and demands the restoration of the conditions to continue with its pedagogical labor. But, on the other hand, the problem is that the network of disciplinary institutions is in crisis.

Now, in Creciendo Juntos they say a different thing: they acknowledge the extent to which they "do not know" and come together with a whole community—teachers, principals, parents and students—to think together. This is an almost unseen event: the school, with all its knowledge, admits that there is something about the sense of the lives of parents and students that it does not know, and that they all have to work through that not-knowing together in order to build, at the same time, a meaning for the institution.

At the school, looting is a difficult issue because the dilemmas posed by it tend to uncover the presuppositions of the institution. Because it questions the dominant image of a model and comprehensive "knowledge," which always portrays itself as capable of exercising a morality, of saying what is right and what is wrong.

The classical school, which does its job of "knowing and educating" without having to go through a profound process of reflection, within itself and with the surrounding community, partakes of the symptoms of a deep autism.

At Creciendo Juntos they begin by openly admitting that the school "does not know." A school that does not know is a complete *novelty* because it really implies an invitation to learn together, with parents and kids, on the basis of a common unknowing. Of course the point is not, in any way, that teachers do not have technical knowledges. It is rather that those knowledges can become mere information if a more encompassing ethical process does not accompany them.

According to Juan J., a founding member of the school: "This is the function of the school we are building together. We might be a little more confident about who will have to teach a given set of knowledges in mathematics or natural sciences, and the challenge is, in that case, how to teach them better. But in everything else, as to which is the position of the school as an institution, the truth is that we are building it."

It is the question of how technical knowledges coexists with "non-knowledge"—about the world, about the meaning of the lives of the kids, about the current situation—what opens this ethical process. The problem for the mathematics or natural sciences teacher may start when he believes that, because he has a punctual knowledge about something, he knows about the life of children and their parents. However, to assume that he "does not know" does not mean for a teacher to abandon his technical knowledge in the classroom, or that he is a bad teacher. On the contrary, to assume, at this existential level, that one does not know, is an ethical attitude that tells us about the decision *not to take the other as object* and to open the door to thought, to the production of situational knowledge, as can be seen in the case of a cinema workshop like the one they are putting together.

According to Oscar: "Since I was a kid I had formed an idea about teachers that changed completely when I met those who were teaching here. For instance, he (Juan) says that he doesn't have a finished idea of what the institution must say about looting and to me, when I was a kid, they always told me that teachers were an example of everything. If it was like that, school should be against looting. And yet, that doesn't happen here, because we all form this school together, with teachers, parents, and children, and therefore it can't be alienated from reality. That is why he (Juan) said that he can teach me math very well, but if I am hungry he can't forbid me to attack a supermarket."

If the school cannot think the depth of the change, it is disoriented. And not only that: it also puts itself in a position of confrontation against children, because nobody will be able to prevent their experiences—the children's—from being very real, more real than any "abstract" or nostalgic value, those which well-intentioned professors try to instill in them. These things have a lot more power than the idealism of a teacher who would like everything to be different.

According to Cristina, the principal of the school, the point is to "change position." Her experience tells her that humility toward children and parents, along with knowing how to listen, opens a new world.

But here we have to look at what the word *position* means. It refers to a change of physical, attitudinal position, and not to a "change of opinion" about a topic.

This position of not knowing what it is that the other has to do removes the school and the teachers from a position of power that cannot but find among children—and parents—two perspectives that make the educational process fail: either resistance—the emergence of an obstacle for learning—or submission. Then, Cristina insists, it is necessary to fight against the "arrogance of knowledge." And to practice dialogue.

But here dialogue means something very specific: to know *how to listen*. It is not dialogue as a democratic technique to fill the head of the other, "progressive" style. No, this is very different. It is about knowing that education is something that happens "with" the other and not something that happens "to" the other.

To listen means to let the others speak, to consider their problems and obstacles as something very different from a "difficulty that tends to failure." Rather, to consider them as a non-arbitrary resistance that hides another knowledge which, if it is not repressed, can multiply and enrich the teaching process. Indeed, ethics begins by not taking the other as *object*: by not knowing "what a body can do." An old polemic of Spinoza on the prophets illustrates this ethics on the basis of the nontransferable character of experience.

According to the tradition of the scriptures, God forbade Adam to eat the apple. In this way, Adam—who represents here the infancy of mankind and man as an infant—is subjected to laws whose foundations he does not understand. God is at the same time the authority who enacts the law and the good father—or teacher—who cares for man. Adam, however, bites the apple. He challenges the law and is expelled from the *Garden of Eden*. Thus, man enters history condemned to be free and to assume his decisions. That is the moral of the story.

Spinoza reveals to us the paradox posed by this classical narrative: either god's decrees are necessary, that is, Adam has enough powers to disobey divine law—which is absurd—or, by eating the apple, Adam is not disavowing any decree. In his *Theological-Political Treatise*, Spinoza tells us that "we must perforce say that God revealed to Adam the evil which would surely follow if he should eat of the tree, but did not disclose that such evil would of necessity come to pass. Thus it was that Adam took the revelation to be not an eternal and necessary truth, but a law—that is, a command arising from reward or punishment, not depending necessarily on the nature of the act performed, but solely on the will and absolute power of a prince, so that the revelation in question was solely in relation to Adam, and solely through the imperfection of his knowledge a law, and God was for him, as it were, a lawgiver and prince."[4]

Adam mistakes divine law (ethics) for human (political, juridical, or moral) law. But God, for Spinoza, is no more than a synonym for the forces of nature. In his empire there are neither prohibitions, nor rewards or arbitrary punishments, unless they are natural consequences. Divested of any anthropomorphic characteristic, God, therefore, did no more than to reveal to Adam the effects that the apple would have on him, so that Adam—the child-man—would know what consequences to expect. But Adam did not know how to understand the nature of those words. Instead of taking them for what they were, a statement, he took them as a prohibition.

Adam's confusion founds an entire pedagogical and moral universe, dominated by the existence of anthropomorphic gods who conduct themselves through imperative signs. Teaching is conceived as a set of prohibitions, rewards, and punishments. The law, which must be respected (or, in any case, transformed) distances itself from any foundation in the real.

Spinoza's critique of the prophets restitutes the ethical dimension: god's law is not moral. It is not about watching over the well being of humanity in spite of itself, but rather it is about an inevitable experience that all men and women have during their existence and that goes beyond any reward or punishment, escaping the "political and moral law." "Divine law"—or ethics—is nothing but knowing the multiple forms of being.

Ethics implies a process of changing position with respect to the other. It implies abandoning any "power over" to begin to share the same ground of *not knowing*. The question is not to act as a moralizing god who always knows in advance what is convenient or inconvenient for the other, but to embark ourselves together in this experiment without certainties.

NOTES

1. This chapter was elaborated from interviews with parents, the administration, and teachers of Comunidad Educativa Creciendo Juntos, municipality of Moreno, Province of Buenos Aires.

2. Around this dilemma, the recent publication of an interview to the Italian philosopher Paolo Virno, who characterized the cacerolazos from classical categories of Italian autonomy such as "exodus" and "multitude," set off among us a polemic of undeniable interest.* The notion of multitude is used in contraposition to that of the people—to emphasize its multiple character—and the idea of exodus sends us to the anti-state path of the process of subjectification of the multitude. Soon after the interview took place, the Argentine philosopher Nicolás Casullo responded to Virno. From Casullo's perspective, the theory of exodus does not function outside the conditions of development and integration in the richer societies of the planet. In fact, in Argentina we are facing a catastrophic withdrawal of the state that turns any anti-state critical position absurd. The concepts of *exodus* and *multitude* in Virno and Negri are closely related to the theory of the *socialized worker*, a figure that emerges from new economic and productive forms hegemonized by immaterial—intellectual and affective—labor, originating in high technology in the most developed countries. On our side, we doubt the convenience of thinking the possibilities of emancipatory struggle in Latin America from this perspective. Nothing really interesting would come up, we believe, from reducing the possibility of action of the Argentine multitudes to the immediate reappropriation of post-Fordist productive powers, as is the case of the demonstrations in Europe and North America. On the contrary, the multitude we can talk about from here is subsumed to a growing process of separation from its productive powers. Not only does the fall of the forms of state regulation not mechanically emancipate the multitude, but, on the contrary, it often operates condemning them to forms of extreme misery. This objection, however, does not intend to refute the Italian autonomist thesis. It rather seeks to discuss two fundamental elements in order to take advantage of its most important conclusions. In this regard, it is not useless to insist, on one hand, that the process of

* Costa, Flavia. "Entre la desobediencia y el éxodo. Entrevista a Paolo Virno," *Clarín*, Suplemento Cultura, January 19, 2002, available in English online at http://www.generation-online.org/p/fpvirno5.htm; Casullo, Nicolás. "¿Y ahora quiénes somos? Réplica a Paolo Virno," *Clarín*, Suplemento Cultura, January 26, 2002. The discussion with Virno continued in an interview with him by two members of Colectivo Situaciones published a few months later by the Spanish journal *Archipiélago*: Sztulwark, Diego and Verónica Gago "General Intellect, éxodo, multitud. Entrevista con Paolo Virno," *Archipiélago*, N. 54, 2002; available in English online at http://www.generation-online.org/p/fpvirno2.htm. (Tr.)

globalization—and foundation of the empire—does not erase structural differences as far as social and economic development is concerned, and, on the other, that the strategy of exodus, or the autonomization of forms from state domination, are not achieved through the high productive level of the socialized worker, but under hard conditions that entail solving basic aspects of social reproduction.

While we were writing this book, Sandro Mezzadra, professor at the University of Bologna and young collaborator of Paolo Virno and Antonio Negri, visited Buenos Aires. Talking about the reach of the polemic, we believe to have arrived at a more balanced formulation of this question: if, on one hand, no theory can aspire to reach beyond a certain limit, in this case given by the very conditions of elaboration, on the other, it is no less true that the subtraction from state and market conditions of domination can today well be postulated as a premise of a politics of emancipation. It is evident, also, that in Latin America the constituent paths of counter-power have developed significantly, producing self-managed experiments in health, education, food production, work, and training. Both Virno and Casullo identify valid aspects of the discussion, but neither seems to perceive the complexity of the problem: in Latin America, exodus consists in the autonomy and self-organization of the social movement. That is why we prefer to investigate these experiments from the point of view of the emergence of a "new social protagonism," whose principle of intelligibility does not fundamentally derive from structural economic processes. To trace the elements of this possible polemic with Negri, see "Entrevista del Colectivo Situaciones a Antonio Negri," in *Contrapoder, una introducción*, op. cit.

3. See the Colectivo Situaciones interview of Comunidad Educativa Creciendo Juntos in the booklet *Borradores de investigación 2: Conocimiento inútil*, Buenos Aires: De mano en mano, 2001.

4. Spinoza, Baruch. *A Theological-Political Treatise*. New York: Dover Publications, 1951, p. 63. Translation modified. (Tr.)

CHAPTER 6

EXPRESSION AND REPRESENTATION

ANOTHER LOGIC: EXPRESSION

THE *PROBLEMS* FACED BY A CULTURE ORGANIZE A CERTAIN *HISTORICAL PE-riod*. To be sure, only in times of rupture is it possible to perceive as a unity that which was once experienced as multiplicity. These are the historical ruptures that allow us to catch a glimpse of how historical periods are never substantial unities, but rather sequences inside a temporality founded by an ensemble of common problems. But this unity is constituted as such only by a rupture that founds a new difference, from which the earlier time appears in its unitary aspect. The same happens with *hegemony*. It registers the problematic elements of a certain epoch.

These epistemological categories allow us to understand the existence of relatively homogeneous modalities within the sequences of political struggles. We insist: there are common problems, and they found historical periods or eras. But these eras are multiple, to the extent that they tend to be taken on and worked out differently by different cultures. And there are different manifestations, even within a culture (the state, arts, philosophy).

This is what characterizes the logic of *expression*. The vast philosophical tradition related to this logic includes in very different ways modern philosophers like Spinoza,[1] Hegel,[2] and Marx.[3] If we turn to the "problem of expression" it is because we are interested in seeing the extent to which it opens for us new perspectives for understanding the power (*potencia*) of the new protagonism.

We argue that beneath the relations of representation—classical to *political subjectivity*—operates an *expressive* dimension. The point, here, is not to propose metaphysical discussions, but rather to inquire into ways of understanding the powers (*potencias*) of the new protagonism, for which—at least our hypothesis—it is necessary to abandon the conceptual apparatus of *political subjectivity*.

Let's begin by affirming that representation works from—and upon—instituted subjectivities—which it itself institutes. What is represented is a presence, an existent, a pre-existent. A lawyer, a politician, or a delegate act by constituting a body to be represented—clients, electorate, citizenry, a group of workers or students. But this pre-existent is internal to the relation of representation and not something that temporarily precedes it. The represented body is not constituted at the margin of the relationship of representation but rather, as Ernesto Laclau affirms, the representative provides closure to the represented body—constituting it—by means of the relationship of representation.

Thus, representation is not *separated* from the represented. Representation implies a specific form, neither innocent nor neutral, of the bond between people.

Market societies are societies of representation.[4] The relationship of representation itself invades everything, at the same time that it separates the representative from the represented to the outmost. The fundamental categories of these societies of representation are those of "consensus," "opinion," "articulation," "explicit networks," "communication," and "agreement." These are all categories of separation, of capitalism. These are societies in which the image, the fragment, the consumer, and the individual dominate. In them, the link between people is produced through the construction of an image that shows and presents as united that which continues to exist as "separated," as Guy Debord said.

The thought of expression, by contrast, functions on the basis of "encounters," "compositions," "disarticulation," "resonances," and "diffuse networks."[5]

Representation as such is a relationship between relationships, but what characterizes the societies of the spectacle is the overemphasis of this relationship, to the point of "making forget" all relations of *expression*. This implies disowning and virtualizing—in a single movement—the exigencies that every historical moment imposes on men and women. And in its place *images* are diffused that replace all possible meaning for our lives with an illusion of fulfillment and fictitious plenitude, preserving the constitutive separation of capitalism. This virtualization that postmodern capitalism practices with the vital exigencies, with respect to every real, is—deeply—embedded in the foundation of the category of the individual.

Expression, by contrast, seeks to take upon itself the problems of *existence*, the possibilities of founding an *ethics*. An ethics provides the possibilities of overcoming separation, at the same time that it sends us back to the link with the real of our situations. To think from the logic of expression makes possible a new theory of justice, namely of politics.

While representation institutes a representational, communicational sphere that totalizes a world of separation in order to, at that point, find the way to present a unity between the separate, expression thinks in a two-step operation. On one hand, it works by subtracting itself from the unified time of the global, representational, and communicative world, and, on the other hand, it works in terms of composition, of the constitution of a time, of forms, and autonomous space for unfolding existence. In this way, expression allows us to explain the production of the world as an "ethics without subject,"[6] that is to say, as the—unconscious, dislocalized—process of production of values of a new sociability, by a multitude of experiments that participate in the production of vital meanings without any kind of conscious and voluntary coordination.

Expression does not imply, then, naïve substantialism. In fact, each experiment, each situation, is radically singular, which in no way negates that this multiplicity operates, each singularity in its own way, upon its sense of time. To say it one more time: expression is the expression of an ensemble of problems that each one assumes in his or her own way. This common problematic only exists in situation. And it exists on the basis of hegemonic elements—capitalism is one of them—that situations very different from one another have to deal with.

But, unlike the logic of representation, the problems that found an era, and the dominant elements that produce conjunctures, do not produce a representational unity that erases the radical singularity of each situation. The global dimension does not acquire its own consistency.

The logic of expression is no more than the possibility of thinking in immanence that which is universal in each situation. This is clear in times of *market societies*, in which there are no state apparatuses organizing a homogeneous space of domination. This reflection allows us then to understand, "beyond representation," a dynamic of social change that no longer operates according to the dominant coordinates of modernity. The production of the world is no longer the work of a consistent and operating subject, capable of directing history at will by knowing its laws scientifically. On the contrary, it is beyond any transhistoric subject, any myth of progress, that we can reach a conception of the production of the values that resignify existence.

The struggle of women in the West, for human rights in Argentina or by the indigenous peoples in Mexico, to pick well known examples, show us how the production of values of justice, equality, and liberty works beyond a single historical subject: in situation, very concrete forms of production of discourses are attained which, referring to themselves—and therefore questioning the discourse that the dominant norm *utters* about them—manage to speak to everybody.

Thus, the place of women has been radically transformed in the course of a generation. But also, and for the same reason, the place of men has changed. This transformation, however, did not have its origin and power (*potencia*) in the apparatus of the state. Which does not mean that these struggles have not been inscribed in a specific legislation. But, by itself, this legislation would not have been able to produce the changes that the struggles of women made possible.

We can say the same about the struggles for human rights in the Southern Cone of the Americas and particularly in Argentina. From the beginning, first the Mothers of Plaza de Mayo, and later the H.I.J.O.S., have spoken to explain for themselves what justice means. Thus, the Mothers said "make them appear alive," preventing both the "disappeared" from being considered dead and the whole set of consequences that ensue from the figure of "disappearance" from being wiped off the map. If there were disappeared, the Mothers demanded, "we want to know why that happened," and this explanation implies laying bare all the concrete mechanisms that operated from the terrorist state, the participation of Western powers and a long chain of civilian participations, the entire logic of the genocide, the squashing of the revolution, and the torture and extermination centers as the ultimate form of reasoning about the lives of men and women by capital. And if this first moment of the struggles for human rights was useful for understanding the more profound functioning of our societies, the *escraches* of the H.I.J.O.S. produced a concrete apparatus for the production of popular justice that gives up on representative justice and, by contrast, turns to the neighbors, the memory of the survivors, and the young people that do not accept any complicity with those who participated in the genocide.

We can say something similar about the struggle of the Indigenous peoples of Chiapas. It is only from a non-capitalist, indigenous subjectivity, capable of preserving forms of traditional communitarian memory, very concrete elements of a subsistence economy, and the exercise of collective decision making, together with the encounter with the history of struggles for liberation in Latin America, that the neozapatistas use words to destitute all the humanizing discourses that the governments and the NGOs of the central countries had "about" them.

However, neozapatismo elaborates a thought that reorganizes each one of those remains of the traditions of previous struggles. On one side, they are a movement of national liberation and, as such, defend their full belonging to the Mexican nation. But, at the same time, they consider that there is no single form of living the nation—one's own—that should be extended to the remaining experiments. Their capacity to speak for themselves puts them in an exceptional place to explain who they are, how they live, and give to the world the knowledges of a negated culture, which confirms our conviction to accept the multiplicity of forms of being in the world. Without a doubt, this is very different from the modern position about how the world ought to be. For their part, the Zapatistas defend their own situation with arms in hand. But this "being armed" no longer maintains a relationship with the guerrilla forms of taking power. The military struggle is rather a defensive one and has an instrumental value. The central thing, they say, is what happens at the level of the indigenous communities and, from that point, of the democratization of civil society, which, of course, does not hinder their ability to demand that the central government recognize their rights, since they are Mexicans.

Thus, these forms of protagonism do not need to "leave their situation" to "articulate themselves" to the rest. Each of these experiments—and we could think of many more, even outside of Latin America—works at the level of what we call a "concrete universal": they deal with universal problematics inside their own situations.

There is something that comes up clearly: where political subjectivity would not see more than dispersion, the new protagonism produces meanings inside itself that rests on multiple forms. That fundamental supposition of political subjectivity, which says that humanity has separated itself from the world in order to understand and control it, finds itself seriously questioned. Nobody lives that way anymore. It is no longer about facing history, trying to determine its meaning, but rather about our integration as concrete human beings in our situation, a situational form of inhabiting the world and asking ourselves about the possibilities that open up from there.

The myth of the global falls apart: the world always exists very concretely, and the responsibility for what one does with it is not—by any means—exclusive to those who operate in "global institutions." The new protagonism manages to speak to all without ever transcending any of the limits of its situation, which is what distinguishes it from the ideology of communication.

Political radicality, then, is a re-encounter with "what happens." Its force is expressive and consists in that it is not separated from the demands that the current times impose on existence. The new protagonism is the contemporary form of an inquiry over the forms of resolving those existential problems once *political subjectivity* has worn out.

The logic of expression allows us, then, to argue that "what happens"—the struggle for justice—"happens also through the political." This "also" is the key, the multiple character of expression. What happens at the level of the obstacles to sense, to existence, expresses itself in art, politics, etc. There is a distinction of status between *that which expresses itself,* the *means of expression,* and *that which is expressed.*

Indeed, following a "logic of expression"—as Deleuze said—we can see how politics—the struggle for justice—expresses itself in multiple ways. One of those "means of expression" is, of course, "the political." And that which is expressed exists as a multiplicity of experiments and forms of social protagonism. Thus, every era marked by a rupture—epistemological and of sense—produces new forms of signifying its practices, new knowledges and concepts, and new forms of intervention in every single instance of existence. And this is the process that has been unfolding for some time as the immediate consequence of the rupture of the fundamental myths of modernity.[7]

In the end, seen under this light, the "crisis of politics" is far from being final or eternal. If what we have been arguing is not too far from what happens in reality, we can affirm then that "the political," as expressive sphere, will gradually adjust following the development of that which expresses itself through it.

But this is very difficult to accept for *political subjectivity,* itself the specific obstacle that frustrates the understanding of this expressive logic and of the transformations it makes viable.

THAT OBSCURE OBJECT OF DESIRE

THE POLITICAL, AS expressive sphere, has peculiarities of its own. Not being, in relation to all the other situations, a productive instance proper, as *political subjectivity* believes, it works as a dimension inside the expressive multiplicity of existence. What "happens," happens *also*—and not privileged—through "the political."

What *political subjectivity* tends to deny is that nature of the political as a multiple among multiples—that is to say, as "*also*" and as "*together with others.*"[8] What does this political illusion argue? That "the political," which draws its consistency from its expressive nature, could deny—forget—this nature in order to affirm itself in its own premises, acquiring its own consistency, and, somehow, its own efficacy. The *political illusion* affirms that politics is not determined—in its expressive character—but rather that it is itself "determinant." Thus, "the political"—the state— would be what the head—consciousness—is to the body: the thought that animates and organizes the physical, extensive parts. It is that which provides meanings, tasks, and functions. Politics becomes that which coordinates and articulates the otherwise dispersed fragments of the social. In one way or another, politics would be the locus of command, the site of the conductor, and also of the philosopher.[9] To do politics would no longer be to ask oneself what to do with "what happens," but rather how to make happen what we desire, by controlling what comes to be the important matter: the "business of power" (*poder*).

The "ethics of the politician"[10]—of convictions or of responsibility, to put it in classical sociological language—begins by renouncing the expressive character of political activity. Politics "ought to" (strictly speaking, we are in a moral register) regard itself as effective cause and as responsible for "the social."[11] There comes into view the actual collision that exists between, on one hand, those who from their "political activity"—the administration of the state and issues that derive from there—assume their work from this *illusion* and, on the other, those who assume the democratic exigencies—presupposed in the idea of *expression* itself.[12] This position leads the latter to accompany the processes that occur at the base, refusing any forcing "from above" proposed by the illusion of the autonomy of the political.

The political *illusion* constitutes itself from a *suture of politics*—as the struggle for justice—and *the political*—as the sphere of state administration. Not happy with this indistinction, it inverts the terms until it places the political struggles as cut across and explained by "the political." The key point of all *political subjectivity*, this *suture* oriented the struggles of the 70s. But in that context, at least, the weaving of the state and resistances sustained that *subjectivity* in practice.

Currently, by contrast, this same *suture* seeks to sustain itself in the same way, only this time everything happens as caricature, with absolutely opposite conclusions to those that were articulated with revolutionary aspirations and practices: given that the political would be—after all—the privileged place of the social, and since politics would be entirely reduced to it, a social change that does not prioritize the question of central power (*poder*) would also prove to be unthinkable today. This point of view condemns us to sadness and lack of understanding because it leads to the negation of the epistemological—and thus also political—rupture, of which we are contemporaries, and condemns us to an absurd autism in relation to the radical experiments under way.

Indeed, after a decade of uncontested neoliberal domination, struggles sprout everywhere. *Political subjectivity* leaves us perplexed in front of them. In fact, it subjects us to dilemmas that are hard to resolve. Thus, the question regarding the possibility of accompanying from "the political"—from administration—what happens at the level of the emergence of a new social protagonism implies, from the beginning, a very profound reflection with regard to our recent reasoning and political conduct.

A PARADOXICAL SITUATION: THE NEGATION OF REPRESENTATION FROM REPRESENTATION[13]

IN CONVERSATION WITH LUIS ZAMORA*

It is evident that, from the moment we decided to use the system of representation as part of the struggle to question representation, we put ourselves in a paradoxical situation, in which everything is exploration, trial and error—generally more error than success. But, fundamentally, it is thinking and asking as we walk, establishing the stimuli and the obstacles. A very stimulating element has appeared since the 19th and 20th: the population doing politics, as a subject or individual that contributes to the collective. To all intents and purposes, this means refusing to acknowledge that politics is for the few. Even though this movement is very heterogeneous, different perspectives appear: there are those who question being told what to do and those who continue looking for the leader to follow. I believe this is a very embryonic germ of criticism; at the same time, a generalized culture of delegation persists. But what up until recently was an abstract—or merely desired—countercultural battle, today is beginning to become a reality. We have some kind of formula in order to not fall into the trap of the classical organizations: we say in the sphere of the state institutions the same we say as neighbors in the assembly, in a cacerolazo, or in a demonstration. We

---

* Luis Zamora was, during the 1980s, the leading figure of *Movimiento al Socialismo* (Movement Toward Socialism), the largest Trotskyist party Argentina ever had in terms of electoral support. Representing a left front, Zamora served as a deputy to the national congress between 1989 and 1993. He has never, to this day, collected the salary he earned as public official and, after the MAS was dissolved, Zamora, a lawyer by profession, sought to earn a living selling children's books from house to house. In October 2001 he reappeared in political life by running for office for a new party he created with a group of friends: *Autodeterminación y Libertad* (Freedom and Self-Determination). A&L was inspired by principles of autonomy and sought to draw inspiration from the Zapatista rebellion. Zamora and another deputy were elected that year. On December 20th, 2001, Zamora was in Plaza de Mayo and sought to stop the repression using his deputy privileges. His popularity increased notoriously in the first months of 2002. (Tr.)

believe that in this way we promote a counterculture that implies denunciation, radical critique, and thinking aloud alternative ideas. In this sense, the use of spheres of the state, although always in the mood for exploration, seems very interesting to me because one day we may conclude that this is not the way to go. The problem is that I do not know of any movement that has been able to avoid being contaminated to some degree by the state. Even those that do not participate in the elections, pose demands to the state, or aims at addressing the state or directly confronting it.

Some people tie what happened the 19th and 20th to the Santiagueñazo or the Cutralcazo.* The truth is that everything is linked to it, because they are experiences that to some degree accumulate but, from another point of view, someone who establishes the link without highlighting the new takes little benefit from it. Because, for example, the Santiagueñazo was summoned by all the statist organizations. But what happened in December was a different thing: without leaders, without models, without prior planning, without organization, without even word of mouth or telephone calls to meet at the corner. Nothing; it was entirely spontaneous and simultaneous. I believe, as well, that analysis itself, any attempt to conceptualize the events, runs the risk of reifying things. The problem is how to think from inside because listening is not to remain quiet.

I wonder whether on the 19th, in the expression "all of them must go," people retook the constituent power

---

* "Santiagueñazo" refers to a popular uprising that took place in December 1994 in the city of Santiago del Estero, capital of the province of the same name, in northern Argentina. People rioting in the streets burned down the government palace of the province and the houses of several politicians of different parties. "Cutralcazo" is the name given to the uprising of April 1997 in the Patagonian city of Cutral Có, a small town in an oil-producing region. This uprising is generally considered to be one of the first massive demonstration of the unemployed, which at the time were known as "fogoneros" (because they made bonfires to block roads). (Tr.)

(*potencia*) that becomes constituted power (*poder*) when it has been delegated. For example, I went to Plaza de Mayo in the middle of the cacerolazos and, because of the culture that had been created, I was regarded as a model and even as the future president. And beyond that flattery to my ego, there was something that deeply disturbed me. The same happened when in an assembly people wanted me to talk, listen to me, ask me questions, and turn me into the center of the assembly. At times I hid behind the largest person in order to not be seen, but other times I tried to debate, to dialog, to deal with the issue, to discuss avenues that we can explore, and ask ourselves where is the power to confront state power: whether it is in the search for an honest leader or in the construction of a counterpower, that is to say, of a politics in the hands of the population. At that moment, I was no longer just any neighbor. I believe that this is a way of using representation to undermine representation. I think it is helpful to demystify the fact that because I take on an issue it will immediately acquire transcendence, because there is a tendency toward some kind of myth, and the search for a model is desperate.

The other day there was a debate in congress. With support from the majority of the floor, a committee was created to investigate the flight of capital. What we thought was: what would we say in an assembly, if we were among the neighbors? I always imagine that I am not in front of legislators, but rather facing a chamber in which all the neighbors are looking at me. These are things that one appeals to cope with the enormous pressure of those spaces.

I began saying, "do you have any credibility among the population to do the investigation?" I asked them this after the preaching of a Peronist deputy from Junín whose house had been set on fire.* Then, many deputies stood

---

* On the evening of January 23, 2002, a cacerolazo organized by residents of the city of Junín (300 km south of Buenos Aires) stopped in front of the house of the national congress member Mirta Rubini (Peronist). Her son

up and insulted me, something that had not happened in all these months. It was some sort of a return to the Menem era. They yelled at me, they jeered at me; they did not leave me alone. I believe that there is a link between what a neighbor says in an assembly, the "all of them must go," and that day in which I could not finish what I was saying. I believe that it is an example of how one can question representation in the very space of representation, and take advantage of the discussions that this raises. That is something that one can try at any moment, but much more at those moments in which one can refer to something concrete like a neighborhood assembly. For me, "all of them must go" applies to everyone who is there now. That is a watchword I stand up for. But thenceforth, there is the issue of whether it implies questioning also the functioning of the institution and not just those who are part of it. The discourse of changing the honest ones for the dishonest ones is weak, it does not arouse much enthusiasm. That is, for example, the discourse of ARI.* Now, it does not seem to me that that position is generalized. Rather, the mass of the population is explicitly questioning the whole system of representation. It does so in actions, but it seems to me that the idea of instituting something again is very much around us, even if it is something different and new.

For me, the cacerolazo continues to have the force of that which was born from below. It is no longer spontaneous, it is organized but continues to have that force: it is like an arm-wrestling match. Anyone can have the audacity of thinking that "all of them must go" has a literal meaning: all that means state power must go. Not because I see, as other organizations of the left

---

fired a shotgun against the crowd from inside the house, seriously injuring one of the demonstrators. The cacerolazo turned into a riot that burned Rubini's house and SUV. (Tr.)

* Argentinos por una República de Iguales (Argentineans for a Republic of Equals) is a party lead by Elisa Carrió that gained recognition for its investigation of different cases of corruption of state functionaries. The party formed during the De la Rúa administration. (Tr.)

argue, that taking power is close at hand, nor because that is the objective. But I do see it in terms of destruction of state power, along the ways we might explore, even though I do not see it as something close. I do see that there is something new that makes one think that this is possible. Whether someone does or does not leave is part of a larger issue: a discussion about what we are we here for. We began by doing what we said we were going to do when we run in the elections, insisting on appealing to self-determination, denouncing the representative system, denouncing the barbarism of capitalism. Now problems arise in the implementation of these things, when one sees that already in the assemblies there is a political game of parties and apparatuses. What are the assemblies? The assemblies are certainly not there to discuss what to do. Besides, I am under the impression that when the neighborhood assemblies gather in Parque Centenario* the structures and the apparatuses have more weight, because the representative aspect is already there. The organization of the apparatus of the state is repeated with the parties as a basis. Then, how could we sense that the self-organized assemblies show us the way? That is very complex to implement. On the other hand, it is very interesting to see how the eagerness to capture and lead puts in the movement's mouth demands that the movement is not making, even though it is incorporating them into the debate. That was the polemic in Porto Alegre: the rage against self-organization, spontaneity. The question was: why didn't you form a PT?** Why not unite the left? They told us: "you in Argentina have in these moments a responsibility." We have no responsibility, that is not the term that expresses what is happening. We can have challenges, or even opportunities;

---

* Parque Centenario, an urban park in the neighborhood of Caballito, the geographical center of Buenos Aires, was the site where the "Asamblea Interbarrial" (Inter-Neighborhood Assembly), an assembly composed of all the assemblies that met every Sunday between mid-January 2002 and its dissolution about three months later. See next chapter. (Tr.)

** PT stands for Brazil's Partido dos Trabalhadores. (Tr.)

rich moments of which we can be part, enjoy, and suffer also. The question was "we have to organize this."
But not organize it in the sense of self-organization,
because there I also believe that we should advance in
organization, the more diffuse the better, because more
autonomous, but stronger and with richer bonds. When
asked how should the antiglobalization movement organize itself, Chomsky stuttered, and said "organize
this? I don't know. I think we should be happy with an
understanding." I loved the word: an understanding,
something to tune in to. And he added: "it can have
some goals, set some goals." The last part is more traditional, but what interested me was what he said about
understanding. Because in order to organize ourselves,
to self-organize, we need to tune in to each other.

SHORTCUTS

THERE IS A formula that reveals that the expressive character of the
political is forgotten: "seizing the apparatus of the state." It is not a
minor oblivion; it goes to the core of the political illusion: if what the
nation-state represents is a resultant of tendencies produced and organized from the ground up, what the democratic state incarnates is
nothing less than a more or less successful reflection,[14] a resultant of
those tendencies and not an autonomous tendency. This is so at the
cost that any refusal by the state to operate in this way questions it in
its sovereign functions—which, on the other hand, begins to happen
in many places.[15]

On the one hand, the nature of the representations that emerge and
are organized in the body of the state—the resultant—has such a status
of reality that it appears as an intangible for whoever seeks to shape it.
But, on the other, it has a structural root that is impossible to force.
In this way, whoever seeks to substitute the present representations for
others in order to travel the shortcut of taking power is already a candidate to become a tyrant: no pedagogy of power is potent enough to
control, model, and manipulate such representations.

This fantasy of the *shortcut* consists in believing that it would be
possible to modify some representations with others, in direct struggle.
The state could well be managed by other groups: each of which comes

to be distinguished as the bearer of its own ensemble of representations, which it would impose on the whole, from above. There thus emerges an entire dictionary of words that pretend to be knowledges about both the "political spaces" and the struggle for their occupation. This imaginary of a political physics is part of the knowledges of political subjectivity. Its discourses consist, as we have seen—and as is characteristic of all imaginary saturations—in erasing every trace of the real.

Only if the previous reflections over the exhaustion of *political subjectivity* and the emergence of a *new social protagonism* have some power (*potencia*) does it make sense to understand how the relation between "politics"—infinite struggles from the ground up that are productive of values of justice—and "administration" is as inevitable as it is necessary, providing that those who inhabit each of these poles of the relation understand its nature.

When politics tries to supplant administration, it falls into an "elemental idealism." When administration wants to replace politics, it falls into a "vulgar materialism" that does away with the thought and practice of revolution. Therefore, there is not a type of administration that is revolutionary "in itself." Administration, as an ensemble of relations, laws, and different elements of the organization of a society can—in a given moment—be the banner, the historical and conjunctural goal of politics but, at the same time, administration should not aspire to eliminate politics. This is true, also, for any temptation to bring about a "political" saturation of social reality. Indeed, if a political movement does not accept in a given moment to affirm and defend a certain type of administration, an eventual political "saturation" would result in what is known as "ultra-leftism," which in the name of certain, generally positive principles, renounces to assume administration as a reflection, maybe as "shadow" of politics. In those cases, the life of society will also be threatened, since without "administration," a society tends to disappear.

This reflection comes to be of extreme importance inasmuch as it implies, among other things, assessing the experience of the failure of real socialisms and learning from it. If the state is not the privileged place of change, it is also neither a place that is simply suppressible nor a reality that can be negated. It is, indeed, a place that tends to remain in every large and complex society and, before all else, it is at the same time a possible situational standpoint, from one side and the other, an element present in the most varied of situations.

There are situational keys to think the relation with this "state-political" element: on one hand, the affirmation of a situational autonomy that does not consist in detaching oneself, but rather in assuming this relation from one's own time, space, and criteria. On the other hand, to see the different possibilities of relations to the state—cooptation, repression, and ability to work together in punctual issues[16]—and to be able to assume them.

NOTES

1. Among the modern authors, Spinoza is the one who most deeply and profusely worked on the question of expression. The *modes*, according to him, are expressions of the *substance*. To this regard see the work by Gilles Deleuze, *Expressionism in Philosophy: Spinoza* (Zone Books, New York, 1990). It becomes clear that even though *substance* is both the cause and reality of the *modes,* the *modes* themselves are the sole form of existence of *substance*. The *substance* exists neither outside nor separate from the *modes*. It exists only "in" the *modes* and "as" the *modes*. Thus, in Spinoza the whole is "in" the part. This is the materialist and radically immanent ontology that has influenced contemporary authors like Althusser, Negri, and Deleuze in different ways. The latter, for example, elaborated his own philosophy—and his ontology—upon the idea that the substantial—as that which characterizes being—is nothing other than the existent, that is to say, *the same* is always in *the other* or, in his own words, influenced by the Nietzschean eternal return—that *repetition* only occurs as *difference*.

2. In his own way, Hegel is also a philosopher of expression. There has been much discussion in the last decades over the incompatibility of the dialectic and expressive immanentism—Hegel vs. Spinoza. In general, from a "Spinozist" position it is considered that dialectical finalism—transcendentalism—is an insuperable obstacle that makes both philosophies incompatible. There is no certainty that Hegel had been so radical in this respect. As far as we are concerned, we limit ourselves to corroborating that the Hegelian dialectic is composed of an absolute that, from the finality, ends up organizing the meaning of earlier moments—giving them a unity, a consistency, and a necessity *post festum*. At the same time, alongside this "teleologism" there is—at least partially—a certain logic of expression, present in categories such as *spirit*—"objective," of a "people," "absolute"—and *concrete universal*.

3. Marx himself has been read "Spinozistically" by the Althusserians—secretly—and by Negri—openly. To find out about the reading by Althusser consult *Essays in Self-Criticism* (London: NLB, 1976). Negri's reading can be found in *Marx Beyond Marx* (New York: Autonomedia, 1991), *The Savage Anomaly* (Minneapolis: University of Minnesota Press, 1991), and *Subversive Spinoza* (Manchester: Manchester University Press, 2004). But in addition to the properly "Spinozan" readings of Marx, which are, rather, projects of readings, or productive readings, there are innumerable "expressive" moments that can be grasped in the Marxist metaphor of base and superstructure as in numerous passages of *Capital*.

4. In this regard, see the Situationist critique, particularly in the work of Guy Debord, *Society of the Spectacle* (Black and Red, Detroit, 1983).

5. On the question of the explicit—organic—or diffuse network, see chapter eight of this book.

6. Ernesto Laclau proposes a conception of "the political" in which the latter

is not reduced to "reflecting" what happens at the social level, but that rather participates—as a more or less privileged practice—in the social, giving it form and meaning. The political invents the social. Political struggle is a struggle to constitute, under a given hegemony, the—*civil*—society. In this way, political subjectivity finds its most sophisticated arguments, accounting for the difficulty of talking about a classical subject when it comes to thinking the question of politics. The political is still postulated as a space that produces social subjectivities but, at the same time, the politician loses all the qualities of the modern prince. The political, however, still "sutures" the two meanings that characterize *political subjectivity*—struggle for justice and "hegemonic closure" from the apparatus of the state. That is why Laclau proposes the precariousness of the social bond as ontology of the political and radical democracy as horizon of the political. If the social bond is precarious and contingent by *nature*, political representation comes to give form and meaning to the social. The action of the "representative" implies a fortuitous dialectic among representative and represented, in which both terms constitute each other. But there is something difficult to grasp from a position of subject-object separation, which is that "representative" and "represented," copulating passionately, playing this game of paradoxical efficacies, can never say *why* "they do what they do," and "they want what they want"—a game in which, we know well, the represented, once in a while, make representation fail, turning the representative into the one responsible for all misfortune. Thus, the rupture, the uncoupling, and the crisis of representation, against all appearance, is not decided by any transhistorical subject. In the end, beyond the subjective game of representations, there exists a vaster phenomenon of *expressions* that, unlike representations, never depends on conscious subjects.

7. We refer to the separation between subject and object, and to the myths of progress and determinism. To find a development of these arguments, see Miguel Bensayag, *Pensar la libertad*, op. cit.

8. It is not that politics appears later to format the pre-existent: reality is not "previous" to the situations and their elements. Reality is here, from the beginning. What happens is that *that which expresses itself* is always a *real*, a self-affirmed multiplicity that organizes—gives meanings and forms to—reality. In other words: reality is *real* plus *symbolic* and *imaginary* and, while the knot remains untied, *the imaginary* and *the symbolic* will not gain independence. At the same time, the *means of expression*—which to political subjectivity seem to be the causes of all reality; in this case, of the political—act as an ensemble of conditions that make our very experiences possible. But this is no longer about the structuralist—Althusserian—image of the cause and effect game, but about the "logic of expression," which no longer thinks in terms of cause and effect by an independent structural variable—let alone in terms of "creation"—but rather in terms of *that which expresses itself*, the *means of expression*, and *the expressed*, with

the methodological condition that each of these three terms is subordinated to an ontology of the multiple. Thus, politics is as multiple as that which is expressed by means of the political. Finally, the political itself is not a privileged form of expression.

9. We would not be far off if we concluded that the "political illusion" has accompanied those who practice, desire, and think politics at least since ancient Greece. Thus, Plato's *The Republic* would find in the mythical figure of the philosopher king—the helmsman of the ship of the state (polis)—a character apt for such functions to the extent that he "knows" that which is just and convenient for all the polis, and for each of its parts.

10. See Max Weber, "Politics as Vocation," in *From Max Weber: Essays in Sociology* (New York: Galaxy, 1958).

11. See Ernesto Laclau, *Emancipation(s)* (London: Verso, 1996).

12. See Spinoza, *Political Treatise* (New York: Dover Publications, 1951). There he says, "But be it remarked that, by the dominion which I have said is established for this end, I intend that which has been established by a free multitude, not that which is acquired over a multitude by right of war" (314).

13. The argument we present belongs to deputy Luis Zamora. It is a text elaborated on the basis of a conversation we had with him.

14. John Holloway has recently reminded us that this representation is not neutral. On the contrary, this condensation constitutes itself under capitalist hegemony. Thus, the fact that the state expresses, represents, or reflects tendencies does not place it "beyond" the prevailing hegemony. This observation of Holloway's brings us to radicalize the central argument: precisely because states represent the prevailing hegemony, it is an illusion to believe that they can be instruments of a decision that consists in altering the hegemony that gives them their character.

15. *Empire* (op. cit.) can be consulted among the works that have recently theorized the question of national sovereignty as product and effect of a long-reaching cycle of transformations. In it, the authors say: "Our basic hypothesis is that sovereignty has taken a new form, composed of a series of national and supranational organisms united under a single logic of rule. This new global form of sovereignty is what we call Empire" (Hardt and Negri xii).

16. In the case of the MTD of Solano, as in general in the piquetero experiments, the relations with the state cover these three options: the state makes itself present offering, at the same time, attempts to coopt their leaders, periodic repressions, and relief packages. These are, in general, the three possibilities faced by all the situations that reflect upon the form in which the state element is present in them.

CHAPTER 7

NEIGHBORHOOD ASSEMBLIES

FROM 19ᵀᴴ AND 20ᵀᴴ TO THE ASSEMBLY

IN THE EARLY DAYS OF JANUARY EVERYDAY LIFE HAD BEEN COMPLETELY altered. The city, its rhythms, and the forms of inhabiting public places had radically changed. The dizziness of the events clamored for the coming of ideas, concepts, words that might establish possible meanings in a radically uncertain context. Self-organized caceroleros continued to occupy streets and squares.

No government could stand up on this unstable soil. The parade of presidents, economic programs, and ministers seemed endless. Economic depression accelerated the growth of unemployment figures. Consumption fell at a meteoric pace. The country defaulted on its debt.

An invisible line has definitively cut through the country: the one that separates, on the one hand, those who still have time, willingness, and resources to listen to the *voice of the market*, and run from bank to bank trying to protect what they have—or to make a difference—in moments when the International Monetary Fund and the American government have decided to punish Argentina, and, on the other hand, those who have devoted themselves to strange rituals: popular assemblies, pots and pans dances, and mysterious self-organized practices of different kinds.

The assembly movement was taking its first steps. More than a hundred neighborhood assemblies populated Buenos Aires seeking to organize, think, build, and sustain the possible meanings of the rupture of December. A displacement that destitutes the rules of the game bursting their prescriptions. A simultaneous movement of thousands of people who alter all preexisting rules gradually giving rise to a new game.

Sites of elaboration and thought spring up here and there, through resonances, without anybody being able to plan it or stop it. New forms of inhabiting public space emerge. The neighborhood assembly is born as a *dispositif* that both contains and puts to work an heterogeneous multitude: it is a labor of discussion, coordination, and collective thinking that is constituted beyond the classical paths of political organization.

Thousands of neighbors participated in this process. The assemblies are popular forums where each person comes with his/her ideas, questions, and knowledges, and participates in a moment of collective elaboration set off from a heterogeneous starting point. The work of setting common premises, making room for diversity, and harmonizing plural—and not always coinciding—expectations, constitutes a rich process of politicization that leads thousands of people to protagonize—almost always for the first time—their own destinies.

The assemblies have gone through a practical reading of the events of the 19th and 20th. They are an intervention in action that produces the specific operations of thought needed to travel the space of significations opened by the insurrection and, from there, bring into existence the meaning of new forms of public participation. The effects soon became apparent. Streets, corners, and squares were subjectively reconfigured with the production of new dimensions of public space after years of dreadful advance of the logic of the market. Thus, the way of inhabiting the city changed.

The assemblies extended the modalities of occupying urban space invented during the insurrection: bars, squares, and corners became sites of assemblies, workshops, committees, and festivals. Suddenly, a hostile and alienated sociability managed to encounter a latent desire for community. In many neighborhoods, the everyday activities and encounters produced—previously non-existent—relations among neighbors.

Some assemblies occupied unused lots of state property, opening new public spaces.[1] The recuperated places are, invariably, made available for cultural and recreational use. But the same has happened with time. The 19th and 20th opened up a new space in the everyday lives of many people: the night. Removed from intimacy, assemblies and demonstrations take place after the regular workday.

Going against the tradition of union organizing, which unfolded its efforts inside the space of the factory and the working day, the movement grew by stealing hours from sleeping time, and also from the weekends. The change is much more radical if we take into account the fact that, over the last few years, the mainstream of usual behavior was marked by the search for security, privacy, and shelters in front of the dominant hostility. Countless spaces of enclosure had been created, bringing about a subjectivity marked by an authentic *ideology of security*, a decadent disease of our saddened postmodern cities: before 19th and 20th many neighbors had begun to gather... but to watch over the dangers "from outside" their neighborhoods, to request in loud voice a police officer at each street corner, and thus to make sure that their houses were "safe." Many others had fled to private neighborhoods or to gated communities with their own security.

While we write these lines, the assembly process remains alive. Even though their mobilization capacity swings back and forth, and some indicators seem to tell us about an end of enthusiasm (the cacerolazos have lost their mobilization capacity and the assistance to the inter-neighborhood assembly has diminished[2]), the massive presence of assemblies in the last demonstration against the coup d'etat of 1976 was quite noticeable.*

The point, then, is not to foresee the orientation of the development of this movement, but to reflect upon its present transformative power, upon the becomings it opens and the elements of new sociability that can crystallize in it.

THE NEIGHBORHOOD AS SPACE OF SUBJECTIFICATION

ONE OF THE greatest difficulties faced by struggles is to realize that the world is not so easy to modify. Until a short time ago we lacked new ideas to think what to do in the face of these complexities. Moreover, *complexity* itself became an unanswerable refutation for those seeking to start emancipatory struggles.

The ideology of *complexity* tells us of a world that is totally incomprehensible, except for a number of experts and knowledgeable people,

---

* This demonstration, held on March 24th, has been organized in all the major cities of the country every year since the end of the dictatorship in 1983. (Tr.)

for whom the world would be transparent, without secrets and therefore manipulable. Under the illusion that a few men and women know
the keys to what really happens, the rest of our contemporaries remain
locked up in the postmodern paradox of the "age of knowledge": precisely at the moment when knowledge is the source of all productivity,
the vast majority of human beings radically ignore the mechanisms by
which our societies function.

The *discourse of complexity* acts, then, as a call to passivity. Things appear "too complicated" for anyone to seek to transform them. But, certainly, this technicist fiction could not work unless there is "something
true" about it. Technology—like economics—is a practice founded in
a set of autonomous combinations that has radically gained independence from the control of the institutions in charge of regulating it to
the point it has become a true process of domination "without a subject." Nobody controls its designs, even though there are always some
who make themselves comfortable in them.

The illusion does not consist in the existence of this *complexity*, but in
how it is assumed. On one side it tells us about a group of experts—scientists and economists—who control the complexities of the world without, at the same time, being controlled by them. On the other side, the
ideology of complexity tells us also about the men and women who have
found in the economy and the sciences the limit to every possible truth.
It is a true historical determinism. Our world will no longer be comprehensible or thinkable and, therefore, it will not be transformable either.

Complexity thus acquires a singular status: not only does it designate
the existence of very real structures of domination, producers of values
that organize society, but it also acts as true alibi for thought, making
the case for giving up all militant research and all social struggles. What
is blocked by means of this mechanism, then, is the peoples' capacity to
reappropriate their own conditions of existence.[3]

The assembly process acquires its full meaning when the intelligence
of the resistances is conceived from this perspective. Indeed, in the assemblies people put forward practical hypotheses of reappropriation—
no matter how partial—of the living conditions.

Although it is true that the assemblies will not fix all the problems—and what would?—it is no less true that they also transform
their participants in a fundamental sense: they abandon the passivity
that is justified from the position of the *victim*. The assemblies display
the neighbors' manifest will to establish forms of sovereignty over
their own resources and possibilities. This passage from impotence to

power (*potencia*) is key: there is where it dodges a first big obstacle. But the assemblies can also be thought as dispositifs of experimentation of an immediately territorial counterpower. In this sense, the *communal* territory has become a terrain of dispute or, perhaps, the site of a *subjectification*.

Communal action resurfaced in times of destructuration of the bonds that had been constituted under state conditions, as the neighborhood correlate of the interpellation of the modality of the *consumer*: the person who has taken refuge in her privacy after the fall of the law, politics, and state regulation. The figure of the *neighbor* is now constituted by retreat, fear of exclusion, and consumption in the home.

In conditions of radical domination by the forces of the market, the public places that until a couple of decades ago constituted spaces of civic socialization have become "unsafe," sites where the presence of the *excluded* operates as permanent threat. *Communal action* can be thought about, then, as one of the names adopted and developed by the conversion of the *citizen*—occupying public space—into *consumer*—retreated to private space.

From the soap operas[4] and private medicine services to the proliferation of "neighborhood" supplements in the most important newspapers and the generalization of virtual networks, the interpellation to the *customer in his house* is a symptom of the withdrawal from the public into the private.

But, as we said, the neighborhood is again[5] a terrain of subjectification. The hypothesis can be formulated in this way: a process of production of social bonds has taken place, in the last years, on the *neighborhood* territory. This subjective operation has transformed the shape of urban neighborhoods, from passive forms of occupying them to active—and multiple—modes of inhabiting them.[6]

The assembly functions as a machine that produces and verifies practical and affirmative forms of resistance, pointing to the recuperation of the social conditions of existence.[7] In them, neighbors of all ages meet to take on common problems, such as the occupation of public places that until December 20th were in the hands of private companies, the re-opening of bankrupt neighborhood institutions—as it is the case with Atlanta Club, in Villa Crespo,[8] where there is now a community eatery—the creation of soup kitchens, collective grocery purchases, newsletters, employment bureaus, barter clubs, cultural, artistic, and recreational initiatives, and even committees dedicated to bargain the price of the services provided by the privatized public utility companies.

The assembly has become a space of experimentation on the possibilities of producing popular and autonomous forms of administration. As such, they are going through a process of collective re-elaboration of the current modes of emancipation. It is a thought that cannot be reduced to explicit statements or to the *conscious*[9] level of reflection. The thought that circulates in the assemblies is practical, not immediately visible, constituted, on the one hand, by a fabric of fragments of experience and previous knowledges, and, on the other, by the imperceptible existence of actions and individual knowledges that coexist there. The existence of "preexisting knowledges"[10] is an authentic source of resources when attempting trajectories alternative to the paths proposed by state power and market forces.

Far from operating from a moral exigency or from being an arbitrary invention, the communal strategy of horizontal and democratic forms of elaboration constitute a practical need to maximize the embodied thought of the assembly.

POLITICAL DESPERATION

THE ASSEMBLIES ARE a place of practical research. An elaboration is going on there. For that reason, because this is the value of experience, there is not a greater danger than falling into the illusion of conceiving of them as "alternative power."

As we already saw, "politics" continues to function under the imperatives of the ideology of inclusion, without considering the profound alteration of the conditions of social, political, and economic reproduction. We have also presented the argument according to that if politics wants to be on a par with true thought and authentic struggles for freedom, it has to go "beyond politics," understood as mediation of social struggles and the system of representations that have the state as their cohesive center. The question now is to understand how the subjectivity of the political class operates as a specific obstacle in front of the new protagonism of the assemblies, and how the movement constructs the meaning of its slogans in this polemic.

Political subjectivity—parties, militants, intellectuals, and groups with vanguardist vocation—acts with the secret belief that the assembly movement lacks a correct direction. It considers that the concrete projects that emerge from the groups of neighbors are secondary with respect to strategic orientations and programs.

It considers the assemblies themselves not as singular experiments, which transform their participants and the neighborhood, but as popular institutions that play a role foreseen by revolutionary plans. According to most of those plans, the assemblies ought to subordinate every task to the requirements of the "power question," the true *measurement* of the adequacy of the assembly to the party.

This perspective heightens confrontation as the top level of consciousness and radicalization, without paying attention to the self-affirmation presupposed by the process. In the end, it does not consider the assemblies in their interiority. It only trusts and values them from the standpoint of a general thinking, which, following a partisan rationality impermeable to the course of the events, identifies objectives only to subordinate the assemblies to them. Indeed, this position instrumentalizes the assembly movement. The assemblies have value only as vehicles toward the fulfillment of a new order, organized according to criteria that are as external as they are neatly ranked.

The desperation with which the movement is perceived is acutely depicted by Luis Mattini: "One way or another, the anguish for the future and that stubborn tossing and turning with the past without assuming it, makes it impossible to live the present with the intensity of surprise and the beauty of creation. We suffered in the past and will suffer in the future and both sufferings prevent us from enjoying this *here and now*."[11]

But the desperation of political subjectivity extends to the supreme slogan of the movement: "all of them must go, not a single one should remain." The paradoxical character of the slogan is interpreted in a more or less direct way, appealing to the inconsistency of its literality in order to complete it with an implicit concept. Thus, the "all of them must go" could not be carried out, since "somebody" would remain. And that "somebody" is, of course, the one who is in position to state that the rest have to go.[12] *Political subjectivity* believes itself to be in a privileged position to explain who that "somebody" is and therefore who those "all" are, without abandoning, not even for a minute, the literality of the slogan.[13]

Such *cunningness* can only be sustained by adopting the position of the one who remains after "all have gone." *That* is precisely what politics is about. The novel and multiple character of the movement is effaced again. The assemblies will be brandished as *representation* and not as phenomenon. They talk in the name of—and in spite of—the assemblies. Politics consists in "saying what the assemblies would say if they were politically conscious."

This is how the movement is constituted as a *majoritarian dispositif.* As Deleuze defined it, the *majoritarian* is not a problem of quantity or massiveness, but of the establishment of a model to conform to. Thus the *majority* supposes the subsistence of the relations of domination and serialization, and in no way announces emancipation.[14] Not only does this majoritarian fancy obscure and disavow the infinity of becomings at hand, but it obdurates the true singular value of the assembly experiment itself.

Political subjectivity acts by obstructing the functioning of assemblies as instances of an effective counterpower—producer of changes and alternatives—in the neighborhoods, becoming a bureaucratic obstacle in the name of an abstract "politicization."

Against this "politicization," the assemblies rely on other resources to interpret the paradox of their slogans. Strictly speaking, "all of them must go" functions to postulate place of enunciation that is *radically heterogeneous* with respect to *politically instituted* discourses. This is not a simple confrontation between the instituted and the instituent. Destitution does not operate as a condition for the institution of a new power. Powers (*potencias*) act destituting previous political representations, as a premise to affirm a non-representational becoming. This opening implies renouncing all literality. "All of them must go" does not need interpreters to read what the text suggests, but practices that navigate what this statement lays open.

"All of them must go," then, is both self-affirmation and work of weeding. It is an attempt to liberate a terrain, a time, and the possibility of radically practicing the experience of the social bond; an attempt to demarcate the line from which any effectuality acquires practical consistency. The question, then, is no longer of composing a unified time that articulates and gives consistency to the neoliberal fragmentation, but of creating singular space-times to experiment the production of a new logic of *sense.*

While *political subjectivity* starts from an already "totalized totality," the new protagonism acts according to a "subtractive" non-knowledge about the situation. It is not a simple ignorance, but an even deeper knowledge, which begins by admitting the inexistence of a *universal knowledge* that is suitable for different situations. The new protagonism acts by destitution, self-affirmation, and production of meanings. But to affirm "there is not a party line" does not mean that there is nothing to be done. On the contrary, it only indicates that the current practices have to be capable of assuming how much in this quest is novel and uncertain.

Once they have overcome the classical perspectives, the struggles and experiments that produce new forms of social and individual existence are divested of all guarantees; but also of every abstract knowledge about *what is to be done* and any traditional form of thinking. We have thus arrived at a ground in which creations are the order of the day.

BEING THERE

AT THE COFFEE shop of a gas station in the porteño neighborhood of Floresta, three young men were watching on television one of the nightly street demonstrations that ended in Plaza de Mayo. It was the first massive and spontaneous cacerolazo after the insurrection. Suddenly, the images showed how the multitude severely beat up a police officer. The kids celebrated it. A police officer who was in the coffee shop, when he heard this, pulled out his gun and murdered them.

The next day—2001 had not ended yet—the first neighborhood assembly was born. The neighbors who had gathered there began to evaluate what to do: lists of demands, festivals, gathering of signatures, and government hearings. They were busy doing that when they noticed that the friends of the murdered kids stayed away from the assembly and did not utter a word at all. Instead, they were coming and going, silently elaborating plans destined to raze the police station that was protecting the murderer. The neighbors, very concerned, asked them to intervene and explain what the assembly should do according to them. It was then when one of the kids took the megaphone and pronounced these words: "I am not really interested in what is being discussed at the assembly. What we have to do now is to be here! I don't know how, but we have to be here, every day!"

This anecdote reveals important details about the character of the events unleashed after the insurrection. We are referring to the radical fall of representations, as a premise to access a minimum of sense capable of creating the conditions for collective elaboration. The exigency is deep: to be there, to remain silent, to accompany. It is not about the destitution of the word, but rather about its unreflective uses as a condition to elaborate a situational, nonrepresentational discourse. Nor is it about summoning interpreters or political bosses. What is necessary are neither roundtables nor opinions, but being there, physically, to see what happens.

This exigency tells us about an ethical movement that imposes new procedures of action and understanding. The required ethics implies assuming the extent to which theory is just one of the elements of the multiple that neither commands, nor explains or produces finished representations about the situation. Thus the new protagonism seems to open a rationality that works from this multiplicity, and from the destitution of every conscious center, of every external leadership and every promise of a future or model that organizes the present.

This interiority is the foundation of the spatial and temporal immanence of the assemblies. The labor of thought they carry out is the result of a process of differentiation, division of positions, and production of imbalances, without freezing anybody in definitive positions, avoiding in this way useless ruptures, moved by narcissistic differences of purely imaginary nature. In fact, the assemblies that have "managed" to avoid these obstacles—and that can congratulate themselves for functioning within an easy consensus—become bureaucratized spaces, filled with minuscule powers made-to-measure for "neighborhood tyrants."

The polemic against *political subjectivity* is set forth again: to dominate an assembly is to destroy it. The situational leaderships are, precisely, the ones that operate empowering (*potenciando*) multiplicity and the internal sense of the process, and not the ones that subordinate the situation to external criteria. Responding to centuries of beliefs in the superiority of centralized structures and in the separation between theory and practice, we know today that intelligence crosses through the entire living body and is not concentrated in the brain. Ideas do not flow from a directing center, but depend on a whole sensual and perceptive network.

The same can be thought about the body of the assembly. As a thinking *machine*, the assembly extends toward the social body. The unity of that body is not an abstract slogan, but a reality of the multiple that exists in concrete tasks, such as the creation of spaces, territories, and times that allow the assembly to subtract itself from the interpellations by communication networks, to assume each aspect of the conjuncture—exclusively—from the power (*potencia*) of the movements and the self-perception of the challenges and problems they confront. The autonomy proclaimed by the assemblies—and in general by all the experiments of counterpower—is itself a way of self-production of experience.

ASSEMBLIES AND PIQUETES*

ANOTHER SLOGAN PRODUCED by the movement was: "pickets and pots: the struggle is the same."**

To be sure, the piquetero struggles began to occupy streets and roads much before the emergence of the assemblies. Somehow those road-blocks opened the way, and the assemblies—undoubtedly—learned from that journey. This is the authentic connection between piquetes and assemblies. The piquetes showed what the assemblies today verify: new forms of intervention in the struggle for justice are emerging that, for the most part, no longer happen as a renewal of political parties or governing elites.

Piquetes and assemblies are connecting points of a diffuse network. Both dispositifs work on the exploration of non-traditional avenues of intervention. This is the richness of the present movement. Both have their demands, but at the same time, the movement is not exhausted in the fulfillment of those exigencies. The piquetes do not demand "only" work, food, and rights. They demand something that cannot be enunciated in the language of the demand. The same happens with the assemblies. Beyond the sociological discourse—of politicians, "intellectuals," and journalists—assemblies are constituted around a desire of justice and protagonism that no achievement, as important as it may be, can exhaust.

Will the assemblies and piquetes be able to, effectively, rid themselves of all the burden of traditional political discourses—"revolutionaries" and "reformists," "nationalists" and "citizens"—to regard themselves, without beating about the bush, as a true driveshaft that propels new experiments, as a place of radical creation? What does the *unity* of piquetes and assemblies consist of?

The problem of many of those who clamor for that unity is that they imagine it as a "political alliance." This can only be an illusion, a shortcut. An alliance like this, which pretended to confer "coherence" from above to the multiplicity of the movement, would not be faithful to the power (*potencia*) of the process.

Assemblies and piquetes develop, each of them, under its own conditions. But undoubtedly they have many fundamental points of

---

* Although "piquete" generally refers to "roadblock," here Colectivo Situaciones is using it to refer to much more than the act of blocking roads itself. To avoid narrowing the semantic field of the expression we leave it untranslated. (Tr.)

** In Spanish the two statements form a rhyme: "piquete y cacerola / la lucha es una sola." (Tr.)

convergence. Demands separate them, but the common experience of founding new modes of participation can imply new forms of exchange. Why should that union be only "political"? Why are we to continue imagining that the encounters between piqueteros and asambleistas only happen through the forms of political representation?

Thus, some people talk about "class alliances": the unemployed and the middle classes; roadblocks and pots. Suddenly, those in power analyze all that is going on with a "pseudo-Marxist" language: everything is read in terms of social classes, material interests, and rationalities strongly conditioned by insertion in the economic structure.

The model of "class alliances" obscures the processes at play. It not only impoverishes them, but ends up being used to, on one side, blame the "middle class"—the *included*—for not having demonstrated until "somebody touched their pockets," and, on the other side, to confirm that the *excluded* mobilized themselves before because "they had nothing in their pockets." There even is an incipient re-edition of the social division of "political" labor between assemblies and piquetes: the— "educated"—middle classes would be the "cultural and ideological" head of a movement in which the *excluded* would be the "strike force" or "obedient body."

"Included and "excluded," middle classes and the unemployed—or "poor"—are categories of a way of thinking that conceives politics as an ideological operation of inclusion, forgetting that the norm is always exclusionary and that to desire it is already to impoverish our existence.

Included and excluded are, then, tricky categories. There is no place for the excluded except for, precisely, where they already are: the margins. There is no possible inclusion—current or future—for those who no longer want to passively await the—material, intellectual, and spiritual—impoverishment of life itself. That is why the *classism* that all "the classes" bring to light—"we are the Argentinean middle class;" "workers and their interests"—is a way of impoverishing that which has come into being, reducing the emergent multiplicity to the economic conditions in which it originates. Piqueteros and asambleistas aspire to become figures of an inquiry about the form of building up a real autonomy, irreducible to any economicism.

This reduction of the multiplicity of the process to—economic— *classism* is a condition that power demands in order to *represent* each of these classes in the game of politics—with its parties, candidates, and government officials. Thus, this is the way in which the unleashed energies run the risk of being absorbed.

Beginning in the days of December, something that had been in the making took shape. Now it is completely visible, for everybody, that the struggles we are going through are very intense. They are seeking, above all, to recover a dignity severely affected over several decades.

MEMORY AND NATION
BY HORACIO GONZÁLEZ

One of the stinging points of the current debate in Argentina is where to put all the preceding cultural strata that went through the "popular national" or "social liberal" phase of politics. In this sense, to go to neighborhood assemblies is a dilemma, because the assemblies do not require that question about memory to come together, and maybe this is why they come together. But without that question, it is difficult to argue that they will be able to empower (potenciar) their voice. The assemblies dramatize December 19th and 20th, in which there were no partisan banners, and make their own historical break. But what character should that break have? How thorough should it be?

Each irruption produces a cross section, giving rise to new responsibilities and an abandonment of the past. An opening moment claims to have no obligations regarding the times that preceded it, which is perhaps indispensable as protoform of innovation. But, is that protoform exempted from revising the preceding protoforms? It would not be good that such a thing happened. The problem is how to pose the problem without proposing at each step that there is a previous history to be remembered, because that is what people called to brandish their previous knowledge as the only valid one generally do. There is right there a subtle point in which the needs of the new have to tie themselves up to a certain preceding memory.

In that earlier memory there are Radicals, Peronists, and countless cracked Argentinean identities. That they are cracked does not mean that they were ever in one piece. Today they are, perhaps in exacerbated form, as imprecise as they always were. Peronism and Radicalism are sites of intersection, of transit, regardless of whether the expression that shelters them lasts longer or shorter. In this sense, the interpretation we make of Peronism seems interesting to me. One possibility is to see it as a collection of induced consciousnesses, dragged to the public square by the category of hasty requests, something like the "I want my dollars" but at the level of political commitment; in fact, this is how people are thinking, but I don't think this is a felicitous way of resolving the issue. No consciousness is entirely trapped in the horizon of its immediacy.

Indeed, Peronism is a defeated force that is completing one of its last cycles as a name in Argentina. At the end of its cycle as a name, it would seem that only hasty behaviors emerge from that which Gramsci called "pensioners of history."* The question would then be, whether politics is now the expression of the legitimate interests of, say, the petty investors.** Does this character have the potential to produce a historical break? Evidently not. Peronism had more potential. But what is interesting about the current situation is that a historically fragile character, such as the defrauded investor, claims more

---

* See Gramsci, *Selections from the Prison Notebooks,* (New York: International Publishers, 1972), 280–7. (Tr.)

** In the 1990s, many petty investors or *ahorristas* created bank accounts in American dollars in the hope that the return of inflation would not alter the value of their savings. After the crisis of December 2001, the banks only offered to return them the same denomination in pesos. For instance, anyone who had 1000 dollars would receive 1000 pesos, which had been devalued to 330 dollars. During the reign of the convertibility regime (1991–2002), the value of 1 peso was 1 American dollar. After December 2001 the *ahorristas* became famous for their protests in front of banks, in which they systematically destroyed glass windows and automatic tellers, forcing the banks to replace the windows by steel panels that had to be replaced periodically. (Tr.)

rupture potential than the old Peronist working class, with its mighty unionist spurs.

My question, then, is about what portions of the previous names are set to continue to be interrogated in the present. What is at stake is the judgment that the present makes on the entire preceding era, on Peronism, on Alfonsinism, and also on Menemism. And in this sense the issue of who are the pot-bangers is also valuable; the question concerning the history of the people claiming legitimate rights in front of financial institutions. We should ask ourselves about the history of that class as well. In this sense, it seems unsuitable to say that it is the same middle class that four or five years ago was blindly enjoying its privileges. It does not seem to me that the previous condition invalidates the protest. It is necessary to look for the turning point that drives them to act and go out to the streets, and, at the same time, understand that the "I want dollars" has a history in Argentina that cannot be ignored. That supposes to reassemble a language with which participation in the assemblies would be possible. This is a point of tension that I personally do not perceive being adequately dealt with, in the midst of the relish for the new. But no historical break was ever intolerant with the remains from the past, at the price that these, in their persistent existence, will be buriers of those who believed they were new, but committed the sin of not inspecting the cellar of history.

The media deal with this issue in such a way that the oblivion of history is evident. This is not because of a vocation for irresponsibility, but because of the very structure of their rhetoric. It is the logic of their own procedure. For example, the only history that cannot be told in Clarin is Clarin's own.* And its history is fascinating. It is the political history of Argentina in the last fifty years. A number of people who write for Clarin today

---

* Clarín is the largest newspaper in Argentina. It belongs to a Buenos Aires-based conglomerate that owns several newspapers, as well as television and radio stations, both in Argentina and in other countries. (Tr.)

had tough experiences in the sixties and seventies. The newspaper itself is a sort of large cavern or catacomb of those thoughts, all of them archived and mixed with the language of journalism. Every newspaper has its archives, but this is also a living archive that does not dare to expose itself under pain of becoming extinct. Once in a while those shreds of history come up, but in a cynical way. That is why every communication medium is cynical one way or another, understanding this not as a moral judgment, but as what is done with thought that continues to be strong as a stratum of the past—and which allows itself to inherit all sorts of language resources—but in which nobody believes anymore.

We could think of notorious examples of historicism in the past. On one hand, the way in which Perón tells history. It is a military style. Perón is, thus, a vulgar historicist, because what he tells is the history of strategies, of the battles of all the geniuses of humanity. On the other hand we have the discussion between Rodolfo Walsh and Montoneros, whom he accuses of having a deficit of historicity.* Walsh's historicism also consists in studying earlier strategy, which is why he recommends rethinking the Peronist resistance.**

Finally, there is Cooke,*** who in a segment of a speech says: "in the end, when we look back at all these apparently forgotten events from the moment of liberation,

---

* Rodolfo Walsh (1927–1977) was a journalist and writer, author of several fiction and essay books. Already active in the revolutionary movements of the 1960s, he later joined Montoneros, the largest armed political organization in Argentina. Founded in 1970, it sought to build a counter-hegemonic force within the Peronist movement. Beginning in 1973, it entered a protracted war with death squads organized by the right wing of Peronism, which lasted until the military coup of 1976. The military dictatorship murdered and "disappeared" thousands of Montonero militants and supporters. Walsh, himself died in a confrontation with a commando group of the military Junta. (Tr.)

** The Peronist resistance was a network of social movements and individuals that struggled to bring Perón back to Argentina during the years after the coup overthrew his government in 1955 and sent him to exile. (Tr.)

*** See translators' note #1 in the introduction (Tr.)

they will acquire a different meaning." This is a very challenging phrase by Cooke, because it supposes appealing to a final moment of redemption, as the consolation of the militant who says "this time, we lost." All these ideas about time help to revise the previous political strategies, and force us to expound the formula for temporality we are using.

Today, the Argentinean left preserves a capacity for mobilization and some growth, but still moves within the old temporality. It is not even the temporality of the 18th Brumaire, which is a more complex temporality, of rises and falls. At one point Marx talks of ecstasis and of many recoils of the past. But if there is a problem of time, there is a problem of history. I believe it is a history that elapses without a unified gaze that disciplines it, and with many contributions of quite an extraordinary vigor and disparity. Otherwise, this moment of strong circulation of world ideas might become a mere reception of some texts, which regardless of their originality, can get trapped under another form of temporality.

It is the problem of the reception of issues and texts in the era of so-called globalization. Combined with imperial relations, the relations of submission, economic flows and world hegemony, there arises a new diversity in the incorporation of issues. For example, the dilemma about whether the struggle against globalization must also be globalized comes up. In a recent interview I took pleasure in referring to the "unglobalizable," as if it were a Kantian noumenon. More than resolving debates, one experiments with words. That is the essence of the essay, not as a literary genre, but as a form of opinion in a time full of challenges and turbulence.

Thus, what I mean is the possibility or the experiment* of living a universal, while keeping alive the individual self in order to, then, really participate in it. In the dialectic, this depended on the formula of the passage of time, but it no longer is that way. What would "our singularity" be without nations, cultural traditions, our own autobiographic capacity, and memory? Well, I think that our singularity is already the way in which we experiment it, in the performative manner of the one who receives the name of piquetero because he blocks a road, even though he is not doing that the entire day and his social culture comes from many places, especially from the old working class.

---

* In Spanish, the world "ensayo" translates both as "test" (or "experiment") and as "essay," the literary genre. González plays with the different meanings of "ensayo" in this paragraph and the previous one. This playful use of words is lost when translated into English. In Argentina, González is well known among his colleagues and students for advocating the essay as a political act against the scientistic pretentions of the social sciences. (Tr.)

NOTES

1. The neighbors of Villa Urquiza took over a property ceded to Coto supermarket and founded a square. The neighborhood assembly currently meets there. In that place the neighbors organize cultural activities, built a football field, and meet once a week to discuss the meanings of public space and the ways of constructing it.

2. The inter-neighborhood assembly brings together delegates from all the assemblies of the City of Buenos Aires and its outskirts. It has been functioning at Centenario Park every Sunday for several months. While in a first moment the enthusiasm of those in attendance was noticeable, its reputation has fallen and the presence—and influence—of neighborhood assemblies has diminished, giving way to an increasingly larger participation of parties from the left.

3. This process by which an ensemble of practices "without a subject"—economics, medicine, biology, technological knowledges—become autonomous, expropriating the peoples from their capacity to decide about their own lives, is at the basis of the category of biopower developed by Michel Foucault.

4. In particular those produced by Adrián Suar, after the success of Gasoleros. [Gasoleros was a very popular Argentinean soap opera that ran on a major national network in the late 1990s. (Tr.)]

5. This return to the neighborhood recuperates earlier forms of sociability, such as the murgas and many other artistic and cultural activities.

6. The production of social bonds is particularly evident in young people, among whom the subjective operation has included the production of new circuits of participation and socialization, especially around rock 'n' roll culture.

7. Of course, this is not absolute. That is why we refer to a dispute opened in the *neighborhood* territory. In fact, the insurrection of 19 and 20 existed as the encounter of this process with the dissatisfaction of the neighbor/consumer/petty investor (*ahorrista*) because of the expropriation of her savings. Ahorristas cannot be considered a homogeneous group. Some of them have sought to link their demands to the assembly process and have experienced a greater transformation as a result. But others have constituted their subjectivity around their claims without incorporating themselves massively into the assembly movement. In this sense, *ahorristas* currently constitute an active movement of injured people who have shown a high level of mobilization. But their perspective does not always coincide with the new communal protagonism. In a recent demonstration at the US Embassy, *ahorristas* demanded that the government of that country guarantee the return of the dollars of their savings. Days later an unexpected conversation took place between some demonstrators and the chief of the IMF delegation, who came to Argentina in March 2002 to make a report on the situation. The ahorristas exchanged opinions in a "cordial atmosphere" and then declared to have been taken care of very well by the Fund's envoy.

8. The neighbors from Villa Crespo who participate in the Assembly of J.B. Justo and Corrientes have undertaken the organization of an eatery after observing that families walk the streets of the neighborhood every day checking garbage bags, looking not only for paper and bottles to recycle, but also for something to eat. The asambleistas decided that these people should no longer be considered as passers-by: they had become part of their everyday life and had to be considered as part of the struggles for the neighborhood's needs. For that purpose, the assembly got hold of Atlanta Football Club, a place chosen not only because of its proximity to the Chacarita train station, but also because, for the neighborhood, it is a symbol of the expropriation of the community by corrupt actions. This is how a space of popular belonging was recuperated with the goal of carrying out different social activities. ["J.B. Justo and Corrientes" is a street corner. Most assemblies initially took their names from the landmarks where they held their meetings. (Tr.)]

9. As we saw at the beginning of Chapter 3, conscious thought is only one form of thought.

10. A quick tracking of previous experiences of urban resistance would bring us to the emergence, at the beginning of the twentieth century, of promotion societies, popular libraries, and other autonomous forms of popular culture. Later, with the predominance of institutions based in wage labor, mass consumption, and social regulation from the state, this autonomous culture would be absorbed by institutional actions and state policy. Peronism was the consciousness of this exchange in which autonomy is given away in exchange for workers participation in an inclusive national project.

With the crisis of the *Peronist nation*—during the 1970s—very interesting working class experiments re-emerged, including the factory committees of the industrial belt of Buenos Aires, Córdoba, and Rosario, which unfolded an alternative logic with regard to state-dominated unionism.

In turn, these working class experiments expanded to the neighborhoods and universities, producing in those places autonomous dispositifs such as the Neighborhood Councils, which at that moment were alternative to the Promotion Societies. During the years 1974 and 1975, Villa Constitución was a clear example of this double territorial power structured around the factory. There, "the experiment fructified into the creation of neighborhood committees elected in massively attended assemblies that took in their own hands the solution of problems that affected them. This new organizational form of the people from Villa extended to 34 neighborhoods and even managed to give birth to their own federation." In the Stella Maris neighborhood, for example, the Neighborhood Committee was created to take care of the "works that affect the common good, and which could hardly be carried out without the organized concurrent participation of society, … even when they are rights that we should be able to have just by asking for them…. The committee's Proposed Line of Action includes, among other points, the construction of a clinic and medical attention … and the restoration of the football field." See "La lucha por la democracia sindical de la UOM de Villa Constitución," in *Luchas Obreras Argentinas*, Editorial Experiencia, Year 2, N. 7, March 1985.

11. Luis Mattini, "Después de los piquetes, las cacerolas y las asambleas," http://www.lafogata.org/02latino/latinoamerica1/mattini11_3.htm, (published March 2002, accessed October 2004).

12. A recent poster from Izquierda Unida reproduces this slogan presupposing that "all of them must go" would not reach the groups from the Left, which is something that is rather debated.

13. The search for a literal meaning for this slogan results in extremely simplistic readings. For instance, "all the bourgeois (or the 'corrupt' ones, etcetera) must go."

14. Deleuze, Gilles and Felix Guattari. *A Thousand Plateaus: Capitalism and Schizophrenia*. Minneapolis: University of Minnesota Press, 1987.

CHAPTER 8

THE DIFFUSE NETWORK: FROM DISPERSION TO MULTIPLICITY

THERE ARE STRUGGLES. THEY MULTIPLY AND UNFOLD UPON A STRUCturally fragmented terrain. *Dispersion* is, then, the point of departure for each experiment, the inevitable starting point for any contemporary thought that wants to be critical.

Political temptation brings us to deny the structural character of this fragmentation. Far from assuming it as the common substratum, it proclaims a voluntarism: articulation, the attempt to centralize the experiments, to escape dispersion towards centrality.

According to this conception, the disarticulation of a foundational totality that gives meaning to each experiment is the origin of a weakness that must be reversed. If fragmentation leads to failure, the search for an articulating, totalizing, meaning giving dispositif—in the last instance, the state—becomes the true object of desire.

Trying to overcome the authoritarian and hierarchical forms of classical—party—politics, they seek another type of totalization. From the theories of hegemony and articulation, everywhere people talk about organizing as a *network*. But does this idea of the network really overcome the centralized forms of organization? Do we all think the network in the same way? If the situation is singular, that is to say, universal and concrete, how would it be possible to establish a horizontal relation with other situations without, precisely, losing this singularity?

CONSENSUS AND HEGEMONY

THE COMMUNIST AND socialist tradition organized itself around the national territory upon which it worked. Its consistency was guaranteed by the presence of a national-state that could give coherence to meanings, signify symbolically, and organize tasks and functions that were correlative to its institutions. The classical contestational movement, then, operated upon a preexistent totality—the nation-state. Its task was to "hegemonize," with its—class—points of view the set of the private institutions that constituted civil society.

But modern revolutionaries have always accompanied this task with a preparation for the moment of storming the apparatus of the state by military means. Hegemony and military struggle are the instances in which policies toward the control of the apparatus of the state and the institutions of civil society unfold.

Hegemony and consensus are categories of a politics of "articulation." The final objective is the national state. Why? Because the intuition is that without the state dispositif—which gives unity and coherence, which "forms society"—there is nothing but a collection of fragments lacking political value.

Hegemony functions as a process of "rearticulation" of the "parts"—classes, social groups, institutions, personalities—of a greater whole—society, nation—around a new principle—ethical, political, social, and economic. And for this principle to be effective, the process of reorganization should consist in an effective will to become state. We have called this general reasoning—with variations—"revolutionary politics"—or plain "politics," if we consider that "bourgeois" politics is "postrevolutionary."

Hegemony is class hegemony, as its primary theorist, Antonio Gramsci, worked impeccably and frequently to clarify. But classes do not operate *politically* unless it is by means of institutions that produce hegemony. Among them, the main organizer of class hegemony—both inwards, "producing the class as such" and outwards, producing a "historical bloc"—is the Party. Thus, hegemony is thought of as a particular type of network, a network "with a center": an articulation whose productive motor is the party of the class—Gramsci clarified many times that the party does not have to be exclusively a traditional political party: even a newspaper, for example, can occupy this *function*. Its ultimate task, as we have said, is seizing state power, a goal that is not achieved entirely by the dissemination of an alternative hegemony but rather which, the Italian communist tells us, requires the intervention, in a given moment, of organized military action. Hegemony is completed only through the control of the state apparatus.

Here articulation functions under a centralizing modality. And this *centralizing* action is taken up as an unavoidable effective condition for destroying the dominant center: to eliminate it and replace it with another ethical, intellectual, political and economic principle. The revolution expresses a change in the character of the state. Having defeated the bloc of the capitalists, society reorganizes itself on the basis of the interests of workers and the people. This centralization—coherently continued in the theory of the *dictatorship of the proletariat*—was not, in principle, the manifestation of a pathological desire for hierarchies and classifications, but rather an impeccable logical deduction: no isolated struggle can defeat the power of the state—which operates organizing the resources of the totality against the weak powers (*potencias*) of isolated struggles. Hegemony grows horizontally. And it does so from a center, reinforcing the centralizing tendency. It is the only way of confronting, when the moment comes, the center of power.

This political theory of revolution is effective as long as it manages to think a fundamental operator: the *revolutionary crisis* for Lenin, the *organic crisis* for Gramsci. The reasoning is as follows: while the state continues to dominate over all the constituent parts of society—"repression plus consensus"—there will not be any possibility of constituting an alternative hegemony. All the fractions of classes and social groups will be linked, subordinated, to the prevailing domination. The whole will effectively hold the parts in such way that there will be no possibilities of reorganization based on another principle. The *whole* will be consistent. The struggle will be waged inside this ruling hegemony. There will be no "true political struggles," they will say; there will be—at most—rearrangement of groups inside the power bloc. The movement of the parts generates no questioning of the organizing principle itself.

But, as Marx, Lenin, and Gramsci insist, those moments are not a constant in history. There are economic, political, and social contradictions, and there are limits to the power of bourgeois domination. Hegemony is not given once and for all. In other words: *the whole is not closed, it is not consistent.* This affirmation is the condition of possibility of revolution.

While there is not a consistent whole, there is a constant operation of totalization. That is, a continuous work that goes through moments of extreme fragility, until the arrival of a truly "organic" crisis of the power bloc. In moments like these, struggles radicalize, new perspectives and debates open, streets are taken in defiance of the very repressive power of the state and the final assault on power is prepared. But this cannot be done without a hegemonic accumulation, without a complex tactical game of alliances, of comings and goings, without clear leadership and a mass disposition—parties, unions, journals, "organic" intellectuals, and other class institutions—towards struggle. In other words, crisis is a necessary—essential—but not sufficient condition. "The party"—the political organization—is still missing. The crisis is a fundamental dispositif of politics. It is what permits "launching the offensive." "Crisis" is a synonym for the alteration of the capacities of domination, of all homogeneous temporality, of all normality. It refers to a rupture of the equilibrium upon which the dominance of the state is stabilized. Hence the difficulty of this category: even when it is fundamental, it is not capable of guaranteeing the direction of the revolutionary process by itself. That is why, said Lenin, the existence of a party that can organize the insurrection and knows how to do it is fundamental in order not to miss the opportunity. The crisis must unleash a revolutionary situation. We could summarize: "from the revolutionary crisis to seizing power."

The structural—economic—crisis, Gramsci argued, does not give us anything. The economic crisis becomes political, precisely, when it coincides with the eruption of an antagonistic social force capable of organizing itself "politically," disorganizing the "political" unity of the bloc of the dominant classes—which is, precisely, in crisis. Later, if things go well, and this time from power, the new bloc of classes takes up the task of organizing its dominance—as the dictatorship of the proletariat. As political theory it is frankly impeccable.

It is clear that the network that this political subjectivity presupposes dispersion as a major and exceptional risk. If a society exists as long as there is a domination that organizes it as such, it follows that its consistency is possible only by means of the articulation of consensual and repressive forms, the only way in which the parts find themselves impelled to coexist in society. Only when there is "crisis of domination" do the normally absent possibilities become actual: 1) dispersion of forces and 2) reorganization of these forces around revolutionary hegemony. According to the first possibility there are two alternatives: social disaggregation or the reconstruction of the bloc of classes in power. According to the second, dispersion does not occur because the "parts"—classes and subaltern groups—go from being lead by a class in power to being lead by *another* that comes to occupy a position of domination (thus endorsing a hegemonic principle around the state-form).

There is room for dispersion in this thought only as an exception. And always as the *lack* of an organizing principle that can substitute for the dominant principle of the state. This *lack* is political. It is a defect in "consciousness," in the "will" to produce alternative meanings capable of organizing another order. It is in the end a lack of organization, of direction and of orientation of the struggle. There is no alternative hegemony that does not set out to destitute the dominant one. There is no hegemonic politics, in the end, without seeking to substitute for the organizing principle of society.

The political *task* par excellence is to aim at dismantling the dominant meanings—rationalizations of the interests of the dominant classes—and producing alternative meanings, powerful enough to be able to reorganize the class game in a sense that reverses the present one. The central place of the game, the privileged position, is the apparatus of the state.

THE NEOLIBERAL REVOLUTION

NEOLIBERALISM WAS NOT simply *a policy*. Had it been a policy, we could celebrate its end, at least in Argentina, where its discursive hegemony was conclusive and today is broken. The problem is more complex. Neoliberalism implied a larger transition. A reorganization of the world: a violent reduction of the multiplicity of humanity to purely economic motivations and rationalities.

In this same perspective, Miguel Benasayag argues that this process of autonomization of the economy must be thought as a "process without a subject." In this sense, the macroeconomy is an autonomous combination of elements, self-sufficient and resistant to every attempt by political institutions to regulate it. In neoliberal conditions, we would add, all the discourses of integration and institutionalism that seek to "humanize the economy" break down. Anti-establishment politics is thus under a real risk of becoming a set of moral statements.

It is not easy to take on the consequences that result from this transformation. Capital-flows—the dynamics of the market—have taken the place, in their determinant power (*potencia*), of the primacy of the nation-state when it comes to organizing a specific order in its own territory. Of course, the nation-state does not disappear, but its strategic functions are reorganized in accordance with the imperatives of the new dominant forces. Far from the "death of the state," what appears is a new type of state. In this sense, there have been theorizations of the *post-Fordist state*,[1] *the competitive state*,[2] or *technical-administrative state*.[3]

All these categorizations of the new state modalities coincide in one aspect: fixed forms, internal to the nation-state territories whose attempt to regulate the flows of populations, information, money, goods, and services is increasingly weaker. Thus, these postmodern state forms persist, subordinated to the strength of mercantile flows.

To sum up: the excess of development and the autonomization of the macroeconomy subordinate the totality of social relations that develop under the territory dominated by them. Fragmentation ceases to be an exception. It is not a temporary or contingent politics, but rather an unstable and uncertain ground, on which we are condemned to carry out our lives.

Dispersion is the *ontology* of contemporary capitalism. The fragments of the nation are virtually articulated by economic forces. Increasingly, this new landscape shows the incapacity of the institutions of the nation-state to organize and sustain its sovereignty in the classical terms of the "monopoly of legitimate violence over a territory."[4] What does it mean in this new scenario that struggles are "dispersed"? What would be the forms of overcoming this fragmentation?

Fragmentation is not an effect of a lack, as political subjectivity thought. On the contrary, this dispersion of sense in which our lives today unfold is produced by the affirmation of effective forces: the market approach. Max Weber himself believed that markets were producers of associations and social classes. Of course these classes had no apparent relation with the social classes thought by Marx. According to Weber, classes are associations of separate individuals who—because of their position in relation to the market, and not in production as in Marx— have *common interests*. As structuring source, the market produces individual consumers, who associate themselves temporarily without ever having to transcend their character as individual consumers.

This social "destructuration" is no longer, actually, the effect of a crisis. Or, in any case, the crisis is no longer exceptional. This is the paradox of neoliberalism: it has regularized and normalized an *exceptional situation*. That "crisis is no longer the issue" means that political struggle has altered its foundations. The issue is not anymore the struggle against a repressive state—even though it does repress—nor against a hegemonic totalizing operator that confers roles to each inhabitant of the nation. Dominance based on economics, technology, and the mass media uses the state for domination, but the state is no longer the strategic dispositif for the production of a subjected, dominated, and subordinated subjectivity.

The obvious question seems to be: *how to articulate these fragmented struggles?* That is to say: it seems that the question is no longer how to disorganize the state hegemony, because the fragments "are already loose." Then: how to deploy strategies that, without reproducing hierarchical forms inside themselves, including the classical and centralist form of the party, can coordinate forces, articulate struggles, and give orientation to the political accumulation that has been achieved, with the goal of resolving the question of "who governs"? How to build a power of popular character that, from below and under its hegemony, can produce once again a strong, organized, planner state? How do these struggles communicate? How are they coordinated? These are the questions that organize the political consciousnesses of the present.

EXPLICIT NETWORK AND DISCONNECTION (THE BARTER CLUB)

DURING THE PAST few years, the image of the *network* has been useful to organize and think possible forms of coming together without "creating centers." According to this language borrowed from information science, each one of us is the *node* of a network. This is how the barter clubs, among others, operate: each *node* is the "concrete part" of the network of exchange. The *prosumers*, a figure that designates those who are at the same time producers and consumers, participate in this network. These *prosumers* aspire to maintain the direct and simultaneous experience of being producers of what they offer, and consumers of what they obtain in the exchange.

The network has been the response of the alternative experiences to the question over how to connect dispersion, how to link those people and groups that have been expelled from the central system. Other circuits, other decentralized networks, have detached from the official networks which permit men and women to organize their lives "outside"— a relative but effective "outside"—the *central nodes* of society. Each one can, at the same time, form part of one or more circuits. The development of these networks produces its own consistency. A barter network is not for anybody and, in principle, it does not aspire to organize the other networks.

The *explicit networks*—in this case, the barter networks—draw their force from the fact that they operate a *scission* in the global network of exchanges, thus opening up an inhabitable space for the *prosumer*, who has usually been expelled from the *global network*. But, at the same time, each one of these experiments is permanently at risk of being reinterpreted, absorbed and reincorporated into the *global network*. In the case of the network called "barter club," the boundaries[5] between the uneven network and the global network are marked, for example, by the fact that the "currency" used for the exchange does not accept "parity" of exchange with the monetary system of the global network.

But once an explicit, limited network, such as the example of the barter club, has been set in motion, it can produce phenomena unthought by the organizers themselves and even by the *prosumers*. It is possible, but in no way necessary, that new forms of relation of people with objects grow there, very different from the fetishized forms of current postmodern capitalism. In this type of alternative practices, new forms of sociability, forms of values and bonds that capitalism repressed for centuries, could also flourish. But this is in no way assured. In fact, only an investigation that takes thinking—from the standpoint of the epochal rupture we are witnessing—the new forms of production of the social bond as its task will be able to understand the phenomenology of a new emergent subjectivity.

THE NORM AND THE ETHIC OF SELF-AFFIRMED MARGINALIZATION

EXPLICIT NETWORKS OPERATE in their singularity by establishing customs' barriers to the flow of exchange with the global network. This is its force, and from here it can draw its desirable character for thousands of people that have been *excluded*—either compulsorily or voluntarily—from the central articulation. But this *marginalization* is not evident. It is not just economic marginalization, nor is it a supposed virtue of the marginalized vis-à-vis the *integrated*.

The issue in question is the definition of *integration* and *marginalization* as imaginary terms in relation to a dominant norm with respect to which the spaces of inclusion and exclusion are constituted. There is no reason, we insist, to think inclusion/exclusion fundamentally in economic terms, but it rather covers issues such as sexuality or ethnicity, and, in the end, all those forms of being human that are subordinated to normalized perceptions according to the parameters of the normalization/pathology grid.

We are not talking about the *marginalization* of someone who was described as excluded, but rather of those who deny the central norm only to affirm for themselves their own models of the adequate. Whoever is considered excluded from the perspective of the norm is already included in the system that excludes; in the same way that the included will always be subjected to the perpetual threat of exclusion. Included and excluded are, paradoxically, two places in the same system.

The imaginary character of the norm follows a "fractal" logic, that is, it reproduces itself in every space. In a peripheral neighborhood there are also centers and peripheries. And in these peripheries of the periphery there are also more "secure" zones and others through which it is better not to go, and so on to infinity. The same happens in the "centers": in the most integrated cities there are always different kinds of zones. This "fractal" topology thus sustains the norm, reproducing the same logic in each city, in each neighborhood, in each street.

The marginalization we are talking about here is not that of those who find themselves subjected to the norm—and continue to desire it. Rather, this marginalization implies a subjective operation: refusing what the norm does with us, opposing resistances, and creating our own novel forms of being. These three moments are, at the same time, part of a single movement of "taking the word." Gilles Deleuze made reference to this with the slogan "resistance is creation."

The possibility of an experience—whether collective or personal—of disarticulation from the norm that names it, knows about it, and defines it by its characteristics as normality, presupposes the movement of assuming the situation sovereignly, proposing discourses, knowledges, and criteria whose origin is already situational, that is to say, multiple. This access to multiplicity is, at the same time, refusal and resistance against the knowledge of the norm.

This *self-affirmed marginalization* is one of the principal vocations of the new protagonism. These are the operations that can produce new values of sociability and powerful (*potentes*) situational knowledges. At the same time it is not a struggle "against" the norm, to abolish it or substitute something else for it. It is not a matter of "changing the norm" for another, because what is being refused is not the specific normative content but rather the normative function itself. Nor is it a matter of abolishing it, because the permanence of the norm does not depend on *a* subject but rather on the desires of subjects.

Self-affirmed marginalization is never a level of "exclusion," precisely because exclusion is always already a subordinate position of inclusion. The norm itself includes by excluding.[6]

Self-affirmed marginalization is an *ethical* form composed of two moments. Resistant *subtraction* and creative *self-affirmation*. But the *subtraction* is not an abstract action. It implies a labor of reappropriation of the very conditions upon which this ethical operation works. Such an operation sets out from concrete historical and material determinations and consists in a modification of those determinations. This operation is neither negation nor sublimation, but rather reappropriation: it transforms determination into condition.

While the norm *determines* the sovereignty of the conditions over the possible liberty under the circumstances, the situation, by contrast, takes the conditions as the material and historical ground for the production of an encounter with power (*potencia*). But this *situational reappropriation* has a paradoxical effect on those who continue to desire via the norm: on one hand, it can inspire analogous experiences but, on the other, it can appear threatening to the dominant structures of power, to those rejoicing inside them. This last is what happens in societies that repress homosexuality: the fantasy that the homosexual experiences a greater and more diverse pleasure puts him in a position to threaten the prevailing *normality*. The new protagonism—*self-affirmed marginalization*—implies, by itself, a new politics to the degree that it produces powerful tendencies of a new sociability at the grassroots. However, the norm is currently acquiring a more abstract functioning than that which we have known and criticized during the era of disciplinary society and the hegemony of the nation-state. We insist: in our biopolitical societies the norm has become even more abstract—the economy and technoscience—giving way to a true "process without a subject." The *pathological* and the *normal*, as much as the *included* and the *excluded*, come to be produced more by postmodern networks of biopower than they are by the institutions of confinement theorized by Foucault.

The film *The Closet*, directed by Francis Veber, tells the story of an administrative employee who occupies an indefinite position in the hierarchy within a large company that manufactures condoms. Our friend, an *average Frenchman*, is sadly divorced from the only woman he loves—and bores—and distanced from his son, whom he is unable to seduce. This is the initial picture: a totally normalized man, depressed and indifferent, who can neither manage to catch the attention of his female coworker nor summon the camaraderie of his other coworkers. He is only a number for the board of a company that, for strictly techno-economic reasons, decides to reduce the staff and include him among the personnel to be laid off. Ruined and on the edge of suicide, a new neighbor, older than him and also alone, intervenes by inviting the protagonist to consider a strategy to reverse the work situation: to pretend he is gay, so that the company would be forced to reverse its decision or face a public and juridical outcry for discrimination. Our hypernormalized character would pay a high cost for this decision: he has to choose between having a reputation as a homosexual or face the most feared situation: become unemployed, excluded. Finally, as expected, he chooses the former. Thus, the accomplices send a retouched photo of the protagonist in an indubitably gay atmosphere, which soon circulates through all the offices. The strategy turns out to be a complete success, and immediately the general manager of the company promotes our friend, at the same time the masculine and homophobic members of the board are forced by their superiors to "make friends" with the false homosexual. Quickly everything is turned upside down and his wife and son become vividly interested in the discovery. Even his female coworker almost assaults him sexually during work time. The film then shows us his accomplice: a genuine homosexual who had to endure in another time—in the hardest isolation—being fired from his job, precisely "because of" his sexual condition. As *The Closet* shows us, homosexuality and economic and social exclusion have traded their places. By no means is this progress of French society as a whole, because the recognition of homosexuals is presented as a forced and calculated act of hypocrisy—although probably gay resistance has obtained advances in this respect. Rather, this is something very different: the process of production of values has been displaced towards the development of the economy and technoscience, which, in their own becoming produce, as an involuntary consequence, new criteria of integration and exclusion.

This new fundamental characteristic of the contemporary forms of domination imposes new demands upon radical thought and the forms of self-affirmed marginalization and obliges us to reconsider the *embodiment* or *enactedness, (puesta en acto)* of the ethical operation—multiplicity—under the present conditions of dispersion.

FROM DISPERSION TO MULTIPLICITY

WE ARRIVE, THEN, at the question that runs through a good deal of the concerns of those who participate in the alternative movement. Is multiplicity a problem to overcome through forms of articulation that organize and give efficacy to struggles? Moreover, how can a network of these experiments of new protagonism be organized?

The only possible network among these experiments is the *diffuse network*. The singularity of these experiments consists precisely in that their own operation implies getting out of the global network—from the norm, from the panopticon—and affirming in this "going beyond" a knowledge of itself and its situation.

The explicit network that each experiment produces is, therefore, restricted and interior to its very foundational premises. They affirm their own forms of exchange. They do not isolate themselves, but rather delimit new boundaries with the "exterior." Or, put another way, they appropriate this "exterior" becoming sovereign with regard to the relation.

The diffuse network operates through *resonances*. These presuppose shared epochal problems, certain common obstacles, which make certain knowledges, feelings, and declarations transferable by means of situational compositions. There are no forms of imitation and direct translation that cause the efficacies of those knowledges to become general—and immediately universal.

But those encounters and compositions do not imply the formation of a new global space. An explicit network cannot really link different situations without taking them as "nodes" of the network, which presuppose a virtual space of communication among experiments homogenized by a common property. Thus, the situational singularity attained through the ethical operation finds itself hurt once the sovereignty of a normative dispositif over the experiment itself is again accepted.

Diffuse network and *explicit network* are, then, two names that try to organize the possible connections between the experiments of counterpower from the perspective of the new protagonism. Indeed, the explicit network is presented here as the existence of active connections among points of a network organized by a present sense, which is to say, by a situation. The diffuse network, in turn, is the environment, or the existing situations with which the situation—explicit network—will communicate, precisely, by resonances.

The diffuse network is the perception of the global network from the point of view of the situation. Indeed, while the global network functions by articulating the full extent of possible points under the virtual bond of communication, the diffuse network operates as the collection of resistances with respect to the abstract point of view of the global network. Another way to say this is to consider the global network as the dispersion that is peculiar to the biopolitical domain, while the diffuse network is the capacity to produce a subtraction or, better, an autonomy with respect to the global network. The diffuse network is the point of view that allows us to think the composition of situations starting from the production of a foundation that is common to both. What the diffuse network affirms is the impossibility of explicitly organizing the global network. Composition, then, is only produced from the standpoint of an intra-situational reflection capable of discovering within itself, as an element that weaves and constitutes it, the situation it encounters and composes.

What these experiments share is "neither too much nor too little": they neither subordinate themselves to a common property that assembles them and normalizes their action nor do they exist as a pure unconnected dispersion. Situations exist as concrete totalities. They have nothing to look for outside of themselves. There is no global "environment" from which to extract information. Let alone is there a "global logic" that governs them. Those concrete universals are consistent multiples that reproduce the world inside each situation.[7] Each one of the other situations that live in a given situation as an element, can be activated, tell something to it, or not. As we said, these are resonances, that is to say, effects of a labor in the situational interiority that, by dealing with common problems of our times, inspires active processes of reappropriation in other situations.

Each situation works at the same time as both an explicit network and a diffuse network. As a cutout from the global network and as diffuse network with respect to the rest of the situations. These resonances open avenues to understand what we could call the "change of hegemonies": the emergence of new epochal elements that make themselves present in each situation. Thus, the resonances are forms in which novelties, discoveries, new knowledges, resonate expressively.

The attempt to organize an explicit network always runs the paradoxical risk of recentralizing itself since there are questions that it cannot help raising: which is the criterion to decide who belongs to the network? How to control compliance with this criterion? How to avoid the reappearance of excluded and included in its interior?

There is sufficient cumulative experience in the sense that every alternative grouping, if it crystallizes as such, begins to set its own criteria of belonging and identity, accomplishing, paradoxically, intentions opposite of those desired. But it could also be that the network does not form a totality at any moment. The diffuse network seeks to investigate these possibilities. It could even be the case that the network does not *really* exist as such. We would no longer be talking about the parts of a whole, or fragments that should be articulated, but rather about radical singularities, capable of being receivers of resonances of other universalities for the simple reason that those singularities have the vocation of integrating the world—to the network—within their own concrete universality.

Thus, dispersion acquires a different status. No longer is it the exceptional lack of a "politics" of statist will, and its destiny is no longer centrality. Dispersion is the spontaneous form of "commodity society" and it does not become active and productive if it does not become multiplicity.

The operation of becoming multiple is always perceived from the point of view of an external spectator. This last sees "lack of center," of coordination among the parts, and easily confuses dispersion and multiplicity. But this external spectator is also the one who resists—from the political subjectivity that is typical among academics, political militants, the humanitarians of the NGOs, and the "global" militants—thinking from inside the process of the multiple.

Both figures, the multiple and the fragmented, begin from a common ground. But there is a substantial difference between them: while dispersion can be conceived according to a previous or future unitary sense, the multiple, in its own sense, exists and consists in itself.

Dispersion is, thus, the multiple that has lost all consistency; all meaning. The new protagonism is a multiple that discovers itself as such. It can only appear as pure dispersion from the perspective of the exteriority from which it is observed, or from the perspective of a lack of elaboration internal to the multiple itself.

The situation—multiple among multiples—can speak to the world from its own experience and without speaking "about" the "external" world. This is what, thus far, we have been calling a *concrete universality*.

This contrasts to dispersion in that the whole is in each part. Each element of the multiple, in its extreme singularity, affirms a universality that allows us to think ourselves as part of "the same": "producers of worlds," we would say. This network is, paradoxically, a network that, far from existing outside of each node, exists "in" each "node."

Each explicit network works in the diffuse network without seeking to organize it.

The network does not demand to be articulated. Nobody has to get entangled in the net.* That is why, we say, the network is useful only as a *diffuse network*. The explicit or political network is the form of the passage from dispersion and the fragment to the—statist—totality. The *diffuse network*, by contrast, implies thinking not in terms of passage from one state to another, but rather in terms of the conversion *of the disperse into the multiple*.

The *diffuse network* is the image of singular situations, productive and concrete forms of appropriating the world, of creating it, knowing that there are as many struggles, modes of existence and points of view, as situational experiments can be assumed. *The diffuse network consists in the possible—non-communicative—resonances between these situations.* Because of its character, the diffuse network is not a communicational network: it does not transmit *information*.

The point of departure is the principle according to which every knowledge—and its value—is purely situational, depending on a set of axiomatic premises that make it consistent. To transfer a knowledge that originates in one system of premises to another is to reduce a situational operation to pure "information"; that is to say, to "data." But data does not preserve its value independently of the context of its appropriation, outside the ensemble of referential points from which it is interrogated.

DIFFUSE NETWORK

IN THE LAST years we have seen the birth of a counteroffensive of struggles all over of the world. This counterpower, however, does not always manage to think itself as a diffuse network of the new protagonism. Many of those who have participated in this new radicality think of themselves as part of a global struggle. They seek, then, to organize the resistance by way of *explicit networks*. The question that these experiences sometimes try to answer is: how to reverse the unjust and self-destructive tendencies of humanity while rejecting the terms of global thinking?

The partisans of the construction of explicit networks maintain that "if domination is global, resistance should also be so." Thus,

---

* In Spanish, there is only one word, "red," for both *net* and *network*. (Tr.)

horizontality, pluralism, global coordination, circulation of information and direct action are the principles that orient the attempts to
build "anticapitalist" movements, under the slogan: "think globally,
act locally."

In turn, the multiplicity of the movement does not acknowledge
the emergence of "leading" or "intelligent" centers seeking to be the
place from which the alternative is organized or thought.[8] Multiplicity
is multiple. In the movement of anti-global resistance two tendencies
appear: those who orient themselves toward the constitution of alternative centers, thus organizing the dispersion—under the idea of
opposing a "just" globalization to the present "unjust" one—or, on
the other hand, those who wager on multiplicity, and consider that if
globalization is synonymous with capitalism, then resistances should
seek to "deglobalize."

The globalizing position catalogs the multiple as dispersion in need
of organization, as something "that doesn't make sense": the multiple
thus goes back to being a "lack." From this point of view all the apo-
rias of classical political subjectivity are activated. On the other hand,
this perspective restores the classical separation between the economic,
the social, and the political. "The political" insists in appearing as the
master key against dispersion, subordinating the multiplicity of experiments.[9] But the present counteroffensive to this tendency should not
be reduced. Since the appearance of the EZLN, in Chiapas, a novel
teaching added practical resources to the self-perception of the new
protagomism. Zapatismo carries out very concrete initiatives to prevent
the crystallization of the networks into a center. Recuperating, animat-
ing, and socializing concepts of Foucauldian and Deleuzian origin, the
network that the Zapatistas propose is "a world in which many worlds
fit." Those worlds are neither dispersed fragments, nor "nodes" of a
network, but rather an undirected multiple.[10]

The rejection of the seizure of power by the EZLN implies a repositioning of the state inside the multiple. The state would no longer
be the dispositif that secures unity and meaning to "the parts," but
rather the institution that regulates and administers the resources of
the Mexican nation. This would be formed by diverse experiments—
those of professional, academic, peasants, workers, and women communities—that do not seek to subordinate themselves to each other:
the movement of democratization is conceived as an invitation to an
ethical operation in each situation, rather than as a mechanical support
for zapatismo. Thus, Zapatista thought can be understood—at least by

us—as that of a *diffuse network*: an action that allows for coordination, solidarity, and encounters at the planetary level but that, even so, does not forget its concrete universality. And it is interesting to see the extent to which this situational interiority places the Zapatistas in better conditions of struggle against the global forces of capitalism. Far from isolation, the EZLN and the indigenous communities of the south of Chiapas manage to appropriate all that turns out to be useful to unfold their experiment.

Neo-zapatismo takes up the confrontation to which it is exposed. The indigenous communities seek to save a form of life[11] and of relation with nature that is threatened by the interests of large multinationals[12] in the biodiversity of the Lacandona jungle. The Zapatistas have managed to take up this struggle coordinating it with other indigenous communities, intellectuals, NGOs, and activists from all over the world. But at the same time this action does not imply any "global consciousness of the world." The indigenous do not need to emit universal moral judgments from which to derive the meaning of their actions. Only capitalism seeks to *really* know "the world." For those cultures that manage to affirm themselves on alternative bases there are only situations: it is not easy, save for our western cult of the individual, to conceive of an imaginary place from which to "observe the world."

Existence, as Sartre said, is prior and multiple with respect to consciousness. Gilles Deleuze read this same movement in the work of Spinoza: according to Deleuze, Spinoza's method consists in going beyond consciousness by revalorizing the body: "the model of the body, according to Spinoza, does not imply any devaluation of thought in relation to extension, but, much more important, a devaluation of consciousness in relation to thought: a discovery of the unconscious, of an *unconscious of thought* just as profound as the *unconscious of the body*."[13]

This essentialization that consciousness makes over existence, over the multiple, is activated when one thinks from the global perspective. This method, however, can be found in the heart of communicative processes. The Spinozist-Deleuzian hypothesis affirms that only at the level of existence, that is to say, of the practical corporeal as multiple thought—which always goes beyond consciousness—is it possible to establish a re-encounter of theory and practice, body and thought, living and operative existential unity, refutation of the scission that condemns us to capitalist separation.

SITUATIONAL KNOWLEDGES (THE ESCRACHES)

ACCORDING TO HORACIO Gonzalez, escraches are the specific weapons of the assemblies. If some loot and others picket, the assemblies "do escraches" ("*escrachan*"). Thus, "all of them must go, not a single one should remain," the dominant slogan of the assembly movement, advances, in words, that which it will later materialize in the form of escraches: "not a single one should remain, without getting an escrache" (*sin escrachar*).

It did not go unnoticed by anyone that the escraches have been reinvented in recent years by the group H.I.J.O.S..[14] It has been this work of recuperation and creation of new forms of demonstrating demands that made it possible for the assembly to appropriate a modality of protest, available because of this previous work.

Hence, the escrache has "generalized." Could this be a sample of how a network operates? Do the escraches preserve, in their *generalization*, the same meaning they have when they are undertaken by H.I.J.O.S.? Is it important that this should be so?

The escraches of H.I.J.O.S. can be conceived, in the first place, as a *practical method for the production of justice*. In this sense, H.I.J.O.S. make their denunciations/escraches against people who have been juridically and/or socially condemned. People who, after being condemned, have not served their sentence. The crimes they have committed have remained unpunished.

The escrache was born as a form of *self-affirmation*. Instead of trusting representative justice, the escrache institutes direct forms of "doing justice" without expecting mediations of any type. This is not only about an institutional deficit, but also about something more important: the effects of the escrache are a denunciation of the inefficient functioning of the judiciary only in a second place. The escrache does not work by "putting pressure on the judges to act," even if, eventually, this also happens. The mark of the escrache on the social body is more profound and disquieting. It removes an entire chain of complicities that made the genocide possible and thus summons—in order to do justice—thousands of people, particularly the neighbors of the perpetrators of the genocide, who are the ones taking into their own hands the task of exercising the punishment. Thus, the one who gets the escrache will no longer be "just another neighbor." From this moment onwards, "everyone" knows who he *is* and what he *did*. The punishment passes into the hands of the neighbors by way of a symbolic act, the escrache.

Contrary to what so-called specialists—intellectuals who voice opinions all too easily—argue, the escraches by H.I.J.O.S. are not media events. According to the "reflections" of these "analysts" of postmodern society, the escraches done by H.I.J.O.S. are unforeseen forms of the resurgence of a proto-fascism, of the lynch mob. However, the response of H.I.J.O.S. toward those who killed their parents—do we or do we not see some difference between this and fascism?—is qualitatively different. Without holding any power, unarmed, peaceful, the escraches convoke a festival whose *duration* is not marked by the logic of "harassment" nor by that of the TV newscasts. In fact, and increasingly so, the escraches are preceded by a long process of discussion with neighborhood organizations and neighbors over the *meaning of the act* that is, clearly, absolutely beyond the grasp of the television viewer.

The time of the escrache is opposed of that of waiting. Direct action, making the neighbors of the barrio executors of a permanent sentence: the bonds that H.I.J.O.S. has to build with the neighbors and the action of reactivation/actualization of a memory of popular struggles—without nostalgia and far from any position of "victim"—tinge in a significant way the meaning of this dispositif. On the other hand, is it a minor issue that those who call to support the social condemnation are the "children" of the "disappeared" and hundreds or thousands of young people from a generation that refuses to accept genocide and neoliberal society as a form of sociability? Is it secondary that the escrache appeared when the classic forms of politics had exhausted their potential for transformation and for producing justice? Is it indifferent, in order to think the meaning of the escraches, that direct action was undertaken in moments in which political "representation" and virtualization by the market and the media have shaped social relations to a point never seen before?

Not, it is not superfluous to say that the escraches started in relative isolation and have been repressed numerous times. That is to say, the climate in which they emerged was very different from the present. Now, if all these elements are components of the meaning of the escrache, how could *another experiment* use these same forms of the escrache claiming the same meaning? The hypothesis would be as follows: it is possible to do *other kinds of* escraches, but not to generalize the escraches of H.I.J.O.S. Those who take the escrache as "media savvy and effective technique," that is to say, as a communication tactic, *betray* the meaning of the escrache. But at the same time it is impossible not to betray it, because the meaning cannot be separated from the practical conditions that make them exist in their singularity.

The requirement then is to adopt the escrache—only for those who are interested, of course—as an element that can be part of a production of a new meaning. This implies, certainly, not *reproducing* it from its external features, but rather from a *new singularity*, appropriating the escrache and producing its own new meaning. Thus, assemblies, for instance realize that the escrache by itself does not carry a particular efficacy, but rather produces effects by becoming an operation specific to the situation.

Escraches, assemblies, cacerolas, and piquetes are all forms of struggle that draw their value from a situational production of meanings. Then, there is no generalization, but only the appearance of it. For *generalization—the explicit network*—has a limit: the diffusion of a form of struggle with its original meaning—for example, the escraches done by H.I.J.O.S.—only holds up within certain conditions of production. Outside those conditions of production—which are organized by a meaning (*sentido*)—the meaning of the escrache does not hold up. It is understandable, then, that when they are extracted from the ensemble of premises that gave them meaning, the most expressive forms of struggle no longer say anything.

The incorporation of a form of struggle is not a simple importation, but rather implies a labor of re-elaboration, appropriation, and colonization of the practice in question by a new meaning that will—or will not—give it a determined meaning. The transfer of the practice and its meaning (*sentido*) from one experience to another is improbable. It only occurs as an effect of the ideology of communication, which seeks to reduce everything to the world of image and opinion, the dispositif that produces subjectivities for the network of the market that annihilates all meaning under the force of quantification.

Escraches have the value of a singular nontransferable "operation." Which does not mean that there is only one way of practicing them, but rather each time they are practiced a reflection on the difficulties of mimesis becomes necessary; that is to say, a reflection on the impossibility of importing efficacies from other struggles through the facile process of copying. This reflection on the escraches comprehends an epistemology, because it tells us about the impossibility of mechanically transferring from one situation to another, without a process of re-elaboration, knowledges that have a value within an ensemble of premises. And it is this consciousness of the boundaries that every situation necessarily has that shows the difference between how the explicit network and the diffuse network functions. The former functions within an ensemble of common premises. The latter doesn't. It functions, by contrast, in the complexity of diverse situations and, for that reason, each "passage" demands a profound resignification. The illusion of a world "without borders" cannot be that of a homogeneous and abstract world, with a unitary meaning, or better, without meaning at all.

COUNTERPOWER

León Rozitchner says that the left has extracted dogmas and models from triumphant revolutions. The laws of history are supposed to become apparent in them. They tell us about the possibilities for humanity to know them and manage them. In the end, they fill us with a rational faith in the future. Rozitchner maintains that this faith in progress conceals that these same historical laws that become apparent in triumphs should be taken into account when it comes to understanding the meaning of failed revolutions.

If the fate of successful revolutions is in the mythified modelization, in the invitation to "generalize the recipe," failed revolutions should warn us about the easiness with which success *makes us forget* the twists and turns of history. If the left selects its successes as a source of inspiration, sweeping the lessons of the failures under the rug, the foreseeable result is the underestimation of marginal, peripheral struggles and the knowledges they produce.

However, the wisdom of failed struggles also has something to tell us. And that moment of failure contains a significant historical load. This is the history of modern Argentina: failures whose words are hard for us to bear. Biographies and battles forgotten for one reason or another. Because they did not fulfill their promise or because the partial triumphs do not please those who have a polished vision of the way in which history should unfold. And yet, oblivion is a *reversible position* in a field of counterposed *positions*. That which was forgotten yesterday is reborn today with an unusual force. The layers of discourses, solidarities, knowledges, and meanings put into play in battles, at moments pushed into the background, activate themselves secretly, reorganized when they are effectively summoned, perpetrating their own counterattack in the moment when, like embers covered with ashes, manage to catch fire again, and spread the contagion.

The 19th and 20th of December stand out alongside other possibilities. The interest they attract is also a mystery. But if we had to argue why those dates and not an earlier one, we would prioritize two arguments. On the one hand, *intensity*. The concentration of demands, exigencies, and decisions made in a city by a multitude that until now—appears to be more or less disjointed.* This intensity was loaded with failures that accumulated and with which nobody completely came to terms with. As Walter Benjamin would have said, these defeats seem not to bother for some time, until that time is abruptly interrupted. In this way, the irruption is not ahistorical; rather it is the only effective form of historicization.

On the other hand, *visibility*. The 19th and the 20th worked as a striking call for attention. As if someone had turned the light on in the middle of the night. The warning was given: "*something* is going on here; we cannot keep on sleeping, as if *nothing* happened!" That is to say, the general visibility was altered, the self-perception of the country, the space of public discourse and the discourse of publicness were restructured. As a relapse of the patient in the real of its affection, or as the end of an illusion—depending on tastes and possibilities.

The 19th and 20th were days of fusion, emergence, irreversibility, visibility, intensity, readaptation, and invention. All of them movements carried out "in" and by an evasive history whose caprices are never interpreted once and for all. A long tradition of political readings threaded at the heat of real and imaginary conspiracies that understand historical facts on the basis of constituted groups and consolidated interests, advises us to adopt an eternal methodology: asking ourselves who benefited. This would be the answer to the riddle. Who won and who lost? The effects carry us directly to the causes. Thus the endless confirmation that "the same always win" and "the same always lose." What novelty can history bring us? What authentic freedom can we think about in the case that this history really goes on?

Whatever may have really happened the 19th and 20th of December, no discourse will be able to encompass its final meanings. Forthcoming investigations will illuminate specific aspects, but they will not exhaust the potential for possible interpretations. Like the great insurrections of our history, like that of the 17th of October of 1945, or that of the 29th of May of 1969, the meaning of the 19th and the 20th is open to whatever we can do with them. Hence their irreversibility.

A new type of insurrection, without an author, without owners, that operated by the fusion of minor histories erupted one night, perplexing those who should have been its protagonists, those who had been preparing for years to participate in it and claimed to know very well what to do in moments of great definitions. And it turns out that the

---

* "Until now" refers to the moment of writing the book, between late December 2001 and the end of March 2002. (Tr.)

dreamed insurrections are always more (im)perfect and impossible than the real ones, which do not conform to the dreams of the parodic remainders of a frayed vanguard. Without an organizing center, the multitude was producing the practical and effective forms of empowering (*potenciar*), coordinating, and giving impetus to all those fragments of the past and present, bringing up to date knowledges, memories, and demands that turned out to last longer than what anyone foresaw. The multitude acted as a multiplicity without a center.

Who would be able to find the author of these events, the one who conceived and predicted them? Who can "reduce" the complex weave of cacerolas, marches, pickets, and opposing demands into one single logic, into one single reason? Not even the network of assemblies that grew as an effect of the uprising can claim authorship. When there are so many possible histories, chronicles, chroniclers and historians, it becomes clear that history is so multiple and perspectival that there is not a single and consistent subject of this tale.

The current situation—too much alive to write about it and describe it—tends to settle down again according to the singularities of each experiment. Other struggles are joining the landscape of resistance. It suffices to mention the experience of workers who took over the factories, meatpacking plants, and businesses that went into bankruptcy, keeping the plants running, altering the forms of production and establishing links with radical cultural, artistic, and political practices, and constituting other forms of practicing counterpower. This extensive diffuse alternative network is not new, but it is now visible. It can not be denied that, all of them, and others as well, are changing the composition of the country and increasingly opening new possibilities, experiences, and values, that go far beyond what each of these experiments can plan at a purely conscious level. In fact, by itself each experiment has no other destiny than death. All that lives tends to die. There is nothing strange in this and the end of an experiment does not imply its devaluing. On the contrary, the values are found among those who know how to confront the end. That is why *immortality* is not an end in itself, but rather the effect of the intensity of what each experiment—whether individual or collective— does in life. A full existence alters the possibilities of life, multiplying and extending them. Only in this sense does each radical experiment live beyond itself. This is the irreversible character of the insurrections that marked the modern generations of Argentineans.

The insurrection of December implies an opening to be navigated, signified. A new radicality begins its protagonism in this open space.

NOTES

1. See the work of the so-called *regulation school.*

2. See Joachim Hirsch; *Del estado de seguridad al estado nacional de competencia*; op. cit.

3. Notes from Ignacio Lewkowicz in the archive of materials of the Colectivo Situaciones.

4. Max Weber's classical sociological definition. See his *Economy and Society,* University of California Press, 1978

5. The prosumer knows perfectly well the existence of this border, but nothing prohibits her from crossing it again and again.

6. Giorgio Agamben, *Homo Sacer*; op. cit.

7. See Leibniz, *Monadology and Other Philosophical Essays.* London: Oxford University Press, 1965

8. A good part of the present debate seems to turn around this question. According to a recent article by Michael Hardt, in the second encuentro of the Forum of Porto Alegre there were two divergent positions: "There are indeed two primary positions in the response to today's dominant forces of globalization: either one can work to reinforce the sovereignty of nation-states as a defensive barrier against the control of foreign and global capital, or one can strive towards a non-national alternative to the present form of globalization that is equally global." Hardt goes on describing the concrete functioning that each of these positions amounts to: "[T]he centralized structure of state sovereignty itself runs counter to the horizontal network-form that the movements have developed. Second, the Argentinean movements that have sprung up in response to the present financial crisis, organized in neighborhood and citywide delegate assemblies, are similarly antagonistic to proposals of national sovereignty. Their slogans call for getting rid, not just of one politician, but all of them—*que se vayan todos.*" Finally, Hardt tells us of the concrete political positions of each of these perspectives: " The traditional parties and centralized campaigns generally occupy the national sovereignty pole, whereas the new movements organized in horizontal networks tend to cluster at the non-sovereign pole. And furthermore, within traditional, centralized organizations, the top tends toward sovereignty and the base tends to move away from it." According to Hardt, the hegemony in the organization of the encuentro was on the side of the positions that prioritize the sovereignty of the nation-state, like "the leadership of the Brazilian PT (Workers' Party), which was the host of the Forum, as well as the French leadership of ATTAC," who, "in spite of the strength of those who occupied the center of the stage at the Forum, in the last instance they may have lost the battle" given that the movement of the networks and multitudes is on the winning side. From our perspective, the merit of Hardt's words is not in the characterization of each of the tendencies confronting each other, but rather in the eloquent explanation of the existence of two great tendencies in the radical movement: those who are

for centralization and those who are for multiplicity. [See Michael Hardt, "Porto Alegre: Today's Bandung?," online at http://www.newleftreview.net/ NLR24806.shtml , accessed 10-06-04. The Spanish version slightly differs from the one published in English. (Tr.)]

9. Something like this happened in the Second Encuentro of Porto Alegre. The FARC (Revolutionary Armed Forces of Colombia), the ELN (the Colombian Army for National Liberation), and the EZLN (the Zapatista Army for National Liberation) were not allowed to participate as official panelists. See the interview with Douglas Bravo by Verónica Gago, in Pagina/12; 10-02-02. For us it is not a matter of saying "yes" or "no" to those *revolutionary armies*—so different from one another—but rather of noting how people keep springing up with the power to say, for example, "no violence" or "that group doesn't belong." In this way, multiplicity is absorbed and the criteria of certain groups or people that are without a doubt also part of the movement come to dominate, which ends up centralizing and formatting the potential of these experiments.

10. See Raul Zibechi; *Los Arroyos Cuando Bajan*. Montevideo: Nordan-Communidad, 1995.

11. Carlos Linkersdorf, philosopher, linguist, and author of the first and–until recently–only Tojobal-Spanish dictionary (which required him to live some twenty years in the Totojbal communities of Chiapas) maintains that his work was inspired by a conviction: the need to learn from cultures that were not dominated by the capitalist civilization of the commodity and the individual. These cultures, he suggests, are true information banks on human perspectives and points of view, whose wealth is indispensable when it comes to thinking alternative forms of existence. Lenkersdorf tells of his first Tojobal gathering: "It was in the heights of Chiapas, in 1972, in Bachajon, in a meeting of representatives, women and men, from different communities. They were Tzeltals and, of course, they spoke in their language. Even though I did not understand anything, I constantly and with repetitive insistence heard 'lalalatik, lalatik, lalalalatik, with higher pitch in the last syllable. What could this -tik, -tik, -tik mean? (...) At the end of the meeting I asked a priest who was present and he began to explain that the -tik -tik -tik, which means 'we', is distinctive of the Tzeltal language and of all the people. The *we* predominates not solely in speech, but also in life, in action, and in the way of being of the people." Lenkersdorf reflects the degree to which this *we* structures the entire Tzeltal culture from a narrative that concerns the question of justice in the communities: two young men from community (x) are about to steal a cow that belongs to the neighboring community (y), but they are captured by members of the community (y). Gathered in an assembly, the members of community (y) decide to keep them imprisoned until they pay five thousand pesos. Meanwhile, the members of community (x) also meet in an assembly to discuss this problem that concerned them as well, and not solely the offenders and their families. The decision of the

assembly is to collect among all the families of the community the sum of five thousand pesos. They appoint a committee to pay the money and ask the assembly of community (y) to forgive them. On their return, the offenders are subjected to the discipline of the assembly of their own community, given the fact that what they have done has damaged the entire community: "they have to repay the five thousand pesos through a series of works determined by the community and for the good of it. Also, they will live under the surveillance of members of the community, so that they can show their change in attitude." According to Lenkersdorf, there are three aspects to highlight regarding the justice that operates on the basis of the Tzeltzal "we": first, "the community identifies itself with the wrong-doers because they are members of the community *we*," second, from the "point of view of the *we* the imprisonment does not resolve anything." And third, there is the "attempt to reintegrate the offenders to the *communitarian we*." Communitarian justice is neither "punitive nor vindictive, but rather restorative." Lenkersdorf's conclusion is that "the justice of the *we* is neither idealized nor utopian, but rather represents very demanding social relations. Each and every one of the members of the community has to recognize him or herself in the other members the social whole (*conjunto*) of the *we*. The individualized people of the dominant society would hardly accept such co-responsibility with all that it implies" like the people of the community (x) did. See "El mundo del nosotros," interview by Ana Esther Ceceña with Carlos Lenkersdorf, in the journal *Chiapas*, issue 7, Mexico, 1999.

12. The focal point of the struggle has been *land*. Ana Esther Ceceña—editor of the journal *Chiapas*—has discussed in a recent article—"Revuelta y territorialidad"; in the journal *Actual Marx*, Buenos Aires, 2000—the logic of this struggle in southwest Mexico. The forces of capital conceive the land as a reduction its multiple possibilities to "the sum of its profitable elements or its profitable potentialities or its geostrategic potentialities." The economic and techno-scientific tendencies in operation have produced a new point of view, "nature now is thought of as biodiversity." "The entire southeast Mexico is one of the paramount areas for the preservation and development of life on Earth and constitutes one of the three fundamental genetic information banks in the world." Now, "biodiversity is the basis of top productive activities and biotechnological processes are continuously incorporated into industrial and agricultural processing. It is, without a doubt, the paradigmatic raw material of the technological standard that is being sketched out and, as such, is the strategic resource that will define global hegemony in the future." A good part of the relevance of the events in Chiapas can be presented from the following perspective: as the competition between, on the one hand, the "Fordist technological pattern, of large-scale industrial production, and its current derivatives and adaptations, which privileges the acquisition and monopoly of oil" and, on the other hand, "the standard of biotechnology and of genetic manipulation

or exploitation, ... counterposed to the exploitation of oil, at least in the way it is done today, because of the high depredation and genetic impoverishment that come with it, and promotes policies of conservation and care for the environment." This contradiction reveals the existence of at least "two forces that represent the most powerful sectors of the global economy, confronting each other over the way in which appropriation of the land is carried out. On one hand, there are corporations like Shell, Amoco, or Texaco, and on the other, corporations such as Monsanto, Pfizer, Pharmocogenetics, Bristol Myers-Squibb or Cyanamid. It is a controversy between giants which, nevertheless, coincide in the interest to deepen their control over the region under the protection and the auspices of the American state itself." Both conglomerates find in the Mexican southeast a privileged bank of resources. Ceceña concludes that "what cannot be doubted is that this transnational logic, in either of the two versions mentioned, means aggression against the indigenous populations and an assault on one of the few reserves of the bioshphere that nourishes life, not only in the region but in the whole planet. The territorialities of big capital cause a physical and cultural deterritorialization of the absolute majority of the population of the planet, as well as a deterritorialization of biodiversity." This is the context in which the Zapatista insurrection is situated. For a development of this context and of the meaning of the uprising of the EZLN see the articles by Ana Esther Ceceña in the journal *Chiapas.*

13. Gilles Deleuze; *Spinoza: Practical Philosophy*; City Lights, 1988, p. 18-19.
14. See the journal *Situaciones 1: Conversacion con H.I.J.O.S. sobre los escraches;* De Mano En Mano; Buenos Aires, October 2000.

EPILOGUE

As we said in the introduction, this book is threaded by *urgency*. We want, at the end, to explain ourselves: *urgency* is not, at least for us, *rush*.

Rush belongs to the acceleration of times, it refers to the haste with which we see we are forced to act. As such, speed refers to an alienated temporality in which it is not possible for us to ask ourselves about *sense*.

Urgency belongs to a different order. It has to do with a *lived experience* and a *resistance*: the former refers to the desire to intervene, to think, to commit oneself, and to produce experiments, investigations, social bonds, in the end, that which, since a few centuries ago, has been called *communism*. And the latter—resistance—refers to the ongoing homogenization and colonization by the commodity, which goes by the name of *globalization*.

Rush, however, has not been—unfortunately—entirely foreign to us. Since the events of December we were taken by the maddening temporality of the insurrection. The elaboration of this book, then, was the attempt to make possible, amidst this disquieting chaos, the production of meaning. Indeed, this book is woven by urgencies more than by rush. Its tensions and contrasting tonalities are perhaps the product of the excess zeal with which we wanted to fight against this impulse.

When we began to write these texts we already had an intuition of what today appears to us a possible conclusion: the events of December—which still act upon our subjectivities—will be captured by none of the existing ideological representations. Not because of a lack of attempts to make it happen, and, moreover, it can happen to some extent. Rather, what is at stake is the persistence with which the new protagonism and the logic of the multiple spoil all the apparatuses of capture that are set before them.

If there is no thought outside action, today's exigency seems to be given by the capacity to assume the new role that theory can find inside the movement of the multiple: neither leading nor capturing, but rather thinking—precisely—that which the multitude resolves, as a dimension among dimensions. In this sense, as in many others already discussed, the insurrection of December came to spoil crystallized perceptions and tranquilizing certainties, but also to confuse and condemn to failure those in a hurry.

These texts were engraved by the materiality and the urgency of events that have transformed us. We have a wish: that the active connection between these pages and many others manage to escape the fate of the academic text, the political pamphlet, and all aestheticizing pretension, in order to form part of this moment of foundation of a new social protagonism capable of bringing to life the experience of revolution.

ON THE BARTER CLUB*

THIS SHORT PIECE ON THE BARTER NETWORKS IN ARGENTINA BRINGS together a series of—more or less provisional—hypotheses from an as yet unfinished investigation: they are only *working notes* that we present here as an appendix requested by the publisher Virus. Beyond the improvisation that these notes imply, it is necessary to highlight the complexity and extent of the barter phenomena, which has spread throughout the entire country and concerns seven million people. Thus, it is not a marginal experience, but rather the specific form in which millions of people found a solution to a significant part of their existence. At the same time, it is not only a mode of survival but rather *another* mode of life that seeks to constitute itself beyond the omnipresence of the market and the state. Currently the experience of barter is undergoing a profound crisis as a consequence of the unforeseen growth it experienced after the economic debacle of December. Here we attempt to sketch some of these problems.

---

* This article was written for the Spanish edition, published as *Argentina: apuntes para el nuevo protagonismo social* (Barcelona: Virus, 2003). (Tr.)

1

THE FIRST BARTER club was born on May 1st, 1995, in Bernal, in the south of the province of Buenos Aires. Its founders belonged to a group of ecologists called Regional Program for Self-Sufficiency, which worked toward the end of the 1980s on self-sustainable productive enterprises. The experiment has its founding myth: the story goes that it all began with an abundant squash harvest that was the result of planting a few seeds in a small terrace. Its owner—one of the three founders—began to hand out squash to neighbors who, in turn, began to give him products in exchange.

In 1996 there were already 17 clubs, which became 40 in 1997, 83 in 1998, 200 in 1999, and grew to 400 in 2000. In addition, they incorporated two networks that already existed but which came to be reorganized around barter: on the one hand, the entrepreneurial experience of the Network of Professionals, which helped make new initiatives possible, and, on the other hand, the Network for the Exchange of Knowledges and Social Cybernetics, which made important methodological contributions, incorporating the *exchange of knowledges* as a new modality and emphasizing *permanent training* as condition for the expansion of the network.

Initially, the exchange of products was accomplished by writing down the goods produced and consumed by each *prosumer* onto forms (*prosumer* is a term that synthesizes the fundamental characteristic of those who barter: producers and consumers at the same time), which later were turned over to a computer database with which exchange was regulated. As the experiment expanded this method turned out to be insufficient, not only because the labor and the manipulation of such a complexity of flows and exchanges became almost impossible, but also because there was a tendency to centralize the command of information in the Bernal club, where the accounting had been done since the beginning.

The local barter clubs that appeared in the first place constituted themselves later into a *network* (Global Barter Network) articulated by numerous *nodes* (barter clubs), mostly after the invention of a social currency (credit) that allowed the connection between different nodes. However, nowadays simple or direct barter also exists: English classes are exchanged for clothing or homemade jam for the label design for those same containers.

2001 was the year of the explosion: the nodes multiplied until there were 1800, and between December 2001 and March of 2002 the number reached 5,000. The network spread throughout the entire country. It is estimated that three million Argentineans *live* on the exchanges made in barter clubs and many other millions participate in them occasionally.

Such "enlargement" was unleashed by the economic crisis: the imposition of the financial "corralito" in December, together with the growing recession and the rise in grocery prices, added 5,000 people per day to the network.

2

OUR STARTING POINT is a hypothesis that synthesizes our investigation into the barter networks (it would be necessary to take into account the existence of other processes, both parallel and different, yet related through some elements, such as the collective purchases of groceries at wholesale prices undertaken by some neighborhood assemblies, the different production experiments developed by certain movements of unemployed workers, and the occupation of closed factories by the workers once their owners decide they are unprofitable):

In its multiple forms, the new social protagonism faces a challenge: its social production and reproduction; that is to say, the socialization of doing in the material sense. From this perspective, the development of radical experiments depends today on their capacities to construct alternative networks of material production and establish links with those that already exist. If the process opened during the 19th and 20th instituted a radical negation of the existing forms of politics, the unfolding of this negativity—or, we could say, its positivity—implies the development of other forms of social relations,[1] of other forms of existence not subordinated to capital, beyond capitalist exclusion, forms that seek to not be recaptured of reabsorbed.[2] To summarize: the forms of alternative sociability have before them the problem of conceiving and constructing forms of organization that go beyond collective and democratic discussion—generated and affirmed in the assembly process—and that imply practices that entail a material socialization of doing.

In this sense, the barter networks comprise, through "multi-reciprocal exchange"—one of the many concepts that the phenomenon uses to think itself—alternative practices in the relations to money, objects, and instances of production, circulation, exchange, and consumption. Barter attempts to break with the domination of *normalized distribution* imposed by the market and wagers on the creation of sociabilities of solidarity. In this sense, it is an experience that implies many *more dimensions* than those of pure economic exchange.

While the notion of the *prosumer* pursues the dissolution of the difference between "worker" (subject) and "product" (object), because the *prosumers* seek to maintain the direct and simultaneous experience of being producers of what they offer and consumers of what they obtain in said exchange, the recuperation of the link between production and consumption aims at establishing a regulatory criterion that resists the force of abstraction of the general equivalent (money). In its place, a wager is laid on the production of the social bond, on direct and everyday links, on the putting in common of potentialities and productive capacities, on the generation of a movement of reciprocity and cooperation that does not pursue accumulation, and that appears, rather, as a flow of *giving* and *receiving* not determined exclusively by profit. This is why in the space of the barter club there are, on one hand, periodic encounters of exchange (fairs) and administrative meetings, but also, on the other hand, skill-training, recreation, assistance, and production activities.

Several major problems spring up when it comes to thinking a *parallel* economy: What form of measure rules the exchange in the networks of the alternative economy? Do elements appear within barter that resituate the commodity character of the products as *only one of the dimensions* of the exchange? Is there anything beyond the notion of general equivalent that comes to light, a transcendent value that regulates, measures, and legitimates all other values? What elements of *symbolic exchange* constitute these practices? Is the existence of a social bond—or at least the suspension of the possessive individual—what makes this not strictly utilitarian dimension possible? And in this sense, taking into account the difference made in this book between a society *with* a market and a *market society* (Polanyi), does the economic sphere cease to exist—even partially—in the barter clubs as autonomous from the rest of social existence?

The possibilities of buying with "credits" (the name of the currency of barter) reach practically all the areas of the economy and not, as is supposed, only the most urgent areas. Those who go to the barter club find all types of possibilities for consumption, the same that have become prohibitive in the formal market: clothing, decoration items, psychological counseling, hairdressing, music workshops, and a variety that is reformulated depending on the neighborhood and the specificities of each area. That is to say, the multi-reciprocal exchange can only doubtfully be called simply "survival" or "subsistence." Better, it institutes—as we said—the possibility of another way of life.

In the words of Antonio Negri, the particularization—singular-ization—of the currency by the base refers—in the case of the barter club—to the incorporation of a dimension of the future, implicit in the fact that, in the exchange, a present good encounters with the promise of a future good. For example: pastries are exchanged for two haircuts. One of the haircuts, inevitably, depends on trust and on the survival of the commitment. Negri insists that a *material exodus* needs a project for the future because biopolitics is tied to the real, and, at the same time, to the attempt to recuperate some forms of *utopia*. Marcel Mauss also speaks of the importance of the notion of *time* in scheduling the coun-tergift.[3] The *gift*, according to Mauss, necessarily comprises the notion of credit, since reciprocal exchange is made with the *certainty* that a *gift* will be returned (long-term obligation).

The development of such a vast network of social self-management implied a novel and specific figure of militant activity: *the coordinators*. In the beginning, the *coordinators* were the people responsible for cre-ating a new node—bringing together all the available elements—and taking care of the regulatory functions that sprang up from there. If it was necessary to connect productive points in order to escape from impotence, that is to say, from isolation, the coordinators were the ones charged with carrying out a ferocious struggle against isolation. It is a figure that articulates the *entrepreneurial* capacity, the *managerial* capac-ity, and the *political* capacity. The coordinators are the ones charged with (re)establishing the bonds between productive capacities and com-munity needs, whether it is by shaping a new node of the network or through the modalities that have been set in motion recently, as the (re)construction of pathways for the production and commercialization of food and medicine that connect small producers with social organiza-tions and communities, or as a practical alternative to the multinational networks of production (transgenics).

The coordinators are committed to the self-regulation of prices. It is a complex process with different mechanisms. In some places it consists in the capacity of the node to obtain for itself products from a "basic pool" at a very low price that limits the possible prices. Another exam-ple is that 50% of what each node collects with fundraising activities—fundamentally admission fees at the fairs—is returned to the members through the purchase of raw materials that encourage production.

3

MANY SAY, AND with good reason, that the barter clubs are the scene of cases of corruption, speculation, hoarding, and fraud. But these "impurities"—not surprising in a phenomenon of this scale, especially when it arises from the fragmented ground of neoliberal societies—are unable to explain the reasons for the decadence experienced in recent days by the more comprehensive barter networks.

A key point for understanding the present crisis of the barter networks has to do with what economists call the question of the "backing" of the currency—in this case the credit—that is to say, the relation of correspondence between the volume of the product and the money in circulation. To put it directly: one of the deepest causes of the present crisis of the networks of exchange has to do with the productive deficit[4] in the nodes.

The massification of attendance and the printing of credits was not accompanied by the consequent growth in production—or in variety—which saturated, dried out, and decomposed a good deal of the dynamism displayed by almost all the nodes in operation. It generated an abysmal gap between consumption needs and productive capacity.

At bottom, as is usually the case, the problem is not strictly economic, but rather more comprehensive and simple: the networks of the Barter Club operate upon the production of subjectivity, of social bonds. At the center of the network is the figure of the *prosumer*, who, as we said earlier, seeks to be the synthesis of the positions that the market usually separates: production and consumption. The open character of the network and the invasion of the needs of the population—who began to massively turn to the alternative networks in search of instant solutions to their most basic and urgent needs—altered the constitution of the figure of the prosumer and turned the barter network into nothing more than an extension of the capitalist market.

This phenomenon unleashed the mechanisms—so usual in the formal market—of speculation on scarce and very needed products, counterfeiting of currency, hoarding of currency, political control of nodes, etc. These types of sabotage were always present. They had existed at a secondary level until the moment when, with the crisis, they became central and accelerated the crisis of the experiment.

The experiment of an alternative economy has not ended. On one hand, the barter networks have not disappeared. Certain nodes that were closed in time have managed to survive. On the other hand, the networks as such have not disappeared and find themselves in an intense process of reflection over the forms of self-protection that would make possible relaunching the effort.

But perhaps the most important transformation is to be found in the incorporation of processes and flows that detach themselves from the network of the market and even establish increasingly significant agreements with local state institutions. New phenomena such as the "megafairs" sprang up, where members of different nodes or clubs from different parts of the country come together, and where up to 20,000 people converge to exchange products and services. Networks of community purchases have been set up that establish bonds between all sorts of food producers (of rice, cooking oil, flour, etc.) and the nodes or megafairs. There was an attempt to organize a healthcare network inside the barter network, incorporating doctors, nurses, psychologists, etc. as prosumers. Members of the network founded the first pharmacy with generic medicines in the country, an experiment that is projected to spread to different neighborhoods and seeks, in the short- or medium-term, to have a laboratory to produce the medicines themselves. There have been agreements with various municipal governments of the country to pay municipal taxes with the currency of the barter networks, a revenue that the municipality will use to keep in place employment programs, promote welfare plans for the unemployed, and hire contractors among the productive enterprises in the barter network.

The experiment of the networks of barter clubs was a monumental experience of the masses in alternative economy. This experience has been capitalized. From now on barter, organized as such, will be one of its elements, but no longer the only one. Experiences (knowledges, contacts, etc.) multiply and the incorporation of technical and professional knowledge becomes increasingly more real.

NOTES

1. These new social forms embody the double modality implicit in their being power (*potencia*): power (*potencia*) unfolded as multiplicity, force, act, and also power (*potencia*) as the opening of new potentiality, as that which is not yet realized, and so as having potentialities that are summoned by the possibility of possibility.

2. The capture is capture of power (*potencia*) in the two previous senses: on one hand it is appropriation of the act and force, giving an orientation to multiplicity and conducting energy toward ideal or instituted models, but, on the other hand, it is capture in the sense of that which amputates possible potentialities.

3. Mauss, Marcel. *The Gift: The Form and Reason for Exchange in Archaic Societies*. London; New York: Routledge, 1990.

4. Certainly, what is at stake here is the fact that the networks of alternative economy tend to autonomize effective social production with respect to capitalist command.

CAUSES AND HAPPENSTANCE: DILEMMAS OF ARGENTINA'S NEW SOCIAL PROTAGONISM*

A LITTLE OVER A YEAR AGO WE PUBLISHED A BOOK ENTITLED *19 Y 20; Apuntes para un nuevo protagonismo social.* The effort of writing and editing those notes in a short few months—while the dynamic of events unfolded in the streets—gave way to a reflection whose style was determined by the vocation of writing on the spur of the moment.

Contrary to what is usually taken for granted, that methodological premise stating that things are better seen at a distance is not entirely convincing. What the perspective of distance allows us to see should not claim for itself any superiority. Since, while it can aspire to a serenity that those affected by the unfolding of the events usually lack, those very affections are the ones that constitute the possible real of a situation. Hence the aspiration of what is written "in the heat of the moment" to register a complexity that might become virtual in the future, when possibilities that were not thinkable then are retroactively attributed.

The long year and a half between the insurrectional events of December 2001 and the presidential elections of April 2003 deserves

---

* Originally published as *Cuaderno de Investigación N. 4,* this article appeared in English translation in *The Commoner* N. 8, Autumn/Winter 2004 and later in the French journal *Multitudes.* The translation has been revised for the present edition. (Tr.)

to be thought. Many questions come up: how to understand, in light of the present phase of apparent institutional stabilization, the events of December 2001? What happened to the promise of a radical transformation of the country glimpsed at from the slogan "all of them must go, not a single one should remain," when the electoral process clearly speaks of a notable participation of the citizenry in the elections and when the five principal candidates—all of them from the two main political parties for many decades—receive almost 95% of the votes?

We cannot claim for ourselves the expertise, craft, and dedication of political analysts. Neither the preoccupations, nor the focus nor the assumptions that animate us are connected to those of such analyses. The word of the experts obtains its consistency from a certain capacity to manage information and dispose of a certain technical use of language. Yet politics is not what occurs in the world of pure facts waiting to be sanctioned by the experts, but is rather a matter that concerns the collective: the same "facts" form compositions with the interpretations made of them, prolonging their power (*potencia*) and turning the readings themselves into a field of disputes that, in turn, are offered to interpretations by others.

What follows, then, is a reading done "in the heat of the moment": this text was conceived between the first electoral return and the announcement of the official resignation by Menem, that is to say, between April 27 and May 13. The intention is to examine the events that transpired between December 2001 and May 2003, a lapse of time that separates and communicates the outbreak of an economic and political crisis without precedents and the emergence of a new social protagonism (piquetero movements, assemblies, barter clubs, factories occupied by their workers, etc.) with the pretended normalization whose point of realization should have been the presidential elections. The intensity of this period—no less than its complexity—has remained clouded by those who have proclaimed that the results of the elections constitute the death of the movement of counterpower and the erasure of the processes that opened with the events of December.

THE SURPRISE
(RUPTURE, DESTITUTION AND VISIBILITY)

THE INSURRECTION OF December surprised everyone. The very notion of "insurrection" had to be adapted to the novel character of the events. In fact, during many months the revolt demanded the intelligence of every one of us who was surprised by its occurrence. What was this unexpected event telling us? Each one prioritized one aspect. According to some, the cause of all that happened had to be found in a Buenos Aires' Peronist conspiracy against the weak government of the time. Others believed they could see behind the strings that move the marionettes the implacable organization of certain proven revolutionaries. There were even some who scorned all that happened, attributing it to a middle class whose savings in dollars had been seized. Be that as it may, it is most probable that all these versions are at once as truthful as they are insufficient to give account of the effective dynamic of what occurred.

The insurrection of December had a destituent character. Its overwhelming efficacy consisted—precisely—in its revocatory power. The cacerolas and the slogans covered the entire urban space. The ant-like presence of human bodies, the occupation of the city, and the saturation with noises that not only did not transmit any message, but rather made it impossible to really say anything. The conditions for the institutional elaboration of social demands were radically interrupted.

And when it was possible to speak people insisted: "All of them must go, not a single one should remain." The closure of the space and conditions of communication with the political system rendered evident the rupture of the political mediations, revealed the impotence of parties and governmental institutions, and opened an interrogation (festive and anguishing) over the collective future of the Argentines.

The insurrection unleashed a rupture with multiple effects. On one side—and from the beginning—it became evident that the irruption of the street multitude in the city disturbed in a conclusive manner the functioning of power. Not only were the powers of the state, the repressive forces, and the government functionaries affected by the unexpected irruption of an important segment of the population, but the effects of such alteration were registered in evident movements in the economy, in forms of inhabiting the city, in business decisions, in the relationship with banks, in the communication policy of the large media, in the field of the social sciences, in the form in which politicians, militants, a good part of the artistic and cultural field, etcetera, conducted themselves.

The combination of default, devaluation, and political crisis turned the country into no man's territory, where the daily demonstrations joined defrauded ahorristas with piqueteros and caceroleros together with audacious tourists who came to learn at low price about the becomings of the "Argentine revolution."

Another consequence of the rupture of December 2001 was the visibilization of a heterogeneous set of forms of social protagonism that arose in dissimilar periods and in relation to different problematics and that, until December, were hardly known, taken into account, and valorized.

The root of this new protagonism is, of course, related to peripheral capitalism in crisis. But the new protagonism is not a mere reaction. The power (*potencia*) of Argentina's current events takes root, precisely, in the emergence of these subjectivities that have, for many years, experienced new modalities of sociability in various spheres of their existence.

Although today it seems evident, by those days of December the then vigorous piquetero movement was practically unknown. Despite the fact that their existence built upon many years of struggle in all the territory of the country, only few months earlier had they become widely known because of their coordinated roadblocks. But in those roadblocks they were harassed, and the very parties of the left—that had scorned them for years—desperately constructed their own piquetero movements just a few short months before the insurrection. The initiatives of various piquetero organizations in their respective territories—linked to food, health, housing, education, recreation, etc.—remained, for a long time, completely unknown to a significant part of the population.

Almost as unknown as the piqueteros were the different nodes, networks, and circuits of barter that drew together millions of people in the harshest moments of the crisis. After several years of development, their size was such that some municipalities accepted that the currency of some of the networks as valid for tax payment. The figure of the *prosumer* had not been valued as the subjective experience that sought to combine in the same space productive capacities and consumer satisfaction, displacing financial, bureaucratic, and commercial mediations. The same can be said of the succession of occupations of businesses by their workers (large numbers of factories, workshops, printing shops, bars, etc.) in various cities throughout the country after the owners had stripped them from their assets. These experiments became the object of attention for the institutional left only when the latter believed it had found there the resurgence of an absent working class subject.

All these experiments—to which we could add, among others, the escraches of the group H.I.J.O.S. against the unpunished perpetrators of the genocide of the last dictatorship, or the struggles carried out by the Mapuches* in the Argentine south and the organization of campesino initiatives in the north of the country, such as the Movement of Campesinos of Santiago del Estero—were more or less known, but remained in relative isolation. The events of December provoked a visibilization—as well as a mutual relation and, in some way, a generalization—among them and before those that rose up massively to participate or to learn about those initiatives.

A third virtue of the rupture had to do with the multitudinous emergence of hundreds of assemblies in the urban centers of the country. As thousands of neighbors met to elaborate—in a collective manner—what happened in December, they discovered a space of politicization in the light of the expansion of the new social protagonism. The destitution of the political institutionalism and of the parties as instruments of management or transformation of reality placed before the assembly members the dilemma of elucidating new modalities of instituting collective life and attending immediate necessities. From the beginning, the assemblies—born after the 20th of December—were torn by such tensions as whether to privilege the space of the neighborhood, experimenting there with initiatives linked to the territory, or whether, on the contrary, to try to sustain the revocatory political capacity of the cacerolas, while, at the same time, they debated what to do with the parties of the left that sought to coopt the neighbors' meetings toward the orientations of their own apparatuses.

Strictly speaking, all the possibilities were experimented with: there were those who devoted themselves to the political conjuncture, or to every type of initiative linked to the neighborhood, and there were even those who remained trapped in the networks of the parties of the left, in addition to different combinations between these variants. During

---

* The Mapuche are an indigenous people living in the provinces of Neuquen and Río Negro in southern Argentina (as well as in the neighboring region of Chile). Many Mapuche communities have been expelled from their homes as part of land seizures designed to facilitate the exploitation of the natural gas and petroleum deposits. Mapuche in the Loma de Lata region have been found to have high concentrations of heavy metals in their blood due to water and ground contamination linked to natural resource exploitation. (Tr.)

2002, the assemblies protagonized the creation of popular eateries, took part in solidarity actions with the cartoneros*, participated in confluences with the piquetero movements, inter-assembly experiments, demonstrations, escraches, and, in some cases, became a very rich experience of politicization for their members.

Among the events that generated the rupture one might point out a whole set of circumstances that decisively lead up to its unleashing: experiences of struggle—like those we just described—whose origins can be found in an accumulation of discontents and unsatisfied demands; overlapping memories of lost struggles and frustrated hopes; the helplessness of millions of people by the crude effects of neoliberalism.

But perhaps it is fitting to speak of a second type of historicity, linked to a certain capacity to read the changes operated in the forms of social reproduction and in the efficacy of political mediations that in some way regulated social co-existence. In this way, the rejection of politicians, for example, is not only related to a corporative or neoliberal vision of the world, skeptical about collective actions, but also feeds into the frustrations derived from the promises of the democratic re-opening from 1983 to the end of 2001.

PHENOMENOLOGY OF AN APPARENT RECONSTRUCTION

THE ARRIVAL OF the government of Eduardo Duhalde, in January 2002, set in motion the delicate process of reconstructing governance after the rupture of December. Until that moment, we had witnessed a pathetic succession of presidents elected by the legislative assembly to finish the term of the unseated Alianza president, De la Rua. The arrival of Duhalde implied, in the first place, a hiatus in this crazy dynamic.

The primary objective of the Duhalde government was to calm spirits and prevent more deaths. The second was to reorganize—in time—the conditions of the new system for the reallocation of resources, and to restore the ties with the financial system.

The declaration of default by the prior government of Rodríguez Saá was followed by the devaluation of the peso—that is to say, the end of

---

* *Cartoneros*—literally "cardboard men"—make their living picking through trash, sifting for recyclable and resalable materials. The Argentinean government estimates there may be as many as 40,000 cartoneros combing the streets of Buenos Aires on any given night. (Tr.)

the peso/dollar convertibility—and the immediate upsetting of prices, the debasement of products, the suspension of services, the breaking of all contracts in dollars (debts, deposits, etc.) Poverty and indigence grew in geometric proportions.

The end of the rules of the game in the total absence of a power capable of proposing new regulations, resulted, in the summer of 2002, in a generalized chaos in which, as usually happens, the main benefits were for those who possessed more resources to confront the situation: the banks (compensated by the state for the "pesification"), the large debtors in dollars whose debts were pesified, the large land owners and agrarian producers, and the transnational export consortia for whom the high dollar is a source of enrichment.

The political landscape fragmented around three large blocs. On one side, those who openly promoted dollarization, entry into the FTAA, and the use of the armed forces as an instance for controlling social conflict (Menem and López Murphy being the visible faces of the project). On the other side, the pesification-devaluation bloc, in power through Duhalde (and now the recently elected government of Néstor Kirchner). Finally, the heterogeneous bloc of the forces of the center left, left, alternative unionism, and the more consolidated expressions of struggle that pronounced themselves for a new form of taking political decisions and producing and distributing wealth.

Duhalde's arrival in office was possible fundamentally for three reasons: (a) the collapse of the pact of domination established by Carlos Menem in which hegemony corresponded to the nucleus of privatized businesses and the transnational financial sector; (b) the strength of Peronism in the province of Buenos Aires, whose level of organization and of penetration in the most impoverished strata of the population allowed it to avoid the generalization of the conflict by distributing about two million of unemployment subsidies of about 50 dollars monthly; (c) because in the face of the breakdown of the political powers the strength of Peronism in the province of Buenos Aires allowed it to impose itself with ease as the ultimate guarantor of the remains of the political system.

The fundamental merit of Duhalde's government consisted in surviving the game of crossed pressures and, particularly, the constant threat of the cacerolas. In this respect it is fitting to recall Duhalde's phrase as he just assumed the presidency (having actually lost in the presidential elections against De la Rua): "it is impossible to govern with assemblies."

The second period of the recomposition of the political system occurred at the beginning of the second semester and revolved around three aspects: (a) the arrival of Roberto Lavagna as economy minister, and his unruffled politics of compatibilization of interests together with the first vows of confidence Duhalde collected for that mere fact of "enduring" that permitted to calm down the inflation of the dollar and produce a moderate growth of the benefited economic sectors; (b) the distribution of unemployment subsidies oiled the political apparatuses, which by means of the networks of clientelism achieved the consolidation of a certain social peace; (c) the increasing repression in the neighborhoods, which found its highest point in the massacre of Puente Pueyrredon the 26th of June, 2002.*

It was precisely the scandal caused by this massacre that forced then president Eduardo Duhalde to set a date for the succession of the next government. The admitted impossibility of normalizing the situation in the predicted time frame explains why the elections were brought forward.

Thus, moving up the elections influenced upon the three virtuous tendencies on the basis of which the government proceeded to carry out its program of reconstruction of a minimum of institutionality: (a) the consolidation of the dollar price, and even its reduction, and the inevitable even impetuous recuperation of an economy that did not stop falling for almost four consecutive years. This point was enormously relevant since the ability of the government in this aspect allowed it to achieve—as a victory—an agreement with the IMF and a feeling of gradual exit from the crisis, at the time that it committed the next government—among other things—to obtain an enormous fiscal surplus for the payment of the external debt; (b) the opening of an electoral dynamic, even over the remains of the political parties, and in conditions frankly unfavorable for the candidates, none of whom had even a low level of popularity—the Radical Civic Union** and the Frepaso*** (both making up the Alianza) have virtually disap-

---

* On June 26, 2002, police attacked a group of piqueteros conducting a roadblock on the Puente Pueyrredon Bridge. Police shot and killed two protesters, injured ninety, and arrested over one hundred, sparking massive demonstrations in response. Colectivo Situaciones discusses the significance of this repression in depth in *Hipótesis 891: Más Allá de los Piquetes* (Buenos Aires: De mano en mano, 2002). (Tr.)

** The Union Civica Radical (UCR) is a centrist political party lead by De la Rua. (Tr.)

*** The Frente Pais Solidario or National Solidarity Front is a coalition of

peared; and Duhalde himself prevented the Peronists from presenting one single candidate, forcing the three internal blocs to run in separate tickets. And (c) increasing levels of repression of the experiments of counterpower: on one side, the persecution of young piquetero leaders in the neighborhoods, many times by armed groups without uniforms, and the reactivation, on the other side, of the judicial apparatus, which in a few months ordered—before the first electoral round—the eviction of factories occupied by their workers (the test case, but not the only case, being that of the workers of Brukman*) and of dozens of squats (some of them by neighborhood assemblies), as well as the detention of important piquetero leaders from Salta.

The last months before the elections many began to perceive with worry that the fragmentation of the political system could come to generate something unforeseen: the return of Menem.

Indeed, the slogan "all of them must go, not a single one should remain" seemed, then, to have remained stuck in its own paradoxical nature: given that someone was going to stay, it could be that the candidate to remain would be precisely the one whose insensitivity with respect to the processes of social rebellion was most evident.

The possibility that Menem could come back, sustained by a considerably important percentage of the population—about 20% of the electorate—suddenly turned into a frightening factor for a large majority. One should add that before the elections at least two circumstances took place whose structure anticipated the dynamic that would become visible with the elections.

In the first place was the American, English, Polish, Spanish, etc. invasion of Iraq. On one hand, the concentrated military power decided and executed a war that was scandalous no less for its intentions than for its effects. But in parallel a gigantic movement against the invasion erupted. Both phenomena were able to coexist without affecting each other: each one developed in a parallel path.

In second place, less than a week before the election, a demonstration of some ten thousand people gathered in support of the workers

---

five political parties. In 1999 Frepaso made a coalition (the Alianza) with the UCR in order to challenge the electoral power of the Peronist Partido Justicialista. (Tr.)

* Brukman is a coat factory that was occupied and operated by workers from December 2001 to April 2003. Police forcibly evicted the Brukman workers because, in the words of an Argentinean federal judge, "life and physical integrity have no supremacy over economic interests." (Tr.)

of the recently evicted recovered factory of Brukman was savagely repressed. At only days from the election repression materialized in the downtown core of the city of Buenos Aires, with a savagery radically incompatible with any consideration about the civil rights that were, supposedly, being restored with the elections of April 27th.

And so, the first electoral round comes about in the midst of this climate. In the previous days, the mass media won over the space of public discussion with polls that gave as the winner Carlos Menem and as possible second place the purebred neoliberal candidate—former leader of the UCR—Ricardo López Murphy.

The result of the first electoral round turned out to be a relative surprise: something less than 80% of the electorate voted. The number of blank and nullified votes was not significant. The list headed by Menem was first with 24% of the vote. The pro-government list came after with 22%. López Murphy was third, followed by the Peronist Rodriguez Saá, and falling behind him, Elisa Carrió—also a former leader of the UCR but of the center left tendency.

The parties of the traditional left, all combined, received less than 3% of the votes.

After the first electoral round two effects clearly appeared: on one hand, the politicians obtained a spot in the public sphere almost exclusively by means of the mass media, and, on the other hand, the polls rapidly forecasted that Nestor Kirchner would demolish Carlos Menem with some 70% against some 20%.

Kirchner's performance in the first round reaped a good part of its scarce votes thanks to the Buenos Aires apparatus that Duhalde leads, in such way that only in the second round the official candidate was going to benefit from the support of an anti-Menemist electorate that in the first round split its vote among the other three candidates.

Of the three weeks that separated the election of April 27th from the election that should have been conducted Sunday the 18th of May, the first two were characterized by massive support for Kirchner by leaders of almost every party. Even the support received by Menem in the first round began to migrate toward the quarters of the assured next president. In this context Menem refused to participate in the second round, accusing Duhalde of organizing an electoral fraud, and Kirchner of being a Montonero.*

---

*   Montoneros was an armed organization of young Peronists founded
    in 1970. Its core ideas combined elements of historical Peronism with
    revolutionary Christianity and left-nationalism. In the mid-1970s, after
    merging with other revolutionary organizations, Montoneros became the

In this way, the success that the first electoral round implied for the recomposition of a representative institutionality was interrupted as the second round failed and it was not possible to proclaim a government elected by a large percentage of the electorate. In consequence, the new government appeared burdened with the persistence of the logic of the Mafia-State and without being able to immediately reap its political capital or popularity. This situation should be read in light of the re-configuration of the totality of the political system that will take place this year through the elections of the government of the city of Buenos Aires, of the government of the Province of Buenos Aires, of Cordoba, and of national legislators.

THE BALLOT BOXES AND THE STREETS

PREDICTABLY, THE FIRST strategies of reflection on the relation between the effects of the events of December 2001 and the elections of April— and May of 2003 have begun to go around. These arguments could be gathered in two large sets of conclusions; each one arrived at—with all its nuances—from an opposite perspective.

The first set of arguments sustains the idea that there is no political legacy to the events of the 19th and 20th. The possibility of organizing a political revolution out of that discontent—if that was an authentic possibility—has been definitively exhausted. The political left has been completely neutralized. It is not that there are not great discontents— or that greater ones can not be foreseen—but rather that the existing demands have not been organized from outside the political system, which now permits the restoration of the proper institutional proce-dures for the mediation of such conflicts. It is not that there has not been a profound crisis, or that it has been resolved. Rather, the crisis logically generated discontents, and now it is all about dealing with those issues towards the normalization of social co-existence through political methods. From this angle, the realization of the first electoral

---

largest group of the revolutionary left. First the death squads formed by the Peronist right, and later those created by the military junta, murdered and disappeared thousands of Montonero militants. Many others went into exile. In the 1990s many former Montonero leaders gave support to Carlos Menem's neoliberal administration. Other former Montoneros, dissident of their former leaders, have given support to the government of Nestor Kirchner. (Tr.)

round possesses a very special significance, since it constitutes a very important step in the moderation of spirits. Although frustrated, the second round confirmed a climate of withdrawal of the extremes. The threat of anti-politics was conjured.

If this first strategy of reflection is festive, the second laments the lost opportunity: the events of December were the beginning of a possible revolution. But for that, it was necessary to endow the discontent with a political program, an organization, and a perspective. One can polemicize over the characteristics of these organizational forms or over the scope of these perspectives, but one cannot deny that these are the conditions for the elaboration of a political alternative. The fundamental error of those who participated in the revolt—and above all of those who participated in autonomous experiences—was to become entangled in the paradoxical structure of the slogan "all of them must go, not a single one should remain." In this way, the complexity of the political struggle disappeared from view and everyone ended up hidden in his/her refuge, with an idealist discourse and some abstractly horizontal practices.

Both readings oppose each other in perspective but confirm the same image of what happened: the elections occupied the center of the political dispute and one of the contenders—it seems—simply did not show up, abandoning the battlefield and signing in this way his defeat. If the forces unleashed in December did not show up in the electoral act, it is because that December has already ceased to exist. Thus April-May of 2003 constitutes the evidence of a retroactive defeat of that which could have happened after December of 2001. The lesson appears transparent: the political system is frankly on its way toward resurrection, and the forces of counterpower have become entangled in a foreseeable political infantilism.

Both perspectives share the same reading of the facts of the 19th and 20th as a founding moment and an opportunity for carrying out a political revolution. Only that while the first feared this possibility, the second desired it. And both hold, in striking coincidence, the same image of politics as a game with homogeneous rules involving two players on the same plane: as if they were playing a game of chess. In this way, things are presented as a match in which the Political System, Power or the State was "staking everything" against Popular Power, the Politics of Horizontality or Counterpower. With things set up in this way, the evaluation is unarguable: the experiments of counterpower must mature, learn how to "do politics," begin the long march (as Lula and the PT) that would lead them, sometime, to become an authentic option of power (*poder*).

And yet, ruptures are just that: *ruptures*. A destituent power doesn't necessarily work according to the requirements of that which institutes. December 2001 was not the appearance of a political subject. This is why no such subject has become manifest. It was, indeed, a rupture, and a visibilization of a new social protagonism. But this protagonism is what it is precisely because it does not understand politics the way it was understood a decade ago. This is why it is not wise to grumble that these forces have not acted as if they were this subject.

Yet there is more: the effects of the events of the 19th and 20th were so radical—and enduring—that the elections were completely affected by them. But this does not entitle anybody to establish a direct *a priori* relation between the street struggles and the elaboration of experiments of counterpower and the result of the elections as such.

In fact, the same people that have participated, voting for this or that candidate, are in many cases the ones who later participate in the alternative experiences of counterpower. Or even better, they are not the same, since people are not the same in the polling booth and in the assembly, or the roadblock. Each place is instituted according to heterogeneous rules: if the elections attempt to represent all that exists and, for that reason, decree the nonexistence of that which they do not manage to capture and measure, the experiments of counterpower, to the contrary, exist only in situation, in a territory, a spatiality, a bodily disposition and a self-determined time.

We don't say that there is no relation between the two. We could never deny that both spheres affect each other in a relevant way. We do say, however, that there is not an *a priori* relation between them. We are dealing with two dynamics that are heterogeneous in their constitution. To transfer the power (*potencia*) of a situation to what happened in the elections, leads to the dissolution of the situation. In contrast, to order a situation starting from a global reading of the elections leads to the destruction of the possibilities of such a situation.

We are no longer in the chess game. There is not just one single dimension. There does not exist a single set of given rules. As a friend once said, this is not about the whites against the blacks but about the blacks against the chessboard. While the whites move in a certain manner, respecting certain rules and preserving certain goals, the blacks can very well alter what is expected of them. This can give birth to another operation, create new strategies, destroy all pre-established objectives, and enable the experience of new becomings. It might be said that all this is no more than an impossible flight on the part of some black pieces that would be committing suicide. But this is not true. To escape the instituted does not have to be an idealist trait. In fact, the blacks must consider the board very carefully and above all the movements of the whites. But, this time, according to another game: the one they intend to play, since it is not true that to play our own game we must first win inside a game that we aren't interested in.

To kick over the board, then, is neither to ignore it nor to scorn the consequences. On the contrary, it is only by intending to play a different game that one gets to know the complexity of the power relations. That is why to think of an "a priori non-relation" does not indicate an absence of affection on either side, but rather it shows us that the way in which they affect each other is a clash of forces of different nature. Each of them develops a priori independently (in the sense that the dynamic of one does not depend directly on the dynamic of the other) and has no preconceived type of relation (causal, of correspondence), and, at the same time, there is no reason to discard the fact that their evolution brings them to certain confluences, to march parallel or to clash in a direct way, producing all types of configurations, including unexpected ones.

And in this case it turns out that the political dynamic has fractured. On one side, power institutionalizes itself, seeks to normalize itself. And for that reason it finds itself in an atrocious combat to manage to do what before the rupture of December it accomplished without major · problems: carry out primaries within the parties, select candidates and elect governments that take office with some legitimacy starting from a certain accumulation of votes. On the other side, the forces of counterpower gain time, organize, argue, and carry out different sorts of actions. As it can be seen, the consequences of the 19th and 20th continue to act in permanent manner across the social field, as condition—of destitution—including for those who struggle to play different games.

PHENOMENOLOGY OF COUNTERPOWER

COUNTERPOWER IS NO other than the resistances to the hegemony of capital. It consists in such a *multiplicity* of practices that is not thinkable in its unity (as a homogeneous movement) and, at the same time, in a *transversality* capable of producing resonances—of clues and hypotheses—among different experiments of resistance.

The formula "to resist is to create" speaks of the paradox of counterpower: on one side, resistance appears as a second moment, reactive and defensive. Nevertheless, "to resist is to create": resistance is that which creates, that which produces. Resistance is, therefore, first, self-affirmative and, above all, does not depend on that which it resists.

Indeed, in Argentina several networks have emerged around experiments working on health, alternative education and economy, assemblies, occupation of factories, roadblocks, etc. These experiments are heterogeneous in relation to each other. These networks tend—and not always succeed—to become autonomous with respect to the command of capital to the same extent that capital cannot include or integrate them socially in any way other than excluding them. While the *crisis* is the common ground of these resistances, it is no less true that the subjectivities forged there have given way to dynamics that transcend the times and penetrate the causes of the crisis.

Among the most important characteristics of these resistances are: (a) the *fusion* between vital reproduction and politics; (b) a better understanding of the possibilities of the relation between institutions (the State) and power (*potencia*), and (c) confrontation as a form of protection and as the truth of counterpower.

Since capitalism works by managing life, resistances are precisely bioresistances. There is no sphere of existence in which one does not find practices of resistance and creation.

These networks have a growing capacity of resources to the extent that they develop in expansive dynamics, linking producers with each other, producers with consumers, inventing new forms of exchange not mediated by mafias, etc.

If we have used sometimes the image of a *parallel society* to describe these circumstances, we have done it *in spite of*—and not in virtue of—the association that this image carries with it with respect to a supposed isolation. The experiments of power (*potencia*) are not *small separate worlds*, but rather that which *produces the world*, that succeeds in *instituting experience* where apparently there is pure devastation (*desert*). Far from thinking of separation, power (*potencia*) produces connection, but does it following a different modality from those "centers" (of power [*poder*]) with respect to which, as they tell us, "we should not isolate ourselves" (the State, "serious" politics, the parties, etc). The experiments of resistance are, precisely, the ones inventing new forms of taking charge of the public, the *common*, beyond the determinations of the market and the State. It is not about abandoning politics—in the sense of engendering collective destinies—but about the emergence of other ways of configuring tendencies and influences in society.

And so, what happened to the movement of resistance? Is there, indeed, "a" movement?

We have seen above that power (*poder*) works from its own requirements: subordinating life to the valorization of capital, conquering territories and business opportunities, obtaining cheap labor power, making for itself a legality that allows it to move at full speed without remaining tied to anything or anyone.

Capital combines control of power (*potencia*) and subjectivity, of nature and of the product of science and, in general, of the culture of the peoples with the result of destitution, exclusion, and violence.

It is not possible to combat the hegemony of capital as a social relation as if we were dealing with something purely exterior, which has its roots in the government palaces. Essentially, there is no other way of attacking capital without seeing, at the same time, that its power is that of sadness, powerlessness, individualism, separation, and the commodity. Hence, there is not any combat against capitalism other than that which consists of producing other forms of sociability, other images of happiness, and another politics that no longer separates itself from life.

The problem, however, is when on one side we realize that there is no creation but in situation, but at the same time the confrontation leads us to exit it, to converge with others with whom we must unite in order to develop the struggle.

And, indeed, the development of power (*potencia*), in situation, leads us to strengthen the line of counterpower to defend alternative experiments. Nevertheless, these are not two different things. It is not necessary to abandon the terrain of the situation in order to meet the line of counterpower. The line of counterpower is reached from inside.

The struggles deploy their defensive line at the time that hypotheses develop inside each experiment, and at the time that each of them experiences the appearance of new values and new modes of life.

One of the problems that come up when there is an attempt to "organize the resistances in a single movement" is precisely the flight from the situation in order to organize the struggle. When this happens, everything is reduced to a discussion of organizational models (of coordination/articulation) as if all that mattered was getting it right with an adequate technique, abandoning the organic relation between the situations and their requirements and counterpower as a moment internal to the situations themselves.

This is how the situation is displaced. Counterpower appears organized as a movement whose unity and coherence are put before (and imposed upon) the situations themselves "from outside." The capacity for confrontation appears magnified: everything else "can wait." Or it is proposed that the "work with the grassroots" must be subordinated to—or be organized from—"the conjuncture."

Between centralism and dispersion, however, power (*potencia*) offers a trajectory of composition between the situations: multiplicity can react without being organized from outside. The example of the autonomous piquetero movements is very clear: while in the neighborhoods there are attempts to produce differently, putting together murgas,* workshops for the children, dispensaries, bakeries, and forms of self-government, at the same time that the movements constitute a physical barrier for the protection of all they are producing. There are advances in multiple forms of coordination and circumstantial alliances whose priority is to preserve the experiment.

In light of this discussion, the tragic confrontation of June 26th can be thought of as a point of inflection for the movement of counterpower. This massacre brings back the echoes of a previous one, that of June of '73 in Ezeiza,** equally decisive at the time for understanding what is usually called political *ebb tide*: moments in which what happens at the level of the situation is devalued as a result of the defeats suffered at the level of the coordination (of the *movement*). This is the effect sought by power (*poder*): to measure the forces of counterpower by their capacity of coordination in a determinate moment and to spread this image of the relations of force as a warning to all the experiments.

On June 26th clashed, on one side, the logic of the gang, of the old task groups of the dictatorship convoked now by the private security firms, the logic of hunting and slaughter, and, on the other side, the dynamic of the protection of the column to back the retreat. While from the side of power (*poder*) the clash is sought, from the side of

---

* See footnote on page 75(Tr.)

** On June 20th, 1973, a crowd of half a million people gathered at the highway that goes to Ezeiza, Buenos Aires' international airport, to welcome Juán Domingo Perón, who was returning to the country after having lived in exile since 1955. Elements of the Peronist right set a trap for the radical groups attending the event. As they were trying to escape, hundreds of members of the Peronist youth and other radical groups were killed, while many others were injured or tortured. The Ezeiza massacre was a turning point that signaled the beginning of the repressive backlash against the radical movements. (Tr.)

counterpower the clash is not produced in order to measure forces, or to advance over power (*poder*) by way of force, but rather as self-affirmation, to protect the comrades, to pressure and conquer unemployment subsidies—in order to help sustain the workshops, etc.—and to demand freedom for the imprisoned comrades.

Behind the notion of political ebb tide there is a frustrated expectation of imminent political revolution. Indeed, the 19th and 20th of December were read as the signal that the crisis of neoliberalism opened the course of a political revolution. The demonstrations of the assemblies to the Plaza de Mayo prefigured the next constituent assembly. The march of the piqueteros with their hidden faces was a glimpse into a popular army in formation. The occupied factories revealed the red grassroots of an insurrectional proletariat, and the barter nodes—in case they were taken into account—an alternative to the functioning of the capitalist economy.

Thus, 2002 was a year of hope and frustration: the nodes of barter had to sacrifice the figure of the *prosumer* to assist millions of people, exceeding all prevision and interrupting the reflection that had been brewing in those networks over the role of money and over the forms of self-regulation of the nodes. Inflation appeared, as did shortage of goods, counterfeiting of money, and the incapacity to regulate the flows of credit, people, and products.

The piquetero movement—especially its autonomous versions—was strongly attacked at the same time that it had to face an accelerated increase of its ranks, so fast that it became very difficult for it to assimilate everything to the existing productive dynamic. The assemblies, after attracting thousands of people wore themselves out in eternal struggles with the parties of the left.

In the end, the lines of exploration and situational production that essentially constitute alternative forms of social reproduction, were invaded by the expectation that such practices should become *alternative* (symmetric) *institutions* to those of the market and the State. The projection over these practices of a will to alternativeness and their conversion into global substitutes for the dominant institutions implies neglecting the specific quality of those becomings as well as to interrupt their experimentation in the name of a majority logic that judges them not for what they are—in their multiplicity—but rather for that they should "come to be."

The *political ebb tide* is, then, a mystifying category. The discouragement that announces it arises from a frustrated belief: that the new social protagonism could be conceived as a new politics in the scene of power (*poder*). It is clear that, as a politics, the new social protagonism—or counterpower—would not give place to just one more politics, but rather to one founded in the most positive features of some experiments of resistance such as horizontality, autonomy, and multiplicity. These authentic keys to counterpower were thus taken as universal and abstract answers—an ideology—apt for an a priori resolution of the dilemmas of the every situation.

This is not a question of reclaiming optimism, but rather of revising this mechanism, if there is a will to do it. The *ebb tide* and the disillusionment—if they exist—represent the perception of a lost occasion, of the unfinished political revolution, the failure of a politics. Such representation proves to be even less appropriate if the persistence of the struggles, the emergence of new experiments, and an extended and profound inquiry is established.

Perhaps the 19th and 20th did not as much announce a coming revolution as they do a rupture. It is not that the very idea of revolution is not at stake—there is no reason to renounce it—but that such revolution has appeared as a demand for a new concept: rebellion, revolt and the subversion of *subjective modes of doing*.

THAT DECEMBER...
TWO YEARS FROM
THE 19ᵀᴴ AND 20ᵀᴴ

WHAT REMAINS IN *US* OF THAT COMMOTION THAT WE HAVE CALLED *THE 19ᵗʰ and 20ᵗʰ*, making reference, in this way, to the insurrectional phenomenon of the end of December 2001?

First of all, something is evident: we *are* no longer the same. But perhaps it is not convenient to start from here, maybe this evidence is too worn. And yet, to ask in the first person plural can throw us once again into the language of politics: *who* were "we" before those events? A "dispersed" we, or a we "in formation"? Maybe not even that. Disconnected points, dumb resistances, both growing and voiceless. However, the "we" that arose during those days unfolded, sustained by a rarely exercised neighborliness. And even so it does not make possible the configuration of a clear, linear, and definitive we. Rather, the we it configures is a more sinuous one, sometimes proud of itself, but other times immersed in resignation and fear of dissolution.

Let's continue along this path. We are not the same, things have changed. And this change does not possess a clear, single message. The changes are multidirectional, as multiple as the current spatiality in which we exercise our practices and thoughts. People said "NO," new inquiries opened, struggles gained power (*se potenciaron luchas*), discussions were incited, relations built, questions deepened; politics took place. In a few words: there were ideas and practices, refusals and constructions. The territory became multiple, as it was inhabited in different ways.

But also, people say, *"all that came to nothing."* They say that there was desolation, disillusion, that the bonds that were created were also dismantled, and, after the long summer of 2001, there was an ebb tide and even resentment toward the autonomous modes of doing.

The contradiction here is not necessarily an obstacle. To corroborate the *saddening* of the forces that pursued a linear advance of the modes of popular self-organization should imply neither a mystification of this decline nor a minimization of the relevance of those events: in fact, there is no way to understand Argentina today without considering these modifications, as much as their persistence.

Could things have worked out differently? Should they have done so? Perhaps the good intentions deserved to prevail. Or the good reasons of the brainy prophets. In the end, the becoming of the events should have happened according to different laws, and not under the complex sign of reality. But things are just like that and today we do not have significant keys to give a retroactive sense to the events of those days. We do not have that ultimate corollary of what happened that would allow us to definitively refute the intimate, anguished impression that all was in vain: an unfinished work, a wealth of energy that dissipates, a bunch of false ideas, a collective mirage that did not know how to seriously take on its challenges. Reality plays hard against the *credulous*, but also against the *sage*.

And, still, we are absolutely sure about the rebellious contemporaneity of those events, to the point that following the track of its power (*potencia*) we can access the most profound nuclei of intelligibility of current dilemmas. As happens at any point of inflection, the urgency is not rooted as much—or even only—in analyzing meticulously its causes (which perhaps do not exist separated from the rupture itself), but rather in exploring the new practical possibilities, tracing the necessary links and questioning the new limits of what can be thought.

The grammar of the changes (and not only their possible orientations) once again reaffirms its complex character. To the point that it becomes pertinent to ask whether so many continuities (political, social and economic) are not telling us about the inexhaustible capacity to persist of that which for the sake of convenience we call "reality."

Indeed, it could be the case that the events of December were nothing other than an outburst that is relatively loose for the lack of a needle that could stitch it to other pieces of cloth. Only that the seam exists and leaves its marks. One way to verify the mark lies in the most immediate: the discourses that tirelessly insist in maintaining that "nothing has happened here." There are many of them, too many—that is *suspicious*. Why negate so emphatically something that does not exist anyway? More still: isn't this very negative energy indicative of a certain modification in the field of the discussible, the thinkable, the imaginable?

Indeed, we have the "method of suspicion," the most immediate. And we also have firm realities: the level of dignity attained by radical social movements. Without going too far, all that the discursivity of the current government does is to work inside that legitimacy, that dignity, in order to announce, from there, that those movements "were" very important, but are no longer necessary. Politics *is back* and we are told that this is reason to celebrate. In the name of this *return of politics* the people who have entered into processes of radical politicization are treated as the troops of a demobilized victorious army: "thanks for the services rendered," now go home.

Demobilized and *dangerous*: those who articulated their demands to the organization of struggles and contributed to the opening of an unprecedented social protagonism, are now subsumed in the greatest factory of subjectivity of contemporary capitalism: "in-security." The paradox is set out: *politics comes back to depoliticize*. Now it is a matter of extinguishing the fires spread throughout the country. Politics is politics again: the social should depoliticize itself... anything that has autonomous life must stop and wait for the signal that authorizes it to be a legitimate actor.

The offensive of "politics" becomes particularly shrewd when it seeks to appropriate the meaning of the events of that December. Then, undoubtedly far from not having existed, those days are reclaimed now as essential raw material with which to constitute a new legitimacy. A renewed set of languages and legalities has been activated on the basis of a strong desire for normalization. This system of transactions between the "new" and the "old" feeds a rejuvenated aspiration over the advantages that can be obtained from the recomposition of the power of command.

To the extent that the forces that have taken the articulation of the social in their hands, confident in their capacity to co-opt the most novel elements of the social movement, can not avoid being continually overwhelmed by an openly reactionary tonality.

And it is probably this lack of connection (between the dominant political narrative of the current processes and the disciplinary tonality that attaches to it) that makes it possible to dress the present circumstances in a pathetic "seventy-ish" cloak. Hope thus becomes waiting: the concrete struggles should submit to the more abstract lucubrations over some relations of forces completely detached from the everyday, and rebellion (the experiments of self-organization of radical social movements) ought to adjust to the new "political schedule."

Thus, the map of present-day Argentina is crossed by a normalizing vertical line made from a reinforced and paradoxical tendency toward social fragmentation (all the more paradoxical because its force lies in the promise of integration founded on a hyper-precarious labor market participation) and from certain features of political recomposition. But it is also crossed by a diagonal line, of multiplicity, that works on a countless variety of sites of thought. A polarization crossed through by a transversal of resistance. The cartography of a socioeconomic and cultural polarity, boycotted by a de facto resistance, and founded in precarious diffuse networks capable of becoming explicit time and again.

A form of governability, then, and a strategy of assimilation of some elements of self-government—under the opposite sign; or a new management of the work force employed and unemployed under the promise of jobs for all: from the unemployment subsidies to pittance wages; or the conversion of the unemployment subsidies into the meager wage base of a laughable "neo-Keynesianism." An invitation, in the end, to political and social organization that oscillates between self-government and co-management, to manage the precarity of lives. Purely political exploitation of the work force conducted by a victimizing humanism that subordinates (sacrifices) life by denying it any capacity for autonomous creativity.

Of course, this same formulation could be thought about without much difficulty at a continental level, because this is the current scale of the processes of subsumption of labor and natural resources under the global market. The fourth world war intensifies. That is why it is worthwhile to consider transversality and popular self-organization as lines of defense of maximum relevance.

In the end, the 19th and 20th are dates of *commemoration*. What politics of memory is at stake in these days? What is *forgotten* in this *remembering*? What are these memories made from? What does the present struggle over the commemoration consist of, other than a dispute over the elaboration of new legitimacies, which work from the perspective of an infinitely emptying thematization?

But the initial question was different: what remains in us—or of us—two years after that December? Who are "we" today? In what practices do we articulate ourselves? What ideas make us strong if, as happens to us, we are not interested in the discourses that "come down" clean searching for realities (things and lives) to format? Where do practices, as paths of verification, lead?

After all, from a certain perspective of that December there might be a "we." Perhaps we can discover what "we are" if we are capable of perceiving what has probably been the most radical revelation of those events: the inexistence of any *a priori* guarantee—as well as of any presumed privileged site—of thinking and doing.

DISQUIET IN THE IMPASSE

IMPASSE: TIME SUSPENDED

WE SPEAK OF AN *IMPASSE* IN ORDER TO CHARACTERIZE THE CURRENT political situation. It is an elusive image, hard to theorize but greatly present in the different situations we are experiencing. As a concept we wish to construct, it requires a *perceptive* practice that takes us beyond the representations used by the language of politics, essay, philosophy or social sciences; and a sensibility that will drive us towards this *suspended* time, in which all acts waver, but everything that must be thought of once again occurs.

The notion of impasse aspires to naming a reality whose signs are not evident, and it is put forward as the key to comprehend the atmosphere in which we live. In doing so, we recur to a set of conversations that aim at investigating what articulations of the discursive, affective and political imaginary order enables activity *in* the present. A present that, as we said, is revealed as *suspended* time: between the irony of the eternal return of the same and the infinitesimal preparation of an historical variation.

Impasse is above all an ambiguous temporality, where the dynamics of creation that have stirred up an increasing social antagonism since the beginning of the 90s—whose implications can be witnessed in the capacity to destroy the main machinery of neoliberalism in large parts of the continent of Latin America—have apparently come to a halt.

We talk of an *apparent* halt because, as we shall see further on, it is not true that the antagonistic perspective has been absolutely dissolved, neither is collective dynamism paralyzed, not by far. On the contrary: in impasse, elements of counterpower and capitalist hegemony coexist, according to *promiscuous* forms that are hard to unravel. Ambiguity thus becomes the decisive characteristic of this period and manifests itself in a double dimension: as a time of crisis with no visible outcome; and as a stage where heterogeneous social logics are superimposed, without any single one imposing its reign in a definite way.

The truth is that the feeling that political activity from below (as we came to know it) is stagnating and lying somewhat dormant acquires a whole variety of meanings when we regard reality in Latin America and a great part of the Western world. The complexity of situations, that do not cease mutating due to the global crisis, urges us to consider this impasse as a concept—perhaps momentary, maybe lasting—that is open to all possible shades and drifts.

In impasse, time passes by without faith in progressivism and indifferent to all totalization. *Suspension* corresponds to a feeling of immobilization/incomprehension of time, of an incapacity to seize the possibilities of a time hounded by all kinds of question marks. It is a time moved by a dialectics with no finality. However, while it rejects the argument that we stand before a new *end of history* (as was promoted a decade ago), there spreads a mood in which the *exhaustion of a historical sense* coexists with a splendorous rebirth of the *already lived*.

In what sense do we speak of historic exhaustion? In that possibilities seem to multiply to infinity, but the *meaning of an action* becomes unfathomable, it dissipates. The possibility of opening (the opening of possibility) that is presented 'as close at hand', this attempt at an *absolute* question (a kind of *and why not?*), turns, in the *tempo* of impasse, into a dynamics of stagnation.

Finally, what do we mean when we speak of a return of the *already lived?* A phantasmal economy that drapes the present in memory, so that the past returns as pure remembrance, tribute or commemoration. This *return of the same* as memory presents itself as a *closure* in the face of a question that *opened a new time* and was, nevertheless, left disfigured. Disfigured in the sense that one tried to close it with the historical answers of the already thought, neutralizing it as a space of problematization. And, yet, it persists, latent or postponed as unresolved tension. Thus, an incessant game of frustrations and expectations emerges in the impasse.

GOVERNMENTALITY AND NEW GOVERNANCE

FROM DICTATORSHIP TO the triumph of neoliberalism—as part of a process that can be perceived across Latin America—we are experiencing, in Argentina, the establishment of a new type of government, whose operation no longer depends on the unique and pre-existing sovereignty of the state, but rather overflows in infinite instances of management originating from contingent couplings that can intervene in any hypothesis of conflict. The *novelty* resides in a permanent invention of political, legal, market, assistance and communication mechanisms that are articulated each time in order to deal with specific situations. Foucault calls this form of rooting of the government in society *governmentality*. It is the incorporation of monetary mechanisms, of mechanisms of administration and public opinion, media influence and the regulation of urban life that renders neoliberalism a form of immanent control over lives, their calculation and their market disposition; while, at the same time, it takes the development of liberties and initiatives as a supreme value. However, in Latin America this new government regime presented a singularity: forms of counter-insurgent terror between the 1970s and the beginning of the 1980s had a definitive role in its instauration. From that moment, the state is no longer the most consistent sovereign synthesis of society and blends in as an actor amongst us, inside the operation of more complex mechanisms of government (*governmentalization of the state*).

We believe that due to the collective experiences that emerged in the context of social movements from the beginning of the 1990s until the early years of the new century—and subsequently caused a displacement of the ways of governing in many of the region's countries, in the sense that they forced the interpretation of certain critical nuclei manifested by these new insurgencies—a point of inflection inside the paradigm of neoliberal governmentality was generated.

We will call this inflection *new governance*. It is formed by the irruption of the social dynamics that questioned the legitimacy of hardcore neoliberalism and the subsequent coming to power of 'progressive' governments in the Southern Cone. Governments that were determined, in different ways and intensities, by the impact of the *new social protagonism* in the alteration of the purely neoliberal regime. Here we must stress the sense of sequence: it was the destituting power of these movements that challenged and brought to crisis the financial mechanisms, mechanisms of subordinated social assistance, unlimited expropriation of resources and consolidated racisms (of neoliberal governmentality);

and that, in turn, allowed, in one way or the other, the coming to power of 'progressive' governments. The new governance can be explained by this conjunction of dynamics.

By the neologism *destituting* we have tried to convey the meaning of the Spanish *destituyente*. A power which is, in a way, the opposite of *instituent*: that doesn't create institutions, but rather vacates them, dissolves them, empties them of their occupants and their power.

Amidst this crisis, the movements and experiences of a new radicalism also questioned the neoliberal administration of labor and all things common (resources, land, public possessions, knowledge, etc.). These dynamics brought about an attempt at a—however partial—social *crossing* of the state (as an apparatus, but even more as a *relation*); a state that is already a form-in-crisis. Far from constituting new political models to be copied, the innovations that were put to practice appeared—where they had the opportunity to grow—as what they are: tactical sizing-ups in a dispute for the redefinition of the relation between power and movements.

Because, if amongst us 'hardcore' neoliberalism was able to define itself as the effort to channel and synthesize the social in the sphere of the market (through the general privatization and marketization of existence, nature and the state and institutions through outsourcing), the new social protagonism and its destituting vocation dealt with the violence of this synthesis, returning to the public sphere the political density that the purely mercantile treatment amputated from it, determining the expansion of a true *difference* in the political scene.

So, the new governance presupposes the increasing complexity of the administration of the social, installed since the end of the dictatorship. However, its novelty lies in that social movements aim—with varying success—at *determining* norms, orientations and dynamics of government (state and non-state), in a space that is also permanently disputed. We cannot achieve a definite and irreversible positive assessment of its actions from such a novel character. Rather, we realize that the plasticity and ambiguity of these processes is enormous, for they are subordinated, by nature, to the ups and downs of political struggle.

From this point on, we are interested in analyzing what happens regarding this new governance, the specific processes that limit and/or broaden its democratic dynamics each time. For that, we must take into consideration two dimensions. On one hand, the 'crisis of social movements,' that was formulated at an early stage by the collective *Mujeres Creando* [Women Creating], was translated to a great extent as a difficulty to favor and deepen innovative policies in the institutional sphere and the dynamics of movements themselves. On the other, the new governance insinuated in this encounter of heterogeneous dynamics was based on the partial and paradoxical recognition of the collective enunciations that emerged in the crisis. As a result, these expressions were recoded by institutions as mere demands, defusing their disruptive and transforming aspect.

The excess produced by the more novel social experiences of the last decade has not found enduring modes of *public autonomous expression*. However, a modality of this surplus of invention persists under premises that could possibly be taken into account by various current instances of government. In this sense, the postulate that has inhibited political repression in various countries of the continent becomes comprehensible; likewise the hypothesis that it is not worthwhile to keep appealing to the discourse of adjustment and privatization. Although both can be considered 'negative statements' insofar as they translate as prohibition what had emerged as a destituting opening, at the same time they display the enduring character of their implications when they manage to be perceived as inevitable axiomatic principles.

Thus, the marks that the crisis (with its main actors) has inscribed in the institutional tissue are still visible today, amidst a process of normalization and weakening of the movements themselves. And this persistence is presented as a game of *partial recognitions* with variable effects (reparatory, compensatory, confiscating) that, nevertheless, exclude the specific perspective of the *social reappropriation of what is common* that has emerged from the agenda of movements on a regional scale.

Let us repeat: this moment is characterized by ambiguity. The democratic statements that survive the circumstances from whence they emerged are left submitted to new interpretations by the disputing forces, to the point that their deployment no longer depends on the subjects that conceived them, but on whoever presently acquires the capacity to adjust them to their own purposes. Thus, the scene is like a game of mirrors, in which we all question the fate of such premises, while the positions never cease to multiply. For example, we cannot compare the experiment of the Single Party of the Bolivarian Revolution of Venezuela with the dilemmas that Morales faces with the reactionary counter-offensive; just as situations as fragile as that of Paraguay do not resemble those of other countries—such as Ecuador— that have achieved constituent processes. Neither can we put on an equal footing the military and paramilitary advance in Chiapas, the incapacity of the Brazilian Workers' Party to create a candidacy that is not Lula's, or the narrowing down of the number of interlocutors that leave the political scene of Argentina completely hollow, inside as well as outside the government.

The weakening of the more virtuous tendencies that characterize the new governance has determined the blocking of its spirit of innovation, thus giving way to the time of stagnation in which we are submerged: the impasse.

NEW GOVERNANCE AND GOOD GOVERNMENT

WITH THE SLOGAN 'rule by obeying' *(mandar obedeciendo)*, the Zapatistas sought to redefine, in a fair way, the relation of power from below with the instances of government, once the occupation of the state as a privileged means of social change had been dismissed. 'Rule by obeying' thus turned into a synonym of another formula: that of 'good government.' They were also the first ones to attempt a dialogue with the local and national government following the armed uprising in Chiapas, with the San Andres Dialogues. Under the impression of this failure, the Zapatistas manifested their distrust towards the more recent wave of so-called 'progressive' or 'left wing' governments in the region, and relaunched, with the *Otra Campaña*, their calling to those below, and to the social and autonomous left. What were the implications of the fact that Evo Morales finished his inaugural address by saying that he intended to 'rule by obeying'? What did the use of this political slogan in a situation as different as the Bolivian one mean? Firstly, it pointed out the weight of the social movements that, in their mobilizing and destabilizing power, forced a 'beyond' to representative forms of government. However, secondly, it highlighted the paradox that those same movements that have turned disobedience into their platform of political action, are now the basis of a new governance that has been in formation since then. In Bolivia, 'rule by obeying' was applied to the project of coexistence between, on the one hand, those powerful social movements that have been confronting neoliberalism and racism for decades and, on the other, a set of transnational corporations and political actors that are relevant in the struggle over the exploitation of key (natural-social) resources for Bolivia's participation in the world economy.

So, the content of 'rule by obeying' emerges from the interplay between the 'new governance' and the Zapatista idea of 'good government' that is deployed in the Councils of Good Government. Rather than being two opposed hypotheses, both try to think of the issue of government in relation to constituent power from below, when they are not crystallized as irreconcilable polarities. And they are proof of how a communitarian element such as 'rule by obeying' has turned into an element that is radically contemporary when reflecting on new political hypotheses.

However, the Zapatistas have realized that, in Mexico, this dialectic between governments and movements could not work; this failure thrusts movements into a new phase of silence and, some times, a substantial reconversion of their strategies.

What happens when certain tendencies to 'rule by obeying' allow for a new attempt to permeate the state, inaugurating a dynamics of 'new governance'? We said that social movements (and now we are referring more precisely to specific subjects, organized around embodied experimental struggles) were left without an 'autonomous public expression.' The transversal plane of political production and elaboration that emerged during the more street-located phase of the crisis does not exist any more, or can only be verified fleetingly, impeding the construction of pragmatics that would deploy the conquered premises in an emancipatory way.

So, in impasse we observe the exhaustion of a certain modality of antagonism, be it in its multitudinous and destituting version, or in its capacity to inspire new (post-state) institutions. This decline in antagonistic tension allowed for the relegation of a set of dilemmas formulated by struggles regarding waged labor, self-management, reappropriation of factories and natural resources, political representation, the forms of deliberation and decision-making, the ways of life in the city, communication, food sovereignty, struggle against impunity and repression. This can be considered a sign of the relative incapacity of the 'movements' (that means, *us*) to play in a versatile way in the new situation. Versatility that not only (or fundamentally) refers to an eventual participation in the 'political/conjunctural' game, or to insisting on a clash with no destination (in the sense that it lacks anchorage), but above all to the possibility of creating independent areas from which to read the process in an autonomous way. To this end, only the political maturity of the movements can provide the tactical capacity to render autonomy a lucid perspective during moments of great *ambivalence*, and put its multiple dimensions to play. However, the democratizing potential of social movements has remained suspended, a prisoner to the canons of *economicism* (that consider the increase in consumption as the only element to be taken into account) or confined to a strictly *institutionalist* dimension, with which the new governance has often been identified.

However, the impasse is also constituted by another kind of indefinition that emerges from the exhaustion of the inherited forms of domination and the confirmation of certain invariants that underpin domination as such. Particularly, the repositioning of forms of neoliberal administration of labor under a developmentalist narrative, which not only impedes the better use of the balance that movements have deployed on this issue, but also de-problematizes narratives that coexist very well with new dynamics of accumulation that inhibit the broadening of the democratic possibility of the use of collective goods.

LATIN AMERICA: TRAVERSING THE CRISIS

THUS, THE CURRENT situation in Latin America makes two contributions to the critical reinterpretation of the crisis that affects the global scene. On the one hand, the overflow of images that anticipated the now generalized disaster of neoliberalism (especially in Venezuela, Bolivia, Ecuador and Argentina); and, on the other hand, having exposed the way in which the constitution of a political subjectivity from below allows for the possibility of a 'democratic traversing' of the crisis.

However, this interesting duplicity has been translated in a *neo-developmentalist* way by many governments of the continent who, while assuming the scenario of crisis, extract from it arguments that promote the reinstatement of a state-national imaginary plagued by the regressive yearning for *wage* forms. (The explicit or implicit critique of the control exercised by the wage over social reproduction being, in our opinion, one of the richest characteristics of the revolt.)

The lack of subtlety in the discourses that shape the current representatives of the ruling party in Argentina can be attributed to their insistence on abstractly opposing elements that are actually not antagonistic: 'liberalism *or* national development', 'market *or* state', 'economy *or* politics.' Although it provides immediate legitimacy and distributes the roles in each scene, this way of expressing conflict entails the risk of re-establishing 'political' neoliberalism by evading all critical reflection on the ways in which institution and competition, private and public, democracy and consumption are articulated. The refusal to construct a singular diagnosis and the incapacity to create original interpretations of the nature of the contemporary crisis lead to policies that cannot describe the current challenge.

Thus, impasse is superimposed on the world crisis of capitalism: while capital tries to redefine new alignments for its reproduction, the global dimension of the debate seems to be focusing on the evaluation of the implications of a renewed policy of state intervention. The renewal of this old binarism implies the absence of rationalities that manage to express the power resulting from successive and recent cycles of struggle.

MYTHOLOGIQUES

THE STRUGGLES FOUGHT against neoliberalism in Latin America during the past long fifteen years are inconceivable without the development of movements that readopt or reinterpret an indigenous world, native cultures and a myriad of mythological elements that, having been subordinated for centuries to the colonial West, form part of a broader potential to *fabulate* the present.

The ambivalent existence of those mythological elements is given by the fact that they simultaneously nurture the imagination with new forms of administrating everything common and the autonomy of the social; and, also, they operate—in *reverse*—as a way of subordinating populations to the national developmentalist paradigm. Neo-developmentalism stimulates an imagery of reconstruction of the social ties linked to full employment, and at the same time it has sustained itself through precarious labor: many mythological elements participate today in complex hybrids that render them functional to these dynamics.

What to conclude from the recomposition of forms of labor regarding economies, such as that of textiles, which are supported by the so-called 'slave labor' of clandestine workshops that mix cooperative relations and methods coming from the native cultures of the Bolivian altiplano with criteria of capitalist valorization? Or the exploitation of the skills and customs of the *quinteras* and *quinteros*, Bolivian migrants that produce a great part of the fruit and vegetables that are consumed in the metropolis of Buenos Aires today?

Are these communitarian (linguistic-affective) elements, in a postmodern (post-communitarian?) assemblage, *reversed* and used as a source of new hierarchies and forms of exploitation? What happens when these same mythical-cultural elements form part of the dynamics of creation of stereotypes and stigmas that justify the policy of the city's social division in new ghettos and areas of labor over-exploitation? Or is it directly included in the calculation of the *cheapening* of labor?

So how do these communitarian traditions coexist with the *modern*, ever strong—and today omnipresent—Argentinean myth of the 'glory years' of import substitution, when at the same time the labor market is currently recomposed by elements that are both precisely *not modern* (hierarchies formed by race and skin color, etc.) and *post-modern* (such as those mobilized in large parts of the service economy)?

In response to the multiplicity of attempts opened by social experimentation faced with crisis, the glorification of labor after the currency devaluation *interprets the 2001 Argentine uprising, and the open situation of 2002-2003, as a catastrophe that must be exorcised,* and once again turns unemployment into a threat and an argument of legitimization in view of the possibility of a new devaluation.

We mentioned that the refusal of labor and the recovery of mythological elements constitute, among others, the ingredients of a political and conjunctural capacity to fabulate. Included as displaced tension in the ambiguities of the present, they form part of processes of constituting subjectivity in the impasse.

Today, that *refusal of labor* (its politicization, its rupture-creating materiality, its other image of happiness) is a vague texture in the peripheral neighborhoods (those who are in the city center as well as in the old 'industrial cordons'). It is included in the urban calculation of many who would rather participate in more or less illegal and/or informal networks than get a stable job. It can be seen in many of the strategies of the youth who do not imagine the possibility of employment, but indeed so many other ways of subsisting and risking their lives. For others, it still persists as a search for self-managing or cooperative solutions in order to solve everyday existence. Likewise, de-ghettoizing and de-racializing tendencies integrate the city's liveliest communitarian and counter-cultural moments. They are *minority* components of an extended diffusion, an active compound that demands great attention.

THE CRAFTS OF POLITICS

So, WITHIN THE promiscuity that characterizes the impasse's muddy terrain, what is happening with radical politics?

Although the most explicit merit of the practices and enunciations that were spread in Argentina at the beginning of this century (autonomy, horizontality, street confrontation, insurrection) was to reveal the inconsistency of the previous political institutions, there was another, equally decisive side to that new social protagonism: the opening of a broad field of experimentation, permeated by all kinds of questions and assertions. That is why today, when we ask ourselves about the present situation of politics, it is essential to keep in mind the extensive process of recoding the social that has caused the relative closure of said experimental space.

One of the layers that form the impasse, perhaps one of the hardest ones to analyze, implies the existence of discursive and identitarian fragments that belong to the memory of struggles with which we have learned to conjugate the verb to *do* politics. This appealing to certain formulas and symbologies of traditions of combat (even the more recent ones) has contributed to the reorientation of processes of extreme conflictuality (openly untamable) according to polarizing dynamics that underestimate the sensible richness of antagonism, reducing the horizon of collective invention. When political difference is reconstituted in terms of binary options, the constituting experience ends up being replaced by a codified representation of the same.

Even so, we can distinguish moments of decodification and attempts at autonomous interpretation parting from efforts of relative subtraction that perforate the polarizing calling. They are not experiences to be idealized, but rather active situations that, producing their own languages, create lateral drifts that try to evade the dominant code, the one that is articulated with the paradigm of government and establishes the monolinguism of capital.

We refer to processes in which the coexistence of a plurality of elaborations of meaning, living territories, and significant ties, lead to unique and unyielding compositions. In this sense, the production of intelligibility overflows the field of discourse and opens up to a much broader diagram (affective, imaginary, bodily), which can be observed at the level of great public and media visibility, as well as on the streets, in domestic-informal economies, and even in our physiological organs (eyes, brain, kidneys).

Antagonism has not disappeared. It has been led to polarization, but at the same time it has been dispersed in mud and promiscuity, to the point of being played as a possibility in every situation. That is why we can insist on the true political value of collectives (the more inadequate they are in relation to the surrounding discourse, the greater this value is) that refuse to dissolve in the common sense that is articulated in the polarizing process.

If it is so hard for us to figure out what political intervention is today, it is because of the ambiguity and the vertigo that make any categorical assertion impossible and render the exercise of evaluation even more complex. We must not react with conservatism, restoring the certainties that remain standing but, rather, immerse ourselves in this ambivalent medium, filled with very real potentialities that never manifest themselves but impede the definite closing of 'reality.'

Perhaps politics is, more and more, this inflection through which we give consistency to the situations in which we find ourselves, discovering the capacity to fabulate on our account. This labor requires a delicate craft.

COMMON NOTIONS is a publishing house and programming machine that fosters the collective formulation of new directions for living autonomy in everyday life.

We aim to translate, produce, and circulate tools of knowledge production utilized in movement-building practices. Through a variety of media, we seek to generalize common notions about the creation of other worlds beyond state and capital.

Our publications include:

Grupo de Arte Callejero, *Thought, Practices, and Actions* (978-1-942173-10-6, $22)

Marcello Tarì, *There Is No Unhappy Revolution: The Communism of Destitution* (978-1-942173-16-8, $18)

CounterPower, *Organizing for Autonomy: History, Theory, and Strategy for Collective Liberation* (978-1-942173-21-2, $20)

Liaisons, *In the Name of the People* (978-1-942173-07-6, $18)

Mario Tronti and Andrew Anastasi, editor and translator, *Weapon of Organization: Mario Tonti's Political Revolution in Marxism* (978-1-942173-22-9, $20)

Silvia Federici, Susana Draper, and Liz Mason-Deese, editors, *Feminicide and Global Accumulation: Frontline Struggles to Resist the Violence of Patriarchy and Capitalism* (978-1942173-44-1, $20)

CareNotes Collective, *For Health Autonomy: Horizons of Care Beyond Austerity* (978-1-942173-14-4, $15)

info@commonnotios.org
www.commonnotions.org

BECOME A MONTHLY SUSTAINER

These are decisive times, ripe with challenges and possibility, heartache and beautiful inspiration. More than ever, we are in need of timely reflections, clear critiques, and inspiring strategies that can help movements for social justice grow and transform society. Help us amplify those necessary words, deeds, and dreams that our liberation movements and our worlds so need.

Movements are sustained by people like you, whose fugitive words, deeds, and dreams bend against the world of domination and exploitation.

For collective imagination, dedicated practices of love and study, and organized acts of freedom.

By any media necessary.

With your love and support.

Monthly sustainers start at $5, $12 and $25.

At $12 monthly, we will mail you a copy of every new book hot off the press in heartfelt appreciation of your love and support.

At $25, we will mail you a copy of every new book hot off the press alongside special edition posters and 50% discounts on previous publications at our web store.

Join us at commonnotions.org/sustain.